479.790

Qualitative Diary Methods

QUALITATIVE RESEARCH METHODS SERIES

Series Editor: David L. Morgan, Portland State University

The *Qualitative Research Methods Series* currently consists of 65 volumes that address essential aspects of using qualitative methods across social and behavioral sciences. These widely used books provide valuable resources for a broad range of scholars, researchers, teachers, students, and community-based researchers.

The series publishes volumes that:

- Address topics of current interest to the field of qualitative research.

- Provide practical guidance and assistance with collecting and analyzing qualitative data.

- Highlight essential issues in qualitative research, including strategies to address those issues.

- Add new voices to the field of qualitative research.

A key characteristic of the Qualitative Research Methods Series is an emphasis on both a *"why"* and a *"how-to"* perspective, so that readers will understand the purposes and motivations behind a method, as well as the practical and technical aspects of using that method. These relatively short and inexpensive books rely on a cross-disciplinary approach, and they typically include examples from practice; tables, boxes, and figures; discussion questions; application activities; and further reading sources.

New volumes in the Series include:

Qualitative Diary Methods
Laura Radcliffe and Leighann Spencer

Qualitative Research Writing: Credible and Trustworthy Writing From Beginning to End
Michelle Salmona, Dan Kaczynski, and Eli Lieber

Crafting Qualitative Research Questions
Elizabeth (Betsy) A. Baker

Narrative as Topic and Method in Social Research
Donileen R. Loseke

Introduction to Cognitive Ethnography and Systematic Field Work
G. Mark Schoepfle

Photovoice for Social Justice: Visual Representation in Action
Jean M. Breny and Shannon L. McMorrow

Hybrid Ethnography: Online, Offline, and In Between
Liz Przybylski

For information on how to submit a proposal for the Series, please contact:

- David L. Morgan, Series Editor: morgand@pdx.edu
- Helen Salmon, Publisher, Sage: helen.salmon@sagepub.com

Qualitative Diary Methods

Laura Radcliffe
University of Liverpool

Leighann Spencer
University of Liverpool

FOR INFORMATION:

2455 Teller Road
Thousand Oaks, California 91320
E-mail: orders@sagepub.com

1 Oliver's Yard
55 City Road
London, EC1Y 1SP
United Kingdom

Unit No. 323-333, Third Floor, F-Block
International Trade Tower
Nehru Place, New Delhi – 110 019
India

18 Cross Street #10-10/11/12
China Square Central
Singapore 048423

Copyright © 2026 by Sage

All rights reserved. Except as permitted by U.S. copyright law, no part of this work may be reproduced or distributed in any form or by any means, or stored in a database or retrieval system, without permission in writing from the publisher.

All third-party trademarks referenced or depicted herein are included solely for the purpose of illustration and are the property of their respective owners. Reference to these trademarks in no way indicates any relationship with, or endorsement by, the trademark owner.

Printed in the United States of America

Library of Congress Cataloging-in-Publication Data

ISBN: 9781071950517

Acquisitions Editor: Helen Salmon

Content Development Editor: Jennifer Milewski

Production Editor: Aparajita Srivastava

Copy Editor: Gillian Dickens

Typesetter: Hurix Digital

Cover Designer: Candice Harman

Marketing Manager: Victoria Velasquez

This book is printed on acid-free paper.

25 26 27 28 29 10 9 8 7 6 5 4 3 2 1

BRIEF CONTENTS

Preface	xiii
Acknowledgments	xvii
About the Authors	xix

Chapter 1:	An Introduction to Qualitative Diary Methods	1
Chapter 2:	Designing QDMs: Addressing Challenges and Ethical Dilemmas *(Coauthored With Hannah Musiyarira)*	19
Chapter 3:	Traditional Diary Methods	51
Chapter 4:	Incorporating the Visual: Photo and Video Diaries	83
Chapter 5:	There's an App for That! Introducing Mobile "App" Diaries *(Coauthored With Joanna Gregory-Chialton)*	127
Chapter 6:	Analyzing Data From QDMs: Thematic Analysis and Beyond	155
Chapter 7:	QDM-Focused Analysis Approaches	185
Chapter 8:	Concluding Chapter and the Future of QDMs	211

Appendix	223
Glossary	229
References	235
Index	261

DETAILED CONTENTS

Preface	xiii
Acknowledgments	xvii
About the Authors	xix

Chapter 1 An Introduction to Qualitative Diary Methods — 1

- What Are QDMs? — 1
- A Brief History of QDMs — 2
- When and Why Should I Use QDMs? — 7
    - QDMs as a Participant-Led Approach — 12
    - QDMs as a Method for Sensitive Research — 14
    - QDMs as a Reflexive Method — 15
- Conclusion — 16

Chapter 2 Designing QDMs: Addressing Challenges and Ethical Dilemmas (Coauthored With Hannah Musiyarira) — 19

- Sampling for QDMs — 20
- Participant Retention and Engagement — 25
- Designing QDMs — 29
    - Diary Designs — 29
        - *Interval-Contingent Diary Designs* — 29
        - *Event-Contingent Diary Designs* — 31
        - *Signal-Contingent Diary Designs* — 32
    - QDM Structure — 35
        - *Using QDMs Alongside Other Methods* — 35
        - *The Pre-Diary Interview* — 36
        - *Post-Diary Interviews* — 39
- Ethical Considerations — 42

Participant Reflexivity	43
Privacy and Confidentiality	44
Balancing Data Needs and Participant/Researcher Well-Being	45
Ending the Researcher–Researched Relationship	46

Chapter 3 Traditional Diary Methods — 51

Traditional Approaches: An Introduction	51
Pen-and-Paper Diaries	52
Potential Challenges	55
Practical Considerations	59
Audio Diaries	66
Potential Challenges	73
Practical Considerations	75

Chapter 4 Incorporating the Visual: Photo and Video Diaries — 83

Visual Approaches: An Introduction	83
Photo Diaries	84
Challenges	91
Practical Considerations	96
Video Diaries	103
Challenges	109
Practical Considerations	114

Chapter 5 There's an App for That! Introducing Mobile "App" Diaries *(Coauthored With Joanna Gregory-Chialton)* — 127

Mobile "App" Diaries: An Introduction	127
App Diaries: Benefits and When and Why to Use Them	128
Challenges	134
Potential Digital Divides	134
Technical Issues	136
Privacy and Personal Boundaries	138
The Paradox of "Cost-Effectiveness" in App Diaries	140
Designing App Diaries: Practical Considerations	141
Adapting an App	142
Tailoring or Creating an App	145
To Adapt, Tailor, or Create an App	149
App Diary Checklist	152

Chapter 6 Analyzing Data From QDMs: Thematic Analysis and Beyond — 155

Analyzing QDMs: An Introduction — 155
Data Management and Preparation — 156
    Pre- and Ongoing Data Collection — 156
    Post-data Collection — 160
Choosing an Analytical Approach: Key Considerations — 161
    What Are Your Ontological and Epistemological Positions? — 161
    Research Question-Analysis Alignment: Why Did You
    Use QDMs in the First Place? — 162
    Are You Integrating Diary and Other Types of Qualitative Data? — 163
Using Traditional Qualitative Analysis Approaches — **164**
    Generic Thematic Analysis Approaches for QDM Analysis — 164
    "Methodologically Wed" Analytical Approaches and QDM Analysis — 167
        Grounded Theory — 167
        Phenomenological Approaches — 168
        Narrative Approaches — 169
    Using Traditional Qualitative Analysis Approaches:
    Strengths and Limitations — 171
Analyzing Multimodal/Visual Diary Data — 173
Integrating Diary and Other Forms of Data — 178

Chapter 7 QDM-Focused Analysis Approaches — 185

Introducing QDM-Focused Analytical Approaches:
Capturing the "Down" and "Across" Benefits of QDMs — 185
    Embracing the "Down": Analyzing QDMs Using
    Event Diagrams Analysis — 187
    Conducting EDA: A Three-Step Process — 188
        Step 1: Conduct a Thematic Template Analysis — 188
        Step 2: Create Event (or Activity) Diagrams — 188
        Step 3: Comparative Analysis Within and Between Participants — 188
    Integrating Event Diagrams With Other Qualitative Data — 189
    Limitations — 191
Embracing the "Across": Analyzing QDMs Using
Thematic Trajectory Analysis — 192
    Philosophical Positioning of TTA — 193
    Conducting TTA: A Four-Step Process — 195
        Step 1: Create Data Display Matrices — 196
        Step 2: Thematic Template Analysis at Micro-, Meso-, and Macro-Levels — 196
        Step 3: Visualization of Thematic Trajectories — 200

        Step 4: Intra- and Intertheme Trajectory Analysis   204
      Integrating TTA Output With Other Qualitative Data   205
      Limitations   205

  Reporting and Interpreting TTA and EDA:
  Reduction Versus Reductive   208

Chapter 8   Concluding Chapter and the Future of QDMs   211

  Recapitulation: Key Points From Previous Chapters   211

  Key Considerations in Developing QDM Research Projects   214
      Research Question and Method Fit   214

  Developments in QDM Research: Looking Back and to the Future   217

  Conclusion   220

Appendix   **223**

Glossary   **229**

References   **235**

Index   **261**

PREFACE

The journey to this book has been as much about our shared passion for qualitative diary methods (QDMs) as it has been about the serendipitous moments that brought us together. For Laura, it all began during her master's dissertation, when she realized how little was understood about daily work–life experiences on the ground and that this evident gap in theorizing required a different kind of methodological approach. As an Organizational Psychology master's student, she struggled to find an approach that might enable her to capture these experiences qualitatively. At the time, the only resource in this field that addressed this need was an insightful book chapter by Professor Gillian Symon, a researcher whose inspirational work continues to influence her own, titled "Uses of Diaries in Research." This chapter sparked Laura's interest in the potential of qualitative diary methods and its ability to reveal new insights.

Despite the challenges of employing a method viewed as fairly different in organizational and management research at the time, with few methodological guidelines and little textbook advice to follow, Laura was fortunate to have the faith, support, and broad qualitative methodological expertise of her supervisor, Professor Catherine Cassell. It was her encouragement that solidified a love for qualitative diaries, a love that would carry her through her subsequent PhD research and beyond. It was during her PhD that she discovered the wealth of qualitative diary methods insights that did exist in other fields, particularly health research, which increasingly inspired her own work.

A few years post-PhD, Laura's journey led her to Liverpool University, where she met Leighann, who was a PhD student at the time. We immediately bonded over our mutual interest in innovative qualitative methods, particularly the possibilities offered by new QDM approaches. It was like finding a kindred QDM spirit—finally, someone else equally geeky about QDMs and willing to engage in endless discussions about their potential! Our shared enthusiasm led to countless conversations, bouncing ideas off one other, exploring the endless possibilities of QDMs.

During this time, we collaborated to build a QDM app for Leighann's PhD research on daily experiences of mistreatment at work. This project presented numerous challenges, from acquiring funding to learning the language of app developers—a language we quickly discovered was as foreign to us as Ancient Greek. We attended National Centre for Research Methods (NCRM) courses together, like "How to Build Apps for Non-Developers," and presented our work at the annual NCRM conference. We also grappled together with the limitations of existing qualitative analysis methods, an area we had each found particularly challenging, which eventually led us to develop thematic trajectory analysis (TTA), a new approach that we hope will serve other researchers as it has served us.

During the development of TTA, we sought funding for workshops from Methods North West (MNW) to introduce and trial our thematic trajectory analysis methodology with other researchers using QDMs. Here, we spent time with researchers across the social sciences, applying this approach to their data—often while huddled around the floor with endless Post-its and large sheets of paper. This collaborative spirit led us to develop further whole-day workshops on using QDMs, which we began delivering annually for NCRM. We thoroughly enjoyed creating interactive materials, meeting other (potential) QDM researchers, and hearing about their exciting work.

These workshops quickly became the springboard for this book. We realized that our materials, which expanded year after year, needed more space than even a whole-day workshop could permit—so a book was the natural next step. This book emerged from our QDM workshops, with our slides serving as the initial blueprint for the chapters you see today. Conversations with other researchers during and beyond these workshops, including with our own PhD students, have shaped and supported us along the way. We've strived to create the kind of book we wished had been available when we first started our own QDM journey as research students—one that offers a comprehensive overview of how these methods have been used across disciplines, alongside practical tips that will be useful for researchers designing their own study, justifying their approach, navigating ethical considerations, and being prepared for QDM-specific challenges, alongside important concrete examples of QDM research materials.

We hope this book will be a valuable resource for current and future QDM researchers, supporting research students and anyone new to using QDMs, regardless of career stage. We also hope it resonates with and is useful to more experienced QDM researchers. Further, for those who have engaged with us so far, whose work we've cited, and who have inspired us in one way or another, we hope you will find this book a unifying resource that brings together QDM researcher and participant voices across social science disciplines. We also hope it might inspire other methods course instructors to add QDMs to their core syllabus, recognizing the exciting potential and growing importance of these diverse methods. As we argue in this book, QDMs represent an exciting range of methodologies with great potential. We hope the exercises provided at the end of each chapter will serve as useful resources for instructors and stimulate thought for research students.

We are eager to continue the conversation with other researchers, and we hope this book will spark new discussions, enabling us all to keep learning and developing together. We look forward to the future of QDM research and can't wait to see what the next phase will bring.

ACKNOWLEDGMENTS

We would like to begin by expressing our gratitude to Hannah Musiyarira and Joanna Gregory-Chialton for their important contributions as coauthors of two chapters in this book. Their expertise and insights, drawn from their own rich experiences as qualitative diary methods (QDM) researchers, not only enriches this book but also advances the broader field of qualitative research in meaningful ways.

We also wish to extend our heartfelt thanks to Mya Kirkwood, an outstanding PhD student who served as a research assistant during the development of this book. Mya's dedication and excellent research skills were instrumental in reviewing the wide variety of exciting qualitative diary studies that exist across social science disciplines. This book would not have been possible without her hard work.

We are deeply grateful to all our fantastic PhD students, past and present, who have employed QDMs in various forms within their own research. Their intellectual curiosity has continually inspired us, pushing us to engage with new and innovative uses of QDMs. We are also grateful to all those researchers who have undertaken exciting QDM research to date. The studies we have cited throughout this book have provided us with ongoing intellectual nourishment and inspiration, shaping the direction of our work.

We would also like to express our gratitude to the National Centre for Research Methods (NCRM) and Methods North West (MNW) for their ongoing support and organization of Qualitative Diary Workshops that were instrumental to the development of this book.

We wish to thank the Sage academic reviewers for their thoughtful comments:

Jason R. Jolicoeur, *Minnesota State University Mankato*
Michael Kreiter, *Boise State University*
Amira Proweller, *DePaul University*
Lisa R. Roberts, *Loma Linda University*

And of course, this book—and indeed all our prior QDM-based publications—would not have been possible without the support and dedication of all the participants in our QDM research studies. We are deeply grateful to them for their willingness to engage with QDMs, to share their experiences, reflections, and journeys with us. We hope that we have honored their stories and that, because of their generosity, we are collectively able to contribute to forging a path toward more inclusive workplaces and societies.

ABOUT THE AUTHORS

Laura Radcliffe is a Reader in Organizational Behavior, an organizational psychologist and qualitative researcher with over 15 years of experience exploring the intersection of work, life, and inclusion. She specializes in theoretically driven research that combines psychological and sociological perspectives to examine how individuals navigate work and nonwork responsibilities, why they make particular choices, and the impact on their lives and employment. Through innovative qualitative methodologies that enable nuanced insights into daily practices, Laura provides in-depth analysis of lived experiences and unfolding processes. Her research has been published in leading academic journals and practitioner outlets, informing organizational policies and practices across the United Kingdom. Laura is the Director of the North West Social Science Doctoral Training Partnership (NWSSDTP), supporting cutting-edge research training for PGRs across the Northwest, and co-leads the Future Families Work network, championing inclusive, flexible, and future-ready workplaces.

Leighann Spencer is an Associate Professor of Organizational Behavior at the University of Liverpool Management School. Her research interests span the dark side of organizations and organizational life, as well as the entanglements of theory and practice. She has a keen interest in qualitative methodologies, notably questions of transparency in qualitative research and the use of qualitative diaries to conduct creative and processual research. Her research has been published in internationally leading journals in organizational behavior and management.

For Ryan, Ella, and Caelan

Laura Radcliffe

For Brian

Leighann Spencer

1

AN INTRODUCTION TO QUALITATIVE DIARY METHODS

This introductory chapter will provide a broad initial overview of qualitative diary methods, including what they are, how they have been used previously, and why their use in research is rapidly increasing. We will also cover motivations for using qualitative diary methods, why they are important, and when and why researchers might use them. This chapter also incorporates a checklist exercise to help you decide on, and be able to justify, the use of qualitative diary methods in your own research projects. By the end of this chapter, you should have a good understanding of what constitutes a qualitative diary and when and why you might use qualitative diary methods in your own research.

WHAT ARE QDMs?

When people think of qualitative diaries, they often initially think of a written, usually pen-and-paper, diary. However, qualitative diary methods (QDMs hereinafter), also known as solicited diaries (i.e., diaries that are written for a specific research purpose), are much more than this. In fact, QDMs are a versatile range of multimodal data collection methods that involve participants recording or capturing events and experiences, as well as associated emotions and reflections, "in the moment" (or closer to the moment than would otherwise be possible), on multiple occasions and over a particular time period.

This might indeed include the traditional, physical pen-and-paper diary, as well as other electronic modes of text-based diary keeping, such as word-processed and email diaries or, more recently, diaries shared via written blogs or text messages. Beyond this, however, they also include visual and multimodal ways in which we might seek participants to capture experiences in the moment and over time, such as photo-, video-, or even app-based diaries that allow for a range of modalities. Over the course of this book, we will cover the diversity of QDM options available to researchers, but first, within this initial chapter, we aim to provide an overview of QDM research, including how their use has evolved, and consider when and why you might seek to use QDMs within your own research projects.

A BRIEF HISTORY OF QDMs

Everyone is familiar with the concept of a diary, whether it is those we use to plan our time, recording daily meetings and to-do lists, or more extensive journals that we maintain to record our personal journeys, important life events, and associated reflections and emotions. As a student or educator, you may have experience completing and/or requesting diary or journal-based assignments, ever popular across education programs due to the acknowledgment that such reflective journals, "logs," or "personal development plans" encourage reflexivity, which has long been considered a vital component of student learning and development (e.g., Vinjamuri et al., 2017; Wallin & Adawi, 2018).

In research contexts, qualitative researchers themselves are likely to be highly accustomed to keeping research journals, with methodological guidance often suggesting that diary keeping by the researcher is an integral part of the qualitative research process. Diaries maintained by researchers similarly aim to encourage reflexivity, a topic that has been written about extensively in the qualitative methodological literature (e.g., Harvey, 2011; Nadin & Cassell, 2006), considered essential in enabling a greater critical awareness of researchers' own impact on the research process, therefore enhancing the quality of qualitative research (Johnson & Duberley, 2003; Nadin & Cassell, 2006). There is therefore a substantial body of research highlighting qualitative diaries as a useful and often important way to record and subsequently reflect on our own personal experiences, thus enabling us to learn more about ourselves, our experiences, our skills, knowledge, and ambitions, as well as our feelings, thoughts, behaviors, and decision-making processes. When we consider such well-researched benefits of, and outcomes associated with, the practice of journaling or keep a daily diary, it is fairly easy to consider how diaries completed by participants might have the potential to enable particularly insightful research.

However, when considering QDMs within the broader landscape of qualitative research methods, other key approaches have traditionally been more widely recognized, taught, and employed, each offering unique strengths and chosen based on the research question, context, and objectives. For instance, interviews are arguably the most commonly used qualitative method, enabling in-depth exploration of individual experiences and perspectives on a given topic (Cassell, 2015; Kvale & Brinkmann, 2009), alongside focus groups, which facilitate group discussions that can reveal collective views and the dynamics of interaction within a group (Morgan, 1996). Case studies are another popular approach, within which multiple qualitative methods may be employed, with a focus on a detailed examination of a single instance or a small number of instances, offering deep insights into complex phenomena (Yin, 2018). Ethnography similarly often involves multiple methods but with a predominant focus on immersive observation, which is traditionally conducted by the researcher, within a specific community or context, aiming to provide a detailed, holistic understanding of social practices and cultures (Hammersley & Atkinson, 2019; Madden, 2022). Interestingly, QDMs have been suggested to be particularly useful as part of a broader ethnographic approach (e.g., Zimmerman & Wieder, 1997), as we discuss later in this chapter.

QDMs thus occupy a unique position within this broader qualitative landscape. Unlike interviews or focus groups, which capture participants' reflections at specific points in time, QDMs provide continuous, real-time insights into participants' daily lives and experiences. This temporal dimension makes QDMs particularly valuable for understanding processes and changes over time, often offering a richer, more nuanced picture of the phenomena under study. Furthermore, diaries have been suggested to be less intrusive than traditional ethnographic observation (Zimmerman & Wieder, 1977), permitting participants themselves to document their own experiences, within their own time and space, potentially leading to more authentic data (Bolger et al., 2003) and a more participant-led design (e.g., O'Reilly et al., 2022). In fact, QDMs have also found a valuable place as part of participatory research designs, which emphasize collaboration and active involvement of participants in the research process (Hacker, 2013), as we discuss throughout this book.

Despite being less prominent across qualitative methods textbooks and course designs, diaries as a research method have been used since the very beginning of social science research and are, therefore, not a "new" method as such. Biographers and historians, for instance, have long judged diary documents (or "unsolicited diaries") to be of great importance for our historical understanding of social reality from the perspective of different actors (Corti, 1993). For example, the sociologist Frédéric Le Play (1806–1882) famously used diaries to collect information about family budgets, capturing earnings and expenditures, aiming to express the family's life in figures (Gobo & Mauceri, 2014). Relatedly, time-diary studies appear to date back to before 1900, with such early work focusing on describing social conditions and economic productivity (Bauman et al., 2019). Indeed, it has been reported that solicited diaries have been used in health care research as early as the 1930/1940s, proliferating in this field from the 1970s onward (e.g., Banks et al., 1975; Finkelstein et al., 1986; Follick et al., 1984; Lawson et al., 1985). Evidently, there has been a degree of sustained interest in capturing data via diaries completed by participants, or actors involved in the phenomena researchers are seeking to study, since the very beginnings of social science research.

In more recent social science history, interest in qualitative diary methods has stemmed from ethnographic approaches, in which participant observation is deemed integral to generate a thick description of ongoing social activities in their natural setting, as they occur (e.g., Moeran, 2009). Such detailed and ongoing observation, however, was recognized as highly demanding on the researcher and not always possible depending on the subject of focus (Zimmerman & Wieder, 1977). For instance, while particular organizational settings, such as the 9-to-5 workplace, may lend themselves to regular observation, regular and ongoing observation of a more dispersed group of actors within multiple personal settings (e.g., families) may prove more problematic. Further, the physical presence of the researcher has also been recognized by some as likely to have the potential to play a more disruptive role in terms of the capacity to significantly alter the behavior of the observed within research circumstances or settings in which their presence would be rendered particularly visible and intrusive (again, such as the home domain) (Becker, 1970; Zimmerman & Wieder, 1977). For instance, Zimmerman and Wieder (1977) draw upon an example from Skolnick (1967) to argue that, while the police are unlikely to be free to alter their daily behavior in the presence of a researcher, for example, when kicking in a door in a narcotics raid, an alternative project focused on the housewife enacting her daily work within the home may pose more challenges. Here, they suggest that the housewife (or househusband, or stay-at-home mum/dad to use more modern terminology), who may be frequently alone with their children, is likely to be particularly impacted by the presence of the researcher, which may lead to fairly extensive changes in behaviors. While such behavior change may be interesting to observe, if the focus of the study was on observing usual, mundane, daily practice, this is likely to become more challenging. Ethnographic researchers such as Zimmerman and Wieder (1997) therefore drew upon qualitative diary methods (e.g., the diary-interview approach, which will be discussed later in this book) to emulate close observation within settings in which this was challenging or not feasible. Here, we can again see why, in more recent social science research history, QDMs have also increasingly become invaluable as part of participatory research designs due to their potential to empower participants by allowing them to document their daily lives and experiences in their own words (e.g., Bartlett, 2012). This is evidently well aligned with the principles of participatory research, which aim to democratize the research process and reduce power imbalances between researchers and participants (Hacker, 2013). However, as we will also consider later in the book, the use of QDMs in which we are, in a sense, asking participants to become researchers themselves entails both benefits and challenges.

Despite this fairly long history of qualitative diary-based research, arguably, until recently, the popularity of QDMs has been fairly limited (Hilario & Augusto, 2023; Radcliffe, 2013, 2018), particularly when we consider this in comparison to other methods of collecting data that are frequently drawn upon as part of the qualitative researchers' toolkits, which, as discussed earlier, tend to include methods such as interviews, observation, and focus groups. This can be gleaned from a simple glance at the tables of contents of core research methods textbooks across the social sciences (e.g., Flick, 2022a; Willig & Stainton-Rogers, 2017) or a standard qualitative research methods course syllabus. This lack of training, instruction, or supportive guidance in the use of the broad range of data collection tools that constitute QDMs not only narrows the researcher's toolkit but also limits a more complex understanding of important topics across the social sciences. For instance, Rauch and Ansari (2022) recently highlighted the potential of QDMs for advancing scholarship around societal grand challenges, here focusing on their capacity to illuminate the innermost thoughts and feelings of people at the forefront of grand challenges and in extreme contexts, and to explore the lived daily realities and practicalities engendered within such contexts. Such research is arguably essential if we are to begin unraveling the complexities of sustained habitual practices that contribute in nuanced ways to the multiple, pressing grand challenges we face as a society today. Further, where researchers may come across QDMs themselves, in search of a data collection method more aligned with the aims of a particular research project, without clear guidance, this can be an extremely challenging undertaking with multiple questions, challenges, and complex ethical considerations along the way. In this book, we hope to go some way to addressing this gap, providing researchers with a practical guidebook for the design of their own QDM studies, as well as resources that researchers can use themselves to support this process but that could also be used by those leading postgraduate research training programs to enable better integration of QDMs into such programs.

Despite the apparent neglect of QDMs, there is evidence that they have also begun to rise in popularity. Initially, this was likely due to similar intensifying requirements for more innovative and temporally sensitive research designs across the social sciences (e.g., Radcliffe, 2018; Vantilborgh et al., 2018). As a result, in recent years, QDMs have been used to explore a variety of topics across the social sciences, from stress at work (Crozier & Cassell, 2015; Travers, 2011), helping at work (Fisher et al., 2018), and the interface of work and family (Lowson & Arber, 2014; Radcliffe & Cassell, 2015), to the lived experiences of female refugees (Linn, 2021) and homelessness (Karadzhov, 2021). They have been used to capture disabled young people's experiences of educational institutions (Gregorius, 2016), the educational decision-making (Baker, 2023) and employability practices of students (Cao & Henderson, 2021), and a variety of health behaviors and experiences (e.g., McClinchy et al., 2023; Mupambirey & Bernays, 2019).

Interestingly, the COVID-19 pandemic and sudden requirement for social distancing in many countries around the world (and thus, for researchers, viable remote research methods) has seemingly led to a further increase in the use of QDMs (e.g., Ashman et al., 2022; Bandini et al., 2021; Hennekam et al., 2021; Rudrum et al., 2022; Scott et al., 2021). As Soronen and Koivunen (2022) noted when conducting research during this time, their QDM data collection remained unaffected by the pandemic, whereas the interview elements of their project required revision in order to ensure they could be moved entirely online. The pandemic-friendly nature of QDMs led to a proliferation of such studies during this time, across diverse social science disciplines, from King and Dickinson (2023), who used mobile instant messaging diaries (see also Chapter 5) to examine the lived experiences of leisure practices during COVID-19 pandemic restrictions, to Scott et al. (2021), who used QDMs to investigate the impacts upon young people's mental health and emotional well-being during compulsory lockdowns.

It is therefore evident that, for a variety of reasons, the utility of QDMs is increasingly recognized, and while they have a long history in one form or another, their use in research projects across the social sciences is now on a rapid upward trajectory. With this in mind, alongside the rather limited practical guidance available for researchers who are interested in using QDMs, we now begin addressing this scarcity by next turning to a discussion and consideration of when and why you might use QDMs in your own research projects.

WHEN AND WHY SHOULD I USE QDMs?

As should now be evident, there are a wide variety of ways in which QDMs can be, and have been, used across a broad variety of disciplines and research areas. However, while they have become increasingly popular, and we are clearly advocates for their use owing to the rich, varied, insightful, and unique data they enable you to collect, it is important to keep in mind that QDMs are time-intensive methods of data collection. Therefore, as with any method, there should be a clear justification for their use. Indeed, as is always the case, the method(s) of data collection chosen for any research project should be led by your research question(s). So, in this case, how might you decide whether QDMs are relevant and useful for your own research study?

We will move on to discuss the many benefits of using QDMs, but when deciding whether QDMs are an appropriate data collection method for a particular research project, we suggest that you ask yourself the following two questions:

1. *To answer my research questions, is it important that I capture details of events/experiences/thoughts/emotions "in the moment"?*

One of the most frequently discussed benefits of using QDMs is that they enable participants to record the details and intricacies of their experiences and associated meaning-making "in the moment." Again, it is important to note that while researchers often refer to "in the moment" data capturing as a key benefit of QDMs, in practice, what this actually means is data captured temporally closer to the experience itself when compared with other popular data collection methods (Iida et al., 2012). For example, while interviews enable the collection of rich data and insightful retrospective reflections, and certainly remain a method that we frequently use ourselves (and often in conjunction with QDMs—see Chapter 2), existing research highlights that such retrospective approaches often lead to specific details being easily forgotten. An increasing body of literature from the cognitive sciences draws attention to the complexity of the recall process required when participants are asked to respond to retrospective questions (e.g., Schwarz & Oyserman, 2001). Retrospection can lead to lapses in memory around the specific details of experiences, thoughts, and feelings, which can be especially problematic for studies where the specific details surrounding particular experiences or events are important in answering research questions. In such cases, little useful or relevant information may be available to participants attempting to construct a response to such questions in retrospect. This may lead individuals to draw on personal theories or ideas regarding what they believe is likely to be the case (Christensen et al., 2003). Other research also suggests that there may be a propensity for state-congruent recall (e.g., Bower, 1981), where the participant's present mood can lead them to recollect particularly negative or positive instances. This might risk concealing other experiences that may be important or relevant to a more comprehensive understanding of the topic under study.

Similarly, it is often the case that, during interviews, more extreme examples of a particular phenomenon will be recalled, rather than those that are more representative of typical day-to-day experiences. For example, within Laura's own research, which focuses predominantly on the work–life interface and the impact of daily work–life experiences on (in)equalities in the workplace, she is more frequently interested in everyday work–life experiences, events, challenges, decisions, and emotions. Therefore, while she may sometimes be interested in the more exceptional events (e.g., what happens when we enter a government-enforced lockdown due to a pandemic), she is more often interested in understanding everyday family negotiations and occurrences. This might include instances as "mundane" as trying to leave work on time to collect children from childcare or deciding who takes a child's PE kit to school if they have forgotten it that day, particularly the thought processes, concerns, and challenges associated with these events. Of course, Laura can, and still does, ask about such topics during interviews but consistently finds a strong discrepancy in the level of detail participants are able to provide on such experiences during interviews as opposed to that which can be captured using QDMs. While participants might comment more generally in interviews that they do sometimes struggle to leave work on time to collect their children from childcare, using QDMs, we are much more likely to capture the complex decision-making process and associated internal (and external) negotiations and emotions that regularly accompany such a daily experience. QDMs, therefore, enable richer insight into momentary occurrences and the daily impact they have on participants' lives.

During retrospective data collection, the recall of past events may also be distorted based on knowledge of subsequent events and their outcomes (Robinson & Clore, 2002). For instance, in the moment, you might have considered something to be a bad idea, experiencing strong concerns, worries, and anxieties, as well as exploring other options. However, if this actually all worked out quite well in the end, you might later forget or play down earlier concerns and report the experience as more generally positive, without an appreciation for the more complex journey that was involved in realizing that idea.

Of course, how people reconstruct their versions of reality after the event is often useful and interesting in itself, and where this is the particular focus of your project, interviews are a particularly useful approach. Similarly, where the focus is on reflecting back on larger scale or particularly pertinent prior events or occurrences that do not occur on a daily basis or are no longer occurring, employing QDMs is unlikely to be the most useful approach for your study. However, where the phenomena of interest are ongoing, occurring regularly, and perhaps more mundane, qualitative diary data provide us with a different and additionally insightful kind of data, where in the moment, recall reduces the degree to which participants are able to construct a cohesive narrative. For instance, in Laura's research investigating work–family decision-making in heterosexual dual-earner parents, couples often reported during interviews that they made work–family decisions just because it was what they both wanted. They might even suggest that this simply "just happened," with little decision-making involved, and they also quite frequently suggest that they share work and care rather equally. However, when data are collected on this topic using QDMs, it becomes clear that narratives provided within interviews are often much neater, post-hoc rationalizations of experiences and interpretations that were actually much more complex and nuanced in daily practice. For example, when work–family decision-making is examined using QDMs, we tend to find that couples rarely share care-related tasks equally despite good intentions and that daily work–family decisions are much more complex and emotion-laden than suggested in interviews and often heavily constrained by external challenges (e.g., mothers feeling more able to access flexible working arrangements than fathers; mothers struggle with perceived judgments of other mothers if they are not the ones more actively engaged in daily childcare). Using QDMs has, therefore, enabled us to attain a more complex understanding of how daily work–family events are experienced and navigated in the moment—for instance, gaining novel insights into the role that prior decision-making has on subsequent decision-making and the complex emotions and circumstances involved in deciding how to respond to particular daily challenges (e.g., Radcliffe & Cassell, 2014, 2015; Radcliffe et al., 2023).

In this sense, QDMs lend themselves to capturing the more specific and fine-grained details of daily experiences closer to the experience itself. They enable the collection of more detailed descriptions of the discrete and fleeting moments of everyday life and thereby how different thoughts, possibilities, and emotions interact in that moment, the details of which could easily be forgotten later. QDMs therefore offer real potential in terms of their ability to capture novel insights into often taken for granted, yet meaningful, daily practices, activities, and experiences in their local and temporal context.

2. *To answer my research questions, is it important that I capture how experiences/thoughts/emotions/interpretations change (or sometimes remain stable) over time?*

In addition to the abovementioned, most frequently cited benefit of QDMs in reducing retrospection, another core benefit of QDMs is their ability to capture change (or stability) over time. Not only are they able to capture change over time in terms of observing fluctuations in specific variables, as is the case when researchers employ quantitative diary methods (e.g., Beattie & Griffin, 2014; Hoprekstad et al., 2019), qualitative diary methods are also able to capture contextual and relational details of unfolding processes that provide insight into how one event or experience may influence subsequent events and experiences (Herschovis & Reich, 2013; Spencer et al., 2021).

Such longitudinal or "shortitudinal" data collection tied to QDMs also lends itself to additional comparative approaches. First, QDMs readily permit within-person comparison over time, enabling insights into how, when, and why participants may experience similar events in different ways on different occasions and why this might be the case. Research demonstrates that there is substantial variation in people's daily experiences, including their moods, emotions, experiences, and interactions with others (e.g., Bolger et al., 1989; Eckenrode, 1984; van Eerde et al., 2005). Rather than collecting data at one specific point in time, QDMs therefore enable us to examine unfolding processes and within-person variations. In this way, QDMs allow us to capture the influence of temporal context on within-person changes over time by, for instance, demonstrating the impact of past experiences on subsequent experiences.

For example, in the context of Laura's research, previous literature has highlighted somewhat contradictory results regarding the benefits of organizational flexible working policies and practices, with some studies reporting that flexible working arrangements actually increase, rather than alleviate, conflicts between family and work (Hammer et al., 2005; Lapierre & Allen, 2006). Employing qualitative diaries, Laura also found that those who used flexible working experienced more frequent work–family conflicts (Radcliffe & Cassell, 2015). However, what previous studies had not shown was the longer-term daily impact on the employees themselves and subsequently the organization of these conflicts. Laura's research demonstrated how a lack of flexibility continued to negatively impact participants some time after the conflict event due to the constraints this put on subsequent daily decision-making. Although a lack of flexibility at work often meant that participants were more likely to take part in the work event at the expense of family responsibilities, when faced with a work–family conflict, the "shortitudinal" nature of QDMs enabled Laura to show how such constrained decision-making often led to further challenges on subsequent days. For example, one participant reported experiencing constraints placed upon her decision-making by an inflexible work context that prevented her from being able to start work at 10 a.m. rather than 9 a.m. on an occasion when she was required to work away from home. Her concern about this situation continued to impact her both at work and in her personal life over subsequent diary days. Laura was therefore able to demonstrate the impact that imposing such constraints on decision-making can have over time. Beyond this, the necessity to continuously make decisions under such constraints was shown to lead to individuals leaving their organization or intending to do so (Radcliffe & Cassell, 2015). In this way, capturing immediate, and not so immediate, outcomes are important in terms of understanding the bigger picture. A within-person analysis enables the exploration of both practical and emotional outcomes over numerous days, often leading to deeper insights, here in terms of emotions and the impact that these emotions have on a person over time. The more in-depth recall of specific events and related feelings enabled by the use of QDMs permits the mapping of the impact of such emotions on events occurring on subsequent days. In this way, QDMs particularly lend themselves to examining within-person change over time, providing insights into the ways in which specific events and experiences are inextricably linked to previous and subsequent events, providing an opportunity to capture and explore these links in a way that many other methods are not able to.

Second, QDMs further enable a temporally sensitive and process-orientated, between-person comparison in terms of permitting an examination of how and why processes might proceed or evolve in similar or different ways for different people over time. This, therefore, enables exploration of these multifaceted links in a way that is often limited using other methods. For example, in Leighann's research exploring how experiences of mistreatment at work emerge and evolve over time, QDMs were particularly useful in enabling her to understand the day-to-day experiences of mistreatment, which in turn led to the identification of short-term "rhythms of mistreatment" at work. For example, over the short term, some participants' diaries reported "step-like" patterns that reflected gradual deterioration or improvement of the mistreatment, compared to participants who recorded "zigzag" rhythms, reflecting more frequent daily variations in their experiences, permitting a novel understanding of the impact of these different patterns of experience (see Spencer et al., 2021).

QDMs therefore harness the depth and richness of qualitative data captured in the moment, alongside the "breadth" afforded by adopting a longitudinal approach, which allows a detailed exploration of how (and why) things change over time. We refer to this as the capacity of QDMs to collect rich qualitative data that enable us to capture both the "down" (i.e., in-depth reflections in the moment) and "across" (i.e., change over time) of participants' experiences. Therefore, reflecting on these two questions should enable you to consider the extent to which QDMs are suited to your research project. It may be that capturing experiences in the moment, or temporally closer to an experience or event (i.e., the "down" of QDMs), is essential to be able to provide in-depth answers to your research questions. However, change over time (i.e., the "across" of QDMs) might not be particularly pertinent. Alternatively, you may find that change over time is especially relevant to your research questions or, as may often be the case, that both elements are useful and relevant for your study. Either way, it is important to remember why you made the decision to use QDMs in the first place (i.e., whether this was to capitalize on the "down" and/or the "across" affordances of QDMs), as this will (or should) influence the way in which you analyze your qualitative diary data, as we will go on to discuss in Chapter 7.

While these two benefits of QDMs are arguably the most well known and frequently discussed and are particularly important in deciding whether to use QDMs in your own projects, there are further important benefits of QDMs also worth considering:

QDMs as a Participant-Led Approach

First, since researchers are usually not present during the data collection process, QDMs are argued to be a participant-led approach (e.g., Bartlett, 2012; Hayes et al., 2024; O'Reilly et al., 2022), thereby well aligned with participatory research (Hacker, 2013), empowering participants by giving them control over the research process with the potential to overcome, at least to some extent, researcher/researched power relations (Hayes et al., 2024). In using QDMs to record their experiences without the presence of the researcher, the power to decide what to include lies with the participant and not with the researcher. Further, it removes the pressure that might be experienced by participants from the physical presence of the researcher during other data collection methods, such as interviews, and related demands of maintaining a particular flow of conversation (Monrouxe, 2009). While this also leads to some particular challenges, as we will discuss in Chapter 2, research suggests that participants feel empowered to share thoughts, ideas, and challenges that might often not be shared so readily within other research contexts (e.g., interviews/focus groups) (Busby, 2000).

Hayes et al. (2024), studying international students during the enforced lockdowns instigated by the COVID-19 pandemic, discussed multimodal QDMs as affording a more inclusive data collection methodology, offering a decolonial methodological praxis, by enabling researchers to research with international students rather than about them. They point out how much existing research "on" international students positions the researcher as the only legitimate producer of knowledge, frequently leading to the adoption of a deficit framing and attempts to "fix a problem." Rather than the research being conducted by outsiders and positioning participants as objects of study, they discuss how their particular use of QDMs enabled a participant-led alternative to ethnography, which acted upon the assumption that participants are powerful agents of their own experience and the ultimate experts, enabling them to explore and express their own systems of meanings and interpretations.

Relatedly, Islam (2015) introduces the notion of para-ethnography within participant-led research to explicate the way in which participants, while not in practice "ethnographers," do take an active role in collecting research data and become involved in building their own theories about their experiences, thoughts, decisions, or actions. In this way, they offer insights from the inside-out, rather than from the outside-in, drawing on an intimate knowledge of their own context or culture in a way that enhances collaboration between the researcher and the researched. Given that research participants using QDMs are involved in collecting data on a particular topic without the presence of the researcher and over a period of time, which certainly may lead to their own deeper reflections and theory building, the term *para-ethnography* seems apt when discussing QDM research. Indeed, referring back to our discussion earlier in this chapter, regarding earlier interest in qualitative diary methods stemming from ethnographic approaches (Zimmerman & Wieder, 1977), we can see how QDMs offer a rather different way to engage in participant observation but here through the eyes of, and therefore led by, the participants themselves, thereby also aligning with a more participatory research approach.

QDMs as a Method for Sensitive Research

Relatedly, researchers employing QDMs to examine particularly sensitive topics have suggested that such a participant-led approach, and in particular one that is predominantly private, without the presence of the researcher, can be highly beneficial (e.g., Dawson et al., 2016; Elliot, 1997). For instance, Elliot (1997), in the context of examining sensitive topics in relation to health and illness, highlights that QDMs work particularly well as participants have the freedom and control to edit, share, and discard their diary writings as and when they want. In her research examining mistreatment at work, Leighann also found that having a degree of distance between the researcher and participant, as permitted by the use of QDMs (particularly where QDMs are used alone, see Chapter 2), enabled participants who were feeling particularly vulnerable to express how they were feeling more openly in a diary, without any requirement to speak directly to another person about the challenging experiences they were facing.

In this way, QDMs can, in some circumstances, enable access to harder-to-reach samples, wherein the nature of the topic focus means that some participants may be more likely to take part when they are not required to meet with a researcher face-to-face, whether physically or virtually. In other senses, QDMs are also adept at accessing participants who may be difficult to reach for other reasons, such as those who are geographically dispersed. Considering the aforementioned challenges of traditional ethnographic research and participant observation in such contexts, QDMs lend themselves to a more remote-friendly mode of data collection wherein the research requires some form of "observation" or ongoing engagement with participants within their lived contexts. This utility also offers an explanation for the rapid rise of QDMs during the COVID-19–instigated lockdown, where other such methods often became impossible, and more remote-friendly approaches to data collection were required. Indeed, in certain disciplines, it has been noted that QDMs are in fact popular in research on and/or during pandemics and epidemics more broadly, not limited to COVID-19, but also during particular outbreaks of foot-and-mouth disease and HIV (Thomas, 2006, 2007). For instance, their particular value for distanced research and their capacity to capture fluctuations during "disasters," not only during pandemics but also during other natural disasters such as earthquakes, has been noted (Mueller et al., 2023). In this sense, QDMs are particularly useful for conducting remote research, which may be especially pertinent to consider in the face of pandemics, epidemics, and natural disasters, as well as when trying to attain insights into hard-to-reach communities (e.g., Filep et al., 2015).

QDMs as a Reflexive Method

A further increasingly acknowledged benefit of using QDMs is the way in which they instigate participant reflexivity, defined as "the reflexive considerations of research participants that are stimulated by their involvement in research" (Cassell et al., 2020, p. 750). Cassell et al. (2020) argue that the context of a research study is one in which reflexive thinking is likely to occur, not just for the researcher who is actively encouraged to engage in reflexivity but also for the participants who are part of this study. This is particularly the case when the research is longitudinal in nature and when there is an element of the research that participants are asked to engage in without the presence of the researcher, where they have greater control over the data collected. Considering discussions above regarding the participant-led nature of QDMs and the inherent longitudinality, alongside a broader awareness of the way in which diaries encourage reflexivity in other contexts (e.g., for researchers or for our students), it is therefore not surprising that QDMs are considered particularly adept at encouraging in-depth participant reflections on the topic of study. Encouraging and accessing participant reflexivity can have clear benefits for researchers, enabling a more in-depth, nuanced, and rich understanding of our research topic, and enabling both participant and researcher reflexive thinking to be part of data collection and analysis processes (Cassell et al., 2020). In this sense, accounting for the participants' standpoint when analyzing data encourages greater focus on QDM projects as co-research environments where "researchers and informants [are] working together as a team to co-produce knowledge" (Takhar & Chitakunye, 2012, p. 932). These perspectives emphasize that richer and more nuanced interpretations may be achieved by gaining an insight into the reflexivity of our participants. Reflexivity is also well documented as having positive therapeutic outcomes and being important for personal learning and development (e.g., Hibbert & Cunliffe, 2015; Moon, 2013; Suedfeld & Pennebaker, 1997; Symon, 2004; cf. our discussion in Chapter 2 of potential cautions surrounding instigating participant reflexivity). For example, in her study exploring how young people make decisions about higher education, Baker (2021) explains how, through her qualitative diary study, respondents found the diaries to be an active tool to enhance their decision-making process, something she interprets as a positive and insightful outcome of the research. Therefore, perhaps unsurprisingly, numerous studies employing QDMs also refer to the therapeutic effects expressed by participants (e.g., Bartlett, 2012; Milligan et al., 2005; Progoff, 1992; Radcliffe, 2013, 2018; Suedfeld & Pennebaker, 1997), including, for instance, those who are recovering from illness (Furness & Garrud, 2010;

Milligan et al., 2005). In this way, qualitative research diaries also have the potential to positively impact participants by encouraging self-reflection, self-awareness and subsequent learning, development, and change.

In Laura's research, she also found that participants frequently express how the process of engaging with QDMs "was really useful actually . . . it feels a bit like self-therapy," due to increased self-awareness, encouraging them to "think more about what I actually do" and enabling them to "analyse my motives." In couple-level studies, others also expressed a growing awareness of their partner's roles and responsibilities, "realising more what the demands are on each other." For some participants, this even instigated behavior change. For example, one participant, who worked from home, realized that a great deal of his daily stress emanated from trying to engage in work and home roles simultaneously, explaining, "It causes stress doing something and then going back and checking my emails and then doing something so I'm not doing it anymore." Another participant even discussed how her reflections, instigated by engaging with QDMs, led to in-depth discussions with her partner (who was not a participant in this particular study) about each of their work roles and desires, which actually caused him to seek changes to his work. This further demonstrates the potentially far-reaching consequences of the way in which QDMs influence reflexivity over time potentially even for those who are not directly involved with the research itself. In this sense, it has been acknowledged that diaries can be used not only as a research tool but also as an intervention having the capacity to enable reflection and raise consciousness about a particular topic, allowing a deeper understanding and space for thinking and acting on change (Alford et al., 2005; Plowman, 2010; Radcliffe, 2018).

CONCLUSION

In summary, in this chapter, we have provided an introduction to QDMs, what they are, and also a brief history of their use in social science research. We have considered when and why QDMs might (not) be useful within your own research projects, which involved an introduction to some of the main benefits and affordances of QDMs. Below you will find a checklist based on this discussion to help you think further about whether QDMs are appropriate for your current project and to help you structure a rationale for their use. We hope that having engaged with this introductory chapter, you now have a good general understanding of QDMs. In the next chapter, we will aim to provide a more practical knowledge of how to design your own QDM study, including how to tackle typical challenges and ethical dilemmas faced along the way. This includes a discussion of examples from our own research, and the various research projects of our PhD students, to support further understanding and formulation of project ideas.

> **APPLICATION ACTIVITY**
> **SHOULD I USE QDMS IN MY RESEARCH PROJECT?**
>
> While we are evidently strong advocates for the use of QDMs and the benefits they bring to a wide range of research projects, as we discussed in this introductory chapter, methodological choices should always emanate directly from, and align with, your project research questions. It is also important to consider your target sample and the context of your research more broadly.
>
> The following checklist is designed to help you to start to think about whether QDMs are appropriate for your study but also to have something physical to look back at, and reflect on, when developing and writing up the justifications in your methodological choices within ethics applications, funding bids, and within the Methodology section of your final project write-up.

QDM METHODOLOGICAL EVALUATION CHECKLIST

Project considerations: Is a QDM study suitable?	Y/N
Does your project require you to capture events/experiences in the moment? (e.g., Are there momentary details that are needed that might be difficult to recall at later time points? Are experiences ongoing?) N.B. *If your research involves reflection on prior events that are no longer ongoing, QDMs may be less likely to be useful or appropriate.* AND/OR Does your project require you to capture events/experiences/processes over time? (e.g., Do your research questions focus on how "things" may change (or not) over time?) N.B. *If your research is not concerned with how an ongoing experience or occurrence changes overtime, consider whether QDMs are necessary.*	
Is a participant-led research approach suitable and/or needed for your research? (e.g., Would participants benefit from being able to recall experiences in the absence of the researcher?)	
Is a participant-led research approach suitable for your research? (e.g., Would participants benefit from being able to recall experiences in the absence of the researcher? Is understanding the phenomena through the eyes of participants key?)	

(Continued)

(Continued)

Project considerations: Is a QDM study suitable?	Y/N
Is it appropriate, and feasible, to ask your participants to maintain engagement and continue to reflect on their experiences/events that are of interest to your research project? (e.g., Is enhanced and ongoing participation and commitment from your participants feasible?)	
Do you have the time and resources necessary to collect and analyze voluminous qualitative data? *N.B. If you are conducting a short-term research project spanning only a few months, with a quick required turnaround, QDMs may not be feasible.*	

FURTHER READING

Cassell, C., Radcliffe, L., & Malik, F. (2020). Participant reflexivity in organizational research design. *Organizational Research Methods*, *23*(4), 750–773. https://doi.org/10.1177/1094428119842640

Radcliffe, L. (2018). Capturing the complexity of daily workplace experiences using qualitative diaries. In C. Cassell, A. L. Cunliffe, & G. Grandy (Eds.), *The SAGE handbook of qualitative business and management research methods* (pp. 188–204). Sage.

Zimmerman, D. H., & Wieder, D. L. (1977). The diary: Diary-interview method. *Urban Life*, *5*(4), 479–498. https://doi.org/10.1177/089124167700500406

2

DESIGNING QDMs

Addressing Challenges and Ethical Dilemmas

(Coauthored With Hannah Musiyarira)

This chapter will provide a practical insight into the process of preparing and conducting a QDM associated challenges, as well as provide guidance on how to address each of these. It will begin by considering appropriate approaches to sampling, recruiting, and subsequently retaining participants in QDM studies before considering different QDM diary designs and how these may best align with different research questions. It will also consider the benefits and challenges of using QDMs as part of a broader multimethod study and will provide practical advice on how to consider the management of data overload at the design stage. Finally, it will examine ethical issues particularly relevant to QDM studies and how to manage these at the design stage and beyond. The application activity at the end of this chapter will include a diary design worksheet that readers can complete to carefully consider the design of their own research projects based on the contents of this chapter. By the end of this chapter, readers will have a good understanding of the different practical considerations to think about when designing their own QDM study, including ethical issues and how to plan for some of the key challenges associated with QDMs.

In this chapter, we will take you step-by-step through the QDM study design process, discussing challenges at each stage and some of the different ways we have addressed these challenges across different diary projects. We are writing this chapter collectively with Hannah Musiyarira, an ESRC-funded PhD student whose research focuses on understanding the experience of people with long-term health conditions in the workplace, particularly how they make regular decisions regarding whether, when, and how to work when experiencing health challenges, as well as the ongoing impact of these decisions on their wellbeing. By drawing on Leighann and Laura's experiences across projects over time and drawing on QDM research more broadly, as well as Hannah's current experiences as someone who is presently navigating the benefits and challenges of designing and engaging with qualitative diary research, we aim to provide those of you who are new to QDM research with a range of useful suggestions that will help you on that journey. We will begin at the beginning by first considering sampling strategies and approaches useful for QDM studies.

SAMPLING FOR QDMs

Sampling is undoubtedly one of the most challenging aspects of QDM research. Researchers may therefore quite reasonably approach QDMs with some apprehension, fearing challenges may arise in acquiring and maintaining participants due to the level of commitment required (Bolger et al., 2003). While these concerns are justifiable and should encourage researchers to ensure that diaries are, indeed, the most appropriate method to answer their research questions (see Chapter 1), there are a number of approaches to support you in minimizing these challenges. As with many other methods within social science research, a carefully thought-out plan to locate and recruit participants, informed by a research question(s), is key (see also Hyers, 2018).

The plan to recruit participants should, of course, be informed by the focus of the research, both in terms of the type of participants required and the proposed sample size for the diary element of your study. For example, which groups and individuals should the researcher engage to answer their research question (Alaszewski, 2006)? Often for QDM studies, researchers are aiming to recruit participants who have experience with the phenomenon or behavior they are interested in. Patton (2002) suggests that what we are aiming to explore must also influence our sample size; however, as with all research, issues surrounding what will be deemed credible and what resources are available also play a major part in how many diary participants will be appropriate.

Before moving on to explore the most common sampling methods employed for qualitative diaries, it is perhaps appropriate here to acknowledge that ontological and epistemological orientations will determine both what the researcher is hoping to achieve via their sample and the role of each participant within the diary study. For example, Saunders (2012) emphasizes that certain ontological positions, such as those more aligned with interpretivist positions, would suggest the need for a representative sample to be inappropriate. Researchers with such views would tend to use nonprobability sampling techniques (nonrandom), an approach most common within QDM research. With that being said, it is possible to collect data for qualitative analysis where the participants have been chosen at random (probability sampling); this sampling technique eliminates the researcher's judgment in terms of selecting participants (Kvale & Brinkmann, 2009; Saunders, 2012).

As emphasized, however, in most cases, qualitative research relies on nonprobability sampling techniques to select participants with the research aims in mind throughout. When doing so, Hyers (2018) argues that the role of participants within the diary study must be considered, depending on the researcher's epistemological position. For example, participants may be characterized as informants who provide the researcher with details of their experience. In other cases, where research designs are more participatory, they may be viewed more as coinvestigators who work in collaboration with the researcher (see also Hayes et al., 2024). All of these considerations are included here to emphasize the importance of not only approaching sampling with a clear view of the research aims but also understanding the ontological and epistemological underpinnings of the research to establish requirements from and expectations placed on the participants who will be recruited and the most appropriate way to recruit them.

As one of the biggest challenges in terms of participant recruitment is locating individuals willing to commit to qualitative diaries, it can be useful to begin by using relevant personal contacts and connections wherever possible (Radcliffe, 2013, 2018). It is often noted in existing diary literature that participants are more likely to agree to take part in a study if they have had personal contact with the researcher themselves (Bolger et al., 2003; Radcliffe, 2013). For this reason, convenience sampling can be an appropriate and justifiable approach, whereby the researcher uses their own personal networks and contacts to attain an initial small sample of QDM participants. From this point, snowball sampling can be particularly effective and is, therefore, one of the most common sampling strategies used in QDM research (Radcliffe, 2018).

Snowball sampling involves a participant who has already taken part in the study recruiting members of their network to also take part in the research. This can often occur when a participant has developed an interest in the study and can identify others who may fit the selection criteria (Hyers, 2018). This can be a particularly useful approach as those who have already engaged in the diary, and often found being involved in the research interesting and insightful (Cassell et al., 2020; Radcliffe, 2018), can share their experience of taking part with others in their network, which can garner further interest (Radcliffe, 2018). For instance, in Laura's research with dual-earner couples with children, she began by sharing her recruitment advert on Facebook among existing contacts and connections. From here, a few individuals expressed interest in taking part and discussed this with their partners, which led to the recruitment of two couples initially. Once these couples had taken part, Laura discussed with them how they had found the process and also whether they would be happy to ask relevant others in their network if they might be interested in taking part, reminding them of the inclusion criteria. Throughout the course of recruitment, some participants offered to share this with others, without Laura even needing to ask, often because they had enjoyed the experience or found it useful, could think of relevant others who might be willing to take part, and due to a desire to further support the research. At this point, following interviews and diary engagement over time, a strong rapport is often built with participants, and they also become interested and somewhat invested in the research, which can result in a desire to support further recruitment efforts.

It is important to note here that both types of sampling discussed above are subject to criticisms (e.g., Bell et al., 2022; Biernacki & Waldorf, 1981), particularly with regard to the associated risk of attaining a largely homogeneous sample. However, while it is important to reflect on potential implications of homogeneity in your sample when writing up your findings and considering limitations, this can be justified in cases where challenges in recruitment would otherwise risk preventing valuable data from being collected. For instance, this approach has previously been suggested to be useful and appropriate when seeking access to hard-to-reach samples (Radcliffe et al., 2022; Saunders, 2012) and also more generally where the data would otherwise be difficult to attain, as is often the case with QDM data (e.g., Radcliffe & Cassell, 2014).

It is also important to carefully consider your research aims when designing your sampling strategy and keep in mind instances when the potential homogeneity of your sample may be particularly problematic. For instance, if a vital element of your research project requires recruiting a diverse group of participants, it will be important to consider a more purposeful element to your sampling approach alongside other sampling strategies mentioned above. Here, Saunders (2012) suggests the use of purposive sampling, whereby the researcher uses their judgment to select participants with diverse characteristics to provide as much variation as possible within a data set. Such a purposeful approach often requires being responsive and strategic throughout the recruitment process—for instance, considering where recruitment adverts are shared, as well as intermittently taking stock of the diversity of your sample so far, and subsequently considering different tactics to ensure the diversity you are seeking. Building elements of purposive sampling into your sampling strategy alongside convenience and snowball sampling can also be useful to address some of these challenges. For instance, in their study exploring the intimate lives of asexual people, Dawson et al. (2016) sought to attain daily diaries completed over a 2-week period from both members of a couple. Aware that initial recruitment strategies focusing upon a particular relevant network may risk their participants aligning predominantly with the typical demographics of previous studies (primarily well-educated, middle-class, white, American females), they sought to diversify their sample, by also employing a purposive sampling strategy. They purposefully targeted individuals who did not fit this demographic by using a variety of recruitment efforts, including writing an article for popular media about their research and posting notices in public spaces particularly likely to reach other groups, before being selective of the final number of participants included in the study, keeping demographic diversity in mind. Relatedly, during Hannah's recruitment process, her focus on long-term health conditions led her to recognize the need to capture the nuanced experiences of individuals with both physical and mental health challenges. She employed tailored advertisements, adjusting wording slightly for different platforms—using broader language like "long-term health condition" on social media but specific terms like "chronic" on support pages. This approach highlighted the subjectivity of individual identification, particularly with labels like "disability," ensuring broader outreach and acknowledging diverse perceptions of health conditions (see also Budworth, 2023). Targeted adverts allowed Hannah to be responsive to various sampling needs, for example, to capture both on-site and hybrid/home workers. Therefore, convenience sampling is often used in conjunction with other sampling techniques, which may be iterative in nature and should always strive to align with your research aims.

This combination of approaches (i.e., convenience, snowball, and purposive sampling) can be particularly useful for diary studies whereby cases are difficult to identify. With the increase in the use of social media sites such as Twitter and LinkedIn, researchers can use the convenience element of their personal networks while concurrently taking a more purposeful approach by being explicit about the selection criteria for the study and allowing members of their networks to self-select based on these criteria. In addition to this, snowball sampling, rather than relying solely on participants' recommendations, requires judgment from the researcher to determine whether or not participants are eligible for inclusion and align with the goals of the study (Bell et al., 2022). Importantly, when it comes to recruiting for QDM studies, it is often useful to employ a variety of different sampling strategies to achieve your desired sample and to be sure to build adequate time into overall study design to permit this.

Whichever sampling technique or approach to choosing cases is adopted within a QDM study, the level of commitment required can make it more challenging to achieve an extensive sample. In this case, it can be useful to consider how many participants you actually need to recruit onto the QDM element of your diary study. Depending on your philosophical underpinnings and the publication standards and expectations associated with your particular field of research, there exists strong justification for smaller samples in QDM studies (e.g., Gregorius, 2016; Sudbury-Riley, 2014; Thompson, 2023; Zundel et al., 2018) based on their longitudinal or at least "shortitudinal" nature and relatedly the extensive data that will be obtained. For instance, Chen et al. (2022) discuss analyzing 205 online written diary (blogs) entries from 12 frontline nurses during the COVID-19 pandemic. Consider, therefore, that depending on your approach, it may be that participants are not the unit of analysis but rather that particular "events" are the focus (e.g., Radcliffe & Cassell, 2014). In this case, even where participant numbers are fewer, the number of events for analysis will likely be substantial.

For those grappling with particular expectations of journals with regards to larger sample sizes, even when it comes to qualitative research grounded in interpretivist traditions, you may consider that QDMs are often used alongside other methods (see "Using QDMs With Other Methods" section), such as interviews, where larger samples could be tackled with interview data, with a smaller subsample asked to keep diaries (e.g., Crozier & Cassell, 2016; Radcliffe et al., 2022; Smith et al., 2013; Spencer et al., 2022). In the case of attaining a broader sample of interview participants (or similar) and a smaller subsample of those engaging with QDMs, this also opens up additional recruitment strategies. For instance, using "interviews as a gateway" can be a particularly useful strategy, wherein participants who engage in an initial interview stage of the study are, where relevant (e.g., if they have ongoing experience of the phenomenon under investigation), subsequently invited to participate in a second QDM stage. By using this strategy, you provide the opportunity for rapport building and the important "personal contact" (Bolger et al., 2003), often deemed necessary for QDM sampling, during the preliminary interview stage of the study. For example, Hannah employed interviews as a gateway to select a proportion of her diary participants, a process contingent upon participants' demonstrated interest in the research, alignment with sampling criteria, and a nurtured rapport. Emphasizing the voluntary nature of the study was key here to ensure no participants felt obligated to take part. However, a number of interested participants emerged, driven by their personal resonance with the topic and a heartfelt appreciation for the opportunity to openly share their experiences within a supportive space. This was part of a dual-route recruitment process, taking place in addition to a separate call for diary-only participants using adverts shared on social media and support groups.

Drawing on a combination of the above strategies, in line with your own research aims, should help you to attain the sample you need for your QDM study. Of course, after you have worked hard to obtain your sample, the next important challenge to consider is participant retention over the course of your QDM project. In the next section, we will explore potential reasons for participant dropout in QDM research, challenges around data loss, and, importantly, how these risks can be reduced.

PARTICIPANT RETENTION AND ENGAGEMENT

It is no surprise that retention rates for QDMs are often lower than those for other forms of qualitative data collection since researchers are asking for repeated responses over a period of time, as opposed to a single point in time (e.g., one-off interview or focus group). This evidently places an additional burden on those taking part, which should be acknowledged (Bolger et al., 2003). The groups targeted in your research should also be considered carefully in the design of your diary and in your retention strategies. For instance, are your participants likely to have busy schedules or limited spare time, or will ongoing engagement be particularly emotionally or physically taxing for this group? This can be further addressed in considering the mode of QDM used as we will go on to discuss in subsequent chapters, but it is evidently also important to keep this in mind when considering, and preparing for, retention rates and appropriate supports that can be put in place to make the experience of engaging in your QDM project as easy, flexible, and enjoyable as possible. Therefore, while it is often recommended to aim for a higher number of participants than your planned sample size to account for participants who leave the study (Plowman, 2010), this may be more pertinent in some samples than others. For instance, in Laura's research with employed single parents (and even with busy dual-earner couple parents), the dropout rate, as well as the regularity with which the diary would be maintained, was considered fairly high risk, thereby increasing the importance of reaching out to a larger sample than would actually be required.

Relatedly, it is important to think carefully about the length of time for which you are requesting participants to keep the diary and how frequently you are asking them to record an entry. As with most methodological decisions, this should be based on the research questions you are seeking to answer. Ask yourself, for how long do I need participants to complete the diary to ensure that I will capture sufficient data to answer my research questions? Consider your answer to this question alongside deliberation about the appropriateness of the commitment you are seeking from your participant group. Decisions around the length of the diary study should usually seek to balance these two important issues. Further, it is also important to consider how frequently you will require participants to make an entry to enable you to answer your research questions. For instance, if you are seeking diary entries more regularly than once a day (e.g., event-contingent designs), the chances are that you might be able to reduce the overall length of the study as there will have been more opportunity to collect sufficient data to answer your research questions, alongside considerations regarding participant fatigue and what it is reasonable to ask your participants to commit to for the purpose of your research. Alternatively, if you need to seek diary completion over a much longer period in order to be able to answer your research questions—for instance, if you are seeking to investigate change over a particular period of transition (such as the transition to parenthood)—it is likely to be less appropriate or feasible to expect participants to keep a daily diary (not to mention that you would likely collect more data than you are actually able to analyze! See Chapter 6). Considerations about diary length and frequency of recording are therefore intertwined with the need to reflect on the two concurrently. Regardless of the duration or frequency of diary completion, Hyers (2018) argues that incentive for a diary study is particularly important, suggesting that some kind of compensation is necessary due to time commitments and, often, having to bring materials or correspondence into their everyday space. Hyers recommends that rewarding participants should not be so great it seems coercive but something to be considered by researchers should they have the means to do so, particularly if recruiting participants from a group who may be unable or unlikely to volunteer otherwise. A pertinent point to note here is that incentivization need not always be monetary and, depending on what is most appropriate for your sample or feasible within your own resources, could also offer a focus on an important social issue, the chance to gain skills, or the therapeutic benefits that come with diary keeping. In Hannah's research, monetary incentivization in the form of a voucher was deemed appropriate and was available via her funding route. It was important to acknowledge that offering financial incentives has the potential to impact the type of participants volunteering for the study and their reasons for doing so. However, Hannah felt it important to acknowledge the commitment of participants, who are likely to be individuals with busy work schedules who face daily challenges navigating their work and personal lives alongside a long-term health condition. As such, diary participants were eligible for a £5 e-voucher for every week they took part, up to 4 weeks, and a maximum of £20. Incentivizing in this way acknowledges that participants' time is valued no matter how many weeks they take part in the study but also may encourage longer participation and recognition of those that have committed to a prolonged period of participation.

However, Bolger et al. (2003) argue that monetary incentives and relying on participants' desire to contribute toward science do far less to retain participants when compared to the importance of maintaining contact with them throughout the process. It is for this reason that the ongoing relationship between participant and researcher is so important throughout a diary study. This relationship will allow a participant to feel comfortable enough to reach out should they have any concerns or queries about the study, rather than halting diary completion, providing minimally completed diary entries, making "best guesses" when they have questions, or dropping out of the study altogether. It is, therefore, important to reach out to participants regularly throughout the QDM element of your study, providing you with the opportunity to check how they are finding engaging with the research and providing them with the opportunity to raise any concerns or ask questions (Radcliffe, 2013).

Remaining in regular contact with those completing the diaries is also essential to try to minimize data loss within the study. Unlike most other qualitative methods, the researcher will not be physically present during the collection of data and, therefore, cannot ensure that relevant information and adequate depth in terms of insights are being captured (Radcliffe, 2013). Let us consider the data collection process engaged in when collecting data via qualitative interviews, for example, where researchers will often work to ensure that they are able to sensitively bring discussions back to the topic on which the research is focused, to enable the collection of data that will help to answer study research questions (see Dempsey et al., 2016). Further, where relatively short answers might initially be provided to questions asked during an interview, here researchers will generally use pre-prepared or "on-the-spot" follow-up questions to attain greater depth of insights, particularly important for qualitative research methods more generally where context, complexity, and nuanced details are tantamount to good research (see Robinson, 2023). During the completion of qualitative diaries, beyond the instructions you have provided participants with initially and, in the case of semi-structured diaries, your careful design of the diary questions posed to participants within their diaries, you will usually no longer have any capacity to influence the diary data they record, at least not in situ or in the moment. Plowman (2010) states that close contact with participants during a diary study is key to enabling them to ask questions of the researcher should they be unsure or to notify them if they have missed any entries. Similarly, it is advised that, wherever possible, QDM studies are designed in a way that enables participants to easily share diary entries with the researcher on a semi-regular basis, to allow researchers to pick up on misunderstandings, challenges, and a lack of depth in responses, earlier in the study to enable further discussions between researcher and participant along the way (Radcliffe, 2018). Having the opportunity to be kept informed in this way reduces the chance that the researcher has any surprises when it comes to retrieving diary data. Similarly, piloting QDMs can be particularly useful in ensuring the information given before data collection is clear and provides participants with enough guidance to ensure that data relevant to the research question(s) are collected. We often recommend also trying to keep the diary yourself for at least a few days to see how you find the process on the other side of the diary keeping. This can also be a useful addition to your own researcher reflections, and you can also keep notes in your own researcher journal on how you experienced journaling as a participant. This may sound like diary overload (and we do certainly love our diaries!), but this process does offer valuable insights into how participants are likely to experience completing your qualitative diary.

As alluded to above, the diary instructions that you provide for participants taking part in your study are also of particular importance. Beyond the traditional participant information sheet, which will provide them with an overview of your research and broadly what will be involved if they take part, an additional "diary instruction sheet" should also be created. The careful creation of this document is particularly important considering the aforementioned challenges associated with the lack of researcher presence during the completion of qualitative diaries, making it vital that you provide clear instructions that participants can refer back to in your absence. While the content of diary instruction sheets may vary from project to project (and depending on diary medium), they will usually include a brief statement/reminder of the purpose of the research in lay terms, a bullet point list of prompts or things to keep in mind when recording diary entries, a reminder of when participants should record their entries, and a reminder of the confidential nature of anything they write in the diary. Here, just as on the more usual participant information sheet, it is again helpful to include the contact details of the researcher so that they have these easily to hand should any further questions arise. Over the course of Chapters 3, 4, and 5, you will find examples of diary instruction sheets, which we hope will serve as useful guides as you begin developing your own.

In addition to the above key considerations, more broadly allowing flexibility in how participants may complete their diaries can also reduce the likelihood of withdrawal. Baker (2023) describes how allowing creativity in her diary study, such as using pictures or creating mind-maps, helped to maintain participant engagement. After one participant withdrew from the study early on, stating she did not enjoy writing, Baker was able to amend the criteria to reduce the likelihood of further withdrawals. This example highlights the importance of balancing the needs of the research with what may work best for your participants (see also Budworth, 2023; Hayes et al., 2024). Considering different modes of QDMs is an issue we will turn to over the course of Chapters 3, 4, and 5, where will consider the importance of aligning the type of diary used not only with your research question but also with your sample. However, we also advocate for flexibility in the modes available to your participants wherever feasible within your QDM study, having personally found similar experiences to that of Baker (2021) noted above. We will discuss this further in Chapter 5, where we discuss the flexibility often inherent in app-based diaries. However, it is important to consider whether some degree of flexibility is possible even where technologically mediated diaries might be unfeasible (for an excellent example, see Budworth, 2023).

In thinking about the ways in which we can attain and retain participant commitment in our QDM studies, we have already gone some way to beginning to think through important QDM study design considerations, including the duration and frequency of the diary study and how we might prepare the diary instruction sheet. We will next move on to consider the more practical elements of the design of the actual diaries themselves.

DESIGNING QDMs

Diary Designs

One of the many benefits of implementing QDM's is the flexibility afforded to researchers when it comes to how these diaries are designed, enabling alignment with your specific research project and philosophical underpinnings. With this flexibility, however, come important decisions to determine which design is most appropriate in best supporting you to achieve your research aims. Following on from discussions of length of the diary study and frequency of required reporting, a key diary design consideration is when you will ask your participants to complete their diary or, in other words, what will be the "trigger" for them to make a diary entry. Eckenrode (1995) describes three general categories of diary designs—namely, interval-contingent, event-contingent, and signal-contingent designs—which can act as a useful starting point.

Interval-Contingent Diary Designs

Interval-contingent designs require participants to record their experiences at regular, predetermined intervals of time, which should be communicated to the participant before data collection. In this sense, the "trigger" for diary completion would be the passing of a particular period of time and/or the arrival of a particular time of day, week, or month. According to Bolger et al. (2003), this type of diary design is particularly useful when the researcher feels the phenomenon of interest may vary day-to-day but should be recalled well over the day. If we think back to Chapter 1, where we discussed key reasons for using QDMs, this is likely to align well with studies using diaries because they are interested in examining change over time. For instance, in Leighann's research investigating mistreatment in the workplace, she adopted an interval-based design asking participants to report their workplace experiences and anticipation of going to work the following day at the end of each day. Here, Leighann adopted an interval-contingent diary design because she was interested in not only capturing experiences on days where participants actually experienced mistreatment or negative interactions but also understanding how they experience the workplace even on days where such interactions or experiences do not occur. This, therefore, enabled her to capture the "ebbs and flows" of mistreatment experiences over time.

When using an interval-contingent design, you may choose to ask participants to record once a day for a period of 4 weeks or, if the phenomenon of interest should vary throughout the day and this needs to be captured, ask participants to record several times a day but usually over a shorter period of time. Alternatively, you may ask participants to record an entry at the end of each week or at particular times of the month over a longer time period, depending on your research focus/topic. While it can be useful to agree with participants, before commencing with the diary study, a particular time when they might complete the diary in order to support regular completion, it is paramount to consider that some flexibility may be needed to ensure adequate data are collected and to prevent unnecessary stress for participants. For example, while it might be agreed with participants engaged in a daily diary study that they complete their diary on the train home from work, it is beneficial and more realistic to permit participants some flexibility as to when they record, as participants' schedules are often busy and varied. Bolger (2003) also notes the importance of spacing within interval-contingent diaries. Intervals that are too long can increase retrospection, therefore potentially undermining one of the main benefits of QDMs, which is their ability to capture data as close to the experience of interest as possible. For example, reflecting on experiences, thoughts, and emotions that have occurred over the course of the past month may capture a more general overview of the month, may be influenced by how participants are currently feeling at this point in the month, and may be subject to the benefits of hindsight as discussed in relation to data collection via interview in Chapter 1. Of course, you need to weigh up the risks of introducing further elements of retrospection alongside the time frame that makes most sense for your study, and where longer spacing between diary entries is deemed most suitable, this is something that you can reflect on in the analysis and write-up of your research findings. Arguably, there may be some study phenomena where greater spacing between entries can be justifiable, especially where it is necessary for participants to keep diaries for a longer period of time (e.g., capturing shifting identity experiences across the transition to parenthood) and others where maintaining a shorter time period between entries to minimize retrospection to a greater extent is particularly important (e.g., when capturing particularly transitory thoughts, feelings, and emotions, such as intrusive and negative thoughts, experiences of pain, or feelings of being (de)motivated). As always, when making such decisions, it is important to weigh up the desire for data wherein retrospection is minimized, alongside considering the burden placed on participants, which may be too high where studies require regular recording over short intervals, over a longer time period.

Event-Contingent Diary Designs

An event-contingent design requires participants to record a diary entry whenever a preestablished event takes place. In this case, the "trigger" for diary completion is the occurrence of this particular event. This could be when you think about or discuss a particular topic (e.g., Ferguson & Chandler, 2005; Mooney et al., 2015) or when a specific external event occurs, such as when participants make a particular decision (e.g., Baker, 2021), when a conflict between work and family responsibilities occurs (e.g., Radcliffe & Cassell, 2014, 2015), or when making a transition between two domains or roles (e.g., Chamakiotis et al., 2014). Event-contingent designs are therefore particularly useful when the aims are to record a specific incident or event in as much detail as possible, meaning that an interval-contingent design may risk missing the rich, "in-the-moment" (or as close as reasonably possible to the moment) details of specific, transitory events (Radcliffe, 2013). Here, if we think back to Chapter 1, where we discussed key reasons for using QDMs, this is likely to align well with studies that are employing diaries because they are interested in capturing rich, momentary details of specific events, or routine occurrences, as close to the time at which they occur as possible.

When using an event-based QDM design, clarity of communication regarding the specific event(s) or incidents that you want participants to record is particularly important as any uncertainty surrounding what they are required to record risks leading to important data being missed. For instance, in Laura's research on decision-making processes involved in resolving everyday work–family conflicts, she was particularly interested in capturing daily events that could be considered so routine and mundane by participants that they may not see them as significant enough to record in their diaries (e.g., struggling to leave the house on time for work in the morning or to leave work on time at the end of the working day or deciding whether to take a phone call from a school/family member while at work). In such instances, alongside providing clear, written diary instructions as discussed above, Laura found it useful to discuss the importance of the routine and mundane with participants in pre-diary interviews (see below section on using QDMs with other methods) and even to help participants consider examples from their own daily lives. Similarly, in Hannah's ongoing research on people with long-term health conditions and how they make decisions regarding whether or not to work when they are feeling unwell, an event-based element of the diaries was essential to capture this decision-making process in, or close to, the moment. In the interview stage of Hannah's research, it became clear that some participants with long-term health conditions faced these decisions on such a regular basis that they often didn't view them as decisions at all. It was therefore essential to provide a clear outline of what she was aiming to capture, thereby what constituted an "event" in her diaries.

Signal-Contingent Diary Designs

This type of diary design involves participants recording a diary entry every time they are contacted by the researcher. In this case, the "trigger" for diary reporting is a signal from the researcher to do so. This evidently requires some kind of signaling device to prompt participants to record at either fixed or random points in time or a combination of both (Bolger et al., 2003). With the advances in technology and the prevalence of personal digital devices capable of receiving such signals, such as the use of smartphones, signal-contingent designs are increasingly an option in QDM research (Smyth & Heron, 2013; see also Chapter 5). Here participants are invited via their smartphone to complete a diary entry reporting their current activity and/or experiences at the time of the alert (e.g., Consolvo et al., 2017; Karnowski, 2013; Kaufmann & Peli, 2020). For example, Kaufmann and Peli (2020) used this approach to ask participants to report, when contacted by the researchers, if they were using any media at that time and encouraged to use any or all multimedia options featured by WhatsApp, including pictures, videos, and screenshots (see also Chapter 5 for a specific discussion of WhatsApp diaries). They purposefully chose times to contact participants randomly, so that this would be unanticipated by participants and, therefore, they could not prepare or deliberately choose specific activities in advance, thereby seeking to achieve momentary snapshots of participants' media use. In this way, signal-contingent designs may also align well with studies that are employing diaries because they are interested in capturing rich, momentary details of specific events. However, when taking a signal- rather than an event-contingent approach, you must be fairly sure that the activity or event of interest will occur on a regular basis to ensure that you are able to capture adequate instances to enable you to answer your research questions. Yet, a signal-contingent design may also align with studies using diaries because you are interested in examining change over time. Here, capturing reports of feelings or thoughts about a particular topic, for instance, at random times, over a particular duration, may also lend itself to understanding how these feelings or thoughts change over time, in particular locations, or at particular times of day. This approach may, therefore, have the potential to attain a more comprehensive and authentic picture over time while encouraging enhanced momentary reporting. For instance, Rose (2020) provides the example of understanding how students experience a study-abroad program, highlighting how the anxiety experienced by learners at the end of each day might be very different from in-the-moment anxiety experienced at different times of day, such as when they are attending classes or engaging in social activities. Signal-contingent designs may, therefore, be useful in studies where timing is seen to be an important influential factor on the phenomenon being researched.

However, when considering whether to use a signal-contingent design, it is paramount to carefully consider whether there is a clear rationale aligned with your research questions for requiring this type of diary design, alongside the burden this may place on participants. The feasibility of your particular participant sample being able to complete a qualitative diary entry whenever they are alerted by the researcher is an important consideration. For instance, Kaufmann and Peli (2020) noted advising participants not to reply to their text message signals in situations where the use of smartphones was dangerous or prohibited (e.g., while driving). Of course, such considerations should form part of ethical applications for QDM-based research projects. Here it is important to stress transparency at the point of participant recruitment in terms of how often participants will be contacted and the expectation placed on them regarding how soon they will be required to make a diary entry after being signaled by the researcher. If recording at the time of the signal being received is paramount to the study design, it might be best to consider the most feasible diary modes for participants to report instantaneously (e.g., audio- or photo-based diaries are often considered quicker than written or typed diaries—see Chapters 3 and 4). Rose (2020) suggests that, in such instances, the use of "logs" rather than lengthier journal entries might be most feasible. However, the disadvantage here is, of course, the reduction of rich, detailed information being provided in the moment. It is, therefore, likely to be more feasible, and potentially ethical, for researchers to allow some flexibility in terms of the time frame during which participants can complete their diary entries following receipt of a signal from the researcher.

Alternatively, where feasible for a particular study, participants may be provided with an option regarding a particular window of time when it would work best for them to receive such a signal or reminder from the researcher, such as selecting a particularly convenient day (Kaufmann & Peli, 2020) or time of day (Consolvo et al., 2017). Consolvo et al. (2017) took this approach, letting participants choose what time they would like to receive a reminder that fit with their personal schedule. These researchers caution against assuming that the time that works best for you will work best for others, noting, for example, that some people work night shifts, go to bed much earlier or later on a regular basis, or have other obligations or routines that are likely to vary across participants.

While we have covered each of the predominant diary-design "types" in turn, it is important to point out that we now often suggest that researchers consider the potential affordances of using a mixed design by drawing on a combination of the above designs. For instance, in Hannah's research, an event-contingent design is necessary to capture the decision-making process discussed above. However, another important research aim within Hannah's project is to understand the impact of (not) enacting presenteeism over time and the impact such decisions have on the well-being of these individuals on subsequent days, which lends itself to an interval-contingent design. Therefore, Hannah decided to draw upon a mixed event- and interval-contingent diary design where she asked participants to record a diary entry every time they made a decision surrounding whether or not to work while feeling unwell (i.e., event-contingent), as well as to record an entry every other day, to capture day-to-day feelings in relation to well-being, experiences at work, or experiences taking time off work (i.e., interval-contingent). This mixed design was decided upon to enable Hannah to capture decision-making processes in the moment, as well as the impact of these decisions on well-being and workplace experiences over time. It is, therefore, once again paramount that you carefully consider all elements of your research aims and questions when making decisions regarding diary design.

QDM Structure

Another important element of diary design, beyond considering which type(s) of diary design are most suitable to enable you to answer your research questions, is the amount of structure to incorporate into the diaries. In a similar way to how we consider different types of qualitative interviews, Radcliffe (2013) distinguishes between "semi-structured" diaries, wherein participants are asked to answer a small number of open-ended questions when recording each diary entry, and "unstructured" diaries, where participants are provided with diary instructions, as discussed previously, but without specific questions to answer each time they complete an entry. There are clear benefits and drawbacks to each approach, which center on the desire to avoid leading participants while also ensuring that sufficient relevant information is captured to enable you to answer your research questions. On one hand, adding greater structure to each diary entry might risk hampering one of the main advantages of qualitative diary data collection, which is the ability to capture rich and detailed participant-led data that minimize the extent to which participants' descriptions are led by the researcher. However, on the other hand, using an entirely unstructured approach can lead to predominantly irrelevant information being recorded, as well as being potentially intimidating for participants who might be faced with a blank page (or the equivalent of, depending on diary medium) on which to express their thoughts, feelings, or experiences (Radcliffe, 2013, 2018). Alongside consideration of your sample and what might be most appropriate for them, as well as alignment with your intended overarching research approach and where you sit on the inductive–deductive continuum, we also highly recommend conducting a pilot study to determine how much structure may be appropriate for your study, trialing different layouts and the richness and relevance of the date each produces. In some cases, it can be useful to consider a compromise between the two, with two to four semi-structured diary questions for participants to focus on when recording each entry, as well as the inclusion of a more "unstructured" element via a question that asks them to record anything else that they deem to be relevant (e.g., see Spencer et al., 2022).

Using QDMs Alongside Other Methods

It is common for QDMs to be employed alongside other forms of data collection, from multimethod approaches using QDMs in conjunction with another qualitative method, for instance, focus groups (e.g., Koopman-Boyden & Richardson, 2012; Mooney et al., 2015; Moran-Ellis & Venn, 2007), to studies employing QDMs as one component of a suite of methods used within case study designs or ethnographies (e.g., Balogun, 2004; Plowman, 2010; Vincett, 2018). However, by far the most popular complementary method used alongside QDMs is qualitative interviews and, in particular, employing the diary-interview method first proposed by Zimmerman and Wieder (1977).

As discussed in Chapter 1, the diary-interview method was devised as an alternative to the intensive observation in situ required in ethnographies, which Zimmerman and Wieder (1977), as ethnographers themselves, highlighted as particularly time and labor intensive and also not always practically feasible. They, therefore, proposed the use of qualitative diaries, in conjunction with interviews, as an alternative method to participant observation, wherein the diary was viewed as not only a source of data in its own right but also a "question-generating" and, hence, further "data generating device" (p. 489). Here they viewed the in-depth interviews, situated alongside qualitative diaries, as enabling enhanced understanding by allowing further details of experiences reported in diaries to be supplemented by interview data, as well as providing the opportunity to move beyond the particular events recorded with diary entries to examine how these relate to the broader context, attitude, beliefs, and understandings of the participant.

Since then, interviews have been used as an important accompaniment to QDMs across the social sciences and in a variety of different ways to add value, richness, and context to data collection (e.g., Alaszewski, 2006; Bartlett, 2012; Radcliffe, 2013). While a variety of different approaches exist, building on Zimmerman and Wieder's (1977) diary-interview approach, the most common technique involves both a pre-diary interview and a post-diary interview, as well as the diary keeping itself (Alaszewski, 2006; Radcliffe, 2013). However, as we will discuss, while pre- and post-diary interviews each have their unique benefits, it is also worth carefully considering how they may or may not be most appropriate for your particular project.

The Pre-Diary Interview

A number of important benefits of conducting interviews before employing QDMs have been highlighted, particularly in relation to the opportunity it provides for establishing context, rapport building, and the opportunity to explain, discuss, and answer questions surrounding diary completion in person

(Radcliffe, 2013, 2018). Initial interviews allow insight into the broader world of participants and the broader context in which their daily experiences will be situated. Further, recalling earlier discussions regarding the importance of personal connections and rapport (Bolger et al., 2003) when it comes to attaining and maintaining participants willing and committed to qualitative diary completion, an initial interview provides an excellent opportunity to establish such connections, build rapport, and establish trust.

Another important benefit of the pre-diary interview is that they are a key way to ensure that participants understand what is expected from the qualitative diary element of a research study, during which time the researcher will not be present. These interviews are therefore an excellent opportunity to discuss the pragmatics of diary completion wherein the participant can be verbally provided with as much information as possible regarding the aims of the diary while allowing them the opportunity to ask questions and raise any concerns (Radcliffe, 2013). For example, as previously discussed, in Laura's research on decision-making during daily incidents of work–family conflicts, the importance of recording minor, routine work–family conflicts is emphasized, and she often uses initial interviews to do this, including the discussion of specific examples. As part of this initial interview, she also regularly employs the critical incident technique (CIT) (Chell, 2004; Flanagan, 1954; see also Radcliffe, 2013; Radcliffe & Cassell, 2014, 2015), which involves asking interviewees to recall the last time they experienced the particular event or incident of interest. Therefore, Laura often uses the CIT to explore recent daily work–family conflict incidents experienced by participants and subsequent resolution processes. Using the CIT in this way can be particularly useful within pre-diary interviews, especially those that rely on an event-contingent diary design, as this affords the opportunity to talk through a particular relevant event with participants in detail before diary completion, encouraging them to express the level of detail that you are looking for them to record within their future diary entries and making them aware of the kinds of follow-up questions you might ask, or be interested in, should you be present. This enables clear links between discussions in the pre-diary interview and participants' subsequent recording of such incidents within their diaries, therefore enabling participants to understand not only the kinds of incidents, events, or experiences that it would be important for them to record but also the importance of including relevant rich associated details. However, arguably, in this way, pre-diary interviews can risk being potentially leading in terms of the diary content that they may go on to record, providing more influence of the researcher over the data collection and process, rather than being as heavily participant-led as may otherwise be the case. In addition, where participants have not physically met the researcher before data collection, this may lead to greater feelings of anonymity, as well as further minimizing the influence of the researcher, who at the point of diary completion would remain relatively unknown in terms of identity. Baker (2021), for instance, opted not to collect diaries before the interview stage, which they suggest encouraged participants to respond to diaries more openly. There is, therefore, always a fine balance to strike between the desire to collect data to enable you to answer your research questions and the desire for data collection to be more open and driven by the research process. This means that you must weigh up the benefits of rapport and verbal clarification of the purpose of the QDMs against the desire to have as little influence over the data collection process as possible, keeping both the aims of the research and participant well-being in mind throughout.

Further, interesting data can be attained via the comparison of the narratives people construct in initial interviews and the experiences reported in diaries, which, as discussed in Chapter 1, each provide very different kinds of data. While interviews tend to provide insights into how people reconstruct and internalize their interpretations of reality to produce more cohesive narratives around a particular topic, QDM data provide more "in-the-moment" data that lend themselves to the production of messy, shifting, and often contradictory experiences. Therefore, being able to compare data generated via interviews and QDMs can lead to a more complex understanding of issues under investigation. For instance, in Laura's research with single mothers where she was interested in how they deal with intense competing work and family norms and expectations, she found that during interviews, they often presented a more cohesive narrative of who they were as employed single mothers, but in diary entries, ongoing identity conflict was observed in action, providing insights into the processes involved in how such complexity is navigated to reach and sustain a more cohesive narrative and sense of self and the role of external constraints (see Radcliffe et al., 2022).

One final point to note with regard to pre-diary interviews requires us to recall the sampling strategy options considered earlier in this chapter. In this sense, such interviews, when used initially as a broader sample in which not all interview participants may become diary participants, can also act as a gateway to help identify future relevant potential diary participants, noting that this not only allows insight into participants who might make particularly good diary participants for your study (e.g., they have a current or ongoing experience of the phenomena focused upon in your research) but also that recruiting participants for an interview may often prove easier than recruiting them directly for a QDM study. In this sense, once rapport has been built, it may be easier to subsequently approach relevant participants to enquire whether they might be willing to commit to a second phase of the study. While in some cases, where strong rapport has been established, it might be appropriate to discuss the potential for their participation in the qualitative diary element of your study directly within the interview, in other cases, it can be pertinent to allow some time to pass before issuing such an invitation. For example, in Leighann's research examining mistreatment in the workplace, interviews were often highly emotional and taxing for participants. As such, after several declined invitations to keep a diary, she soon realized that it was not appropriate and/or conducive to ongoing participation to invite participants to keep a diary during/at the end of the interview. Instead, she found that if she waited a week or two, interview participants were more likely to agree to keeping a diary and thereby ongoing participation in the study. This highlights the importance of considering the most appropriate timing regarding requests for participation in qualitative diary elements of your study, following preliminary interviews, particularly when studying topics deemed highly sensitive or even following an interview that might have unexpectedly aroused negative recollections and associated emotions.

Post-Diary Interviews

Interviews following diary data collection and preliminary analysis can also bring a number of important benefits, the most pertinent of which is the opportunity it provides to seek further detail and clarification from participants on the content of the diary entries. As this is arguably the key benefit of post-diary interviews, it is usually recommended that at least an initial familiarization, and ideally a first-pass analysis of diary data, is engaged in before conducting follow-up interviews. Following Zimmerman and Wieder's (1977) advice in the development of their diary-interview approach, it can be useful to develop post-diary interview questions that are specifically based on the contents of the qualitative diary entries, where appropriate. In this sense, diary entries can be considered a "conversational technology" (Gammack & Stephens, 1994, p. 76), or elicitation device, when used in conjunction with post-diary interviews, wherein specific experiences reported within diary entries become the focal point of conversations during the interview. Harvey (2011) describes the use of private diaries in a study exploring participants' intimate everyday experiences wherein the private diaries themselves were not actually shared with the researcher but rather used as a prompt for deeper discussions during follow-up interviews. In this sense, post-diary interviews provide space for participants to reflect more deeply on their entries, providing additional details, as well as their own post-experience analysis, thereby allowing the researcher the opportunity to not only clarify any areas of uncertainty with the participant but also attain additional data based on participants' own analysis and reflections (Radcliffe, 2013; Thille et al., 2022).

However, it is important to note some ethical concerns to take into consideration when asking participants to go over experiences or events reported in qualitative diaries. In some instances, where information is not particularly sensitive, it can certainly be useful to discuss particular reported experiences in greater detail, but in other instances, for instance, where the topic or even just the specific experience reported involves potentially sensitive or upsetting details, this will need to be considered and approached with great care. For example, in Leighann's research on mistreatment at work, she decided not to engage in post-diary interviews since she deemed the topics discussed likely to be highly sensitive. Therefore, going over these experiences with participants and probing for further details may lead to negative implications for participant well-being. Thereby, the desire for further data must be weighed against the real potential of having a negative impact on participants. In Laura's research investigating couples' experiences of navigating conflicting work and family responsibilities and demands, wherein she found conducting follow-up interviews highly useful in gaining further insights into participants' daily decision-making, it remained important to take great care not to ask follow-up questions about any events recorded that may be considered potentially sensitive, such as those that were clearly emotive for the participants, even where further insights may have been useful. Further, given that both members of a couple often completed private qualitative diaries in Laura's studies, ensuring that no questions were asked that may risk indicating any events reported in their partner's diary was also of paramount importance. For instance, where discrepancies or contradictions existed across partner diary entries, while it may arguably have been interesting to explore such discrepancies further, Laura took care not to discuss any such issues within individual follow-up interviews (see also Radcliffe, 2013). Of course, here it is also important to point out that where group or couple interviews may be useful in some studies and could potentially be considered when designing pre-diary interviews (e.g., Radcliffe & Cassell, 2014), this would certainly not be appropriate when conducting post-diary interviews wherein individuals have kept private, personal diaries, and therefore, individual post-diary interviews are strongly advised. Broadly, in line with much ethical guidance, it is always important to balance the desire or need for data against the potential impact on participants, and we would argue that this is especially pertinent to consider when deciding whether and how to use post-diary follow-up interviews. Ultimately, the interests of participants must come before the desire to collect additional data (Gatrell, 2009).

Thille and colleagues (2022) also discuss the importance of choosing the interval between data collection and the time of the interview. Although to some extent, this choice can be driven by the practical needs of the researcher, there should be consideration of the fact that the length of delay ultimately impacts the proximity of the diary data collection to the present. The authors suggest that the value placed on how close the interview is to when the diary was completed should ultimately, once again, be guided by the research questions. Finally, given the time invested by participants in engaging with QDM studies, as well as the participant reflexivity that we are aware this instigates (Cassell et al., 2020), post-diary interviews also arguably provide a potentially much-needed confidential and nonjudgmental space for participants to share their experiences of keeping the diaries, as well as their own reflections and anything that has arisen for them as a result. We discuss participant reflexivity below in more detail within a broader discussion of ethical considerations particularly relevant to QDM studies. However, in relation to considering whether or not to include post-diary interviews as part of your research design, you may want to consider not only the additional data and insights that attaining how participants went about and experienced maintaining their qualitative diaries affords but also the important debriefing space that this provides for participants. Here, we would suggest that, even in instances where follow-up interviews are not deemed appropriate, it is worth offering participants a space, or informal conversation, in which they can debrief, discuss their own reflections, and gain a sense of closure in relation to the research process in which they have been heavily involved over a period of time. Considering all that we have discussed above, when it comes to deciding on the extent to which you embed qualitative diaries within the diary-interview method, we have provided an "at-a-glance" overview of the pros and cons of using QDMs alone, as well as alongside either or both pre- and post-diary interviews (see Table 2.1). We hope that this will help you think through your own QDM study design, as well as support you in developing a sound rationale for whatever approach you choose when writing up your methodology.

TABLE 2.1 ■ Pros and Cons of Different Diary-Interview Study Design Combinations

	Diaries Only	Pre-Diary Interviews Only	Post-Diary Interviews Only
Pros	• Participants may be more open as they have a greater sense of anonymity • Less effort to integrate/combine different data types • Spontaneous event recording (e.g., not influenced by content of the interview)	• Participants may not want to reflect on their diary content in a follow-up interview (e.g., emotive and sensitive content) • Able to explain how to complete diary • Able to establish rapport and trust • Develop interpretive context through interview data	• Able to probe diary contents/events • Sets a clear "deadline" for both researcher and participant • Bookends research (e.g., helps to give boundaries to the research relationship) • Able to gather feedback on the diary-keeping process (e.g., for improving materials, future research, and methodological articles)
Cons	• Diary completion may be poor due to lack of engagement and explanation of how to complete entries • Lack of interpretive context (e.g., background information gathered in an interview)	• Unable to probe diary content, so limited to what is written in the diary (although this can also be a benefit) • Participant may lack closure (NB to have an informal conversation with participants in lieu of an interview)	• Participants may be reluctant to reflect on some of the content included in their entries (e.g., enhanced scope for sensitive and emotionally charged interviews) • Enhanced workload for researcher to ensure diary data are analyzed before follow-up interview

ETHICAL CONSIDERATIONS

While it is beyond the scope of this book to consider all the various important ethical considerations that should be thoughtfully engaged with when designing and conducting qualitative research projects, as intimated above, there are a number of QDM-specific considerations. For instance, we have already discussed the importance of carefully considering the amount of data collected, balancing the desire or need for data against the potential impact on participants, the implications of going over sensitive topics again in post-diary followup interviews, and the importance of building in flexibility regarding when and where participants are asked to record diary entries. We cover some of these in more detail below while addressing others throughout the remainder of the book, which we encourage you to use alongside broader ethical guidelines within your own institutions and discipline-related ethical codes of conduct, as well as engaging with relevant textbooks on ethics in qualitative research (e.g., Iphofen & Tolich, 2018; Miller et al., 2012).

Participant Reflexivity

As noted above and in Chapter 1, one of the additional benefits of QDMs is their capacity to encourage participant reflexivity surrounding the topic(s) of interest (Cassell et al., 2020; Plowman, 2010; Radcliffe, 2018). As we know from broader reflexivity literature, this is generally considered to be predominantly positive as reflexivity is known to be integral to learning and development (e.g., Hibbert & Cunliffe, 2015; Moon, 2013; Suedfeld & Pennebaker, 1997), and providing participants with the space to develop such reflexivity around a particular topic may also support them in feeling less alone with their experiences, with a more nuanced self-understanding, as well as enabling them to feel by a person who genuinely wants to understand their stories (Miller & Boulton, 2007). This can be particularly the case where participants feel that they have not been permitted the space to think about or openly engage in discussion about these topics previously (for a review of the benefits of participant reflexivity, see Cassell et al., 2020).

However, while acknowledging that the opportunity afforded by QDMs in instigating participant reflexivity can be beneficial, researchers must also be aware of related ethical issues. In facilitating the critique of important aspects of their lives, via a research process that instigates participant reflexivity, this may in turn lead to some emotional discomfort for participants (Cassell et al., 2020). The emotive nature of reflexivity and the potential for this to cause some distress for participants, particularly if the topic of the research is sensitive, is well known in existing literature, highlighting how reflexivity is entangled with emotions (Burkitt, 2012; Cunliffe, 2002; Hibbert et al., 2019). For instance, in Laura's research employing photo diaries alongside post-diary interviews, as well as reporting positive experiences of engaging with the study, some participants expressed more challenging emotions and some discomfort, explaining that "some of them provoked emotion" or that they made "me feel a bit apprehensive about the future" or involved questioning, "Do I really want to be reminded of where my failures are so explicitly? It makes me feel quite inadequate." In light of this, we would argue that the researcher within QDM studies has some level of responsibility in terms of supporting participants to explore and develop their reflexivity and emotions in a safe space (Cassell et al., 2020; Hibbert & Cunliffe, 2015).

Hibbert and Cunliffe (2015) suggest that the learning process that accompanies reflexivity needs to move beyond the level of disturbance and doubt to create new forms of understanding. Therefore, ensuring that our participants have the opportunity to develop their reflexivity, which may have been instigated by involvement in our research, within a safe and confidential environment, is important (see discussion above on post-diary interviews). Additionally, prioritizing privacy and participant confidentiality when considering the design and implementation of QDM studies, alongside balancing the needs of the research with the well-being of all involved, is essential. Relatedly, it is important to ensure that you are fully aware of, and have carefully considered and prepared for, the potential challenges surrounding participant reflexivity and prepared to sensitively navigate the emotions and discomfort this may bring, demonstrating empathic behaviors during the interview, for example, through sensitive follow-up questioning, and being prepared with avenues for further support if required. Day and Thatcher (2009) discuss how engaging with sensitive diary responses, which often comprise highly emotive writing, can be complicated for researchers; therefore, preparation, discussions within your research or supervisory team, and having the appropriate support in place for yourself in advance, should you need it, are also advisable. Finally, we would recommend ensuring that participants are also aware of the reflexivity that engaging in a QDM study is likely to instigate. While we would reiterate that this is frequently a positive experience enjoyed by participants, by being upfront about this in participant information sheets (i.e., stating that taking part in qualitative diaries is known to encourage reflexivity, which can lead to interesting but also potentially emotive insights), participants are also more fully aware of what the research process entails.

Privacy and Confidentiality

Diaries, by their very nature, are personal, and although the level of detail and sensitivity of the data collected will vary depending on research aims and topics, having access to this data comes with a considerable amount of responsibility. Even where the topic discussed may not necessarily be deemed highly sensitive, as discussed above, the process of recording a diary regularly and reflecting on personal experiences of any nature has the potential to raise unexpected emotions. It is, therefore, paramount that participants feel safe when agreeing to take part in a diary study and that care is taken to support privacy and confidentiality (Plowman, 2010). Formally, this would be achieved through well-designed and thorough data management and security procedures, which would be outlined in participant information sheets and consent forms, emphasizing the importance of anonymity and confidentiality, thereby helping to create a safe space for participants.

However, when participants are keeping private diaries over a period of time, support should also be provided in terms of helping them to carefully consider their own management of their personal data during this time (i.e., while the data are still with them). Here, considering their own local context, as well as the diary medium, and, where relevant, where or how they will safely store their diary during the period of completion, is also important. This can be especially pertinent when using traditional pen-and-paper or physical diaries, as we will discuss in more detail in Chapter 3. For instance, in research such as that conducted by Laura, in which families living within the same household are completing private diaries, it becomes evident how supporting participants to think about where they will store their data to ensure confidentiality is good practice, to ensure they remain private within the context of their own home and family. Further, considering diaries that may be completed within public spaces, such as in the workplace, may require similar careful data storage plans, as well as support from yourself as the researcher to ensure that diary mediums used are as unobtrusive in this environment as possible. For instance, if diaries might be completed during the working day, how might the diary be designed to ensure it remains as discrete as possible? Consider, for instance, an inconspicuous work-style notebook if a physical pen-and-paper diary is required. With the advent of app diaries and the increased functionality of password-protected smartphones, ensuring the confidentiality of participant data during diary completion may arguably be becoming less challenging (see Chapter 5 for further discussion of app diaries and privacy), yet this should still be considered carefully, for instance, in the context of their own households where passwords and personal mobile devices may be more readily shared.

Balancing Data Needs and Participant/Researcher Well-Being

As intimated above, qualitative diaries are fairly unique in the fact that they often require participants to engage in data collection within their own personal space over an extended period of time (Plowman, 2010). This extended engagement with the research process not only requires additional time and commitment from participants but also has time implications for researchers, who must maintain contact throughout this period and who will also have a great deal of data to manage and analyze subsequently (see Chapter 6). This additional time commitment requires you to think carefully about how you can best balance the needs of the research and your desire for interesting qualitative diary data, with both your own well-being and that of the participants. For instance, in the example provided earlier in this chapter, Laura elected not to further discuss or examine particularly sensitive issues raised in diaries or discrepancies and contradictions across partner diary entries, within follow-up interviews, to protect individual privacy and well-being (see also Radcliffe, 2013). As we have discussed, it is important to carefully consider whether QDMs are necessary to answer your research questions, whether pre- and/or post-diary interviews are each important, useful, or challenging in your particular study context (see Table 2.1), and to consider how long you will require participants to complete their diaries. Seeking diary completion for longer than is completely necessary has ethical implications for both participant and researcher well-being. For example, in a study exploring daily stressors of university students, diary entries could be collected over a 16-week-long semester to capture experiences throughout the duration of the semester. However, when considering participant burden, the extent of data that would need to be effectively analyzed should participants continue to engage over this time period, and what is actually required to attain important insights into "daily" university stressors, a 2- to 4-week duration seems adequate and, therefore, more ethical. Plowman (2010) also notes the importance of being clear with participants from the outset about what it is that you, as the researcher, are looking for in diary entries, using carefully designed diary information sheets (see examples provided in Chapters 3 and 4) and, where appropriate, pre-interview briefings. This, again, helps to reduce participant and researcher burden by reducing the amount of data recorded that may not be relevant to your study.

Ending the Researcher–Researched Relationship

As is the case within any qualitative research, debriefing participants at the end of engagement is important and, given the ongoing and more intensive investment of participants in QDM research, especially important. Due to the issues emphasized throughout this chapter, particularly in considering participant reflexivity, it is essential to be prepared to provide participants with details of where to access support if needed and, where engaging in post-diary interviews is not deemed appropriate, to offer participants an alternative opportunity to discuss how they have experienced taking part in the research, to gain feedback on the diary process as a whole, and to enable a sense of closure (Cassell et al., 2020; Radcliffe, 2013). It is also usual that a particularly strong rapport and even a sense of friendship has been established over this time between researcher and participant as a result of continuous engagement over time, which can make it especially important to establish a clear end point to data collection, something that may be usefully achieved by a final interview or debriefing session, as appropriate. This may be particularly the case in research exploring sensitive topics and experiences, such as in Leighann's research focused on workplace mistreatment, where it was not uncommon for participants to reengage contact and provide updates on their circumstances. You may also consider ways in which you can use your research to give something back to your participants, such as feeding back an overview of your findings and/or developing, potentially collaboratively, tools or resources that can support the communities involved in your research. For more detailed discussion/reflections on ending the researcher–researched relationship, please see Batty (2020) and Morrison et al. (2012).

We frequently hear that engaging in QDM research has been a positive experience for our participants, and we hope that by highlighting some of the ways in which we can best support both ourselves and our participants throughout the diary process, you will also find your study participants report similarly positive experiences and that it is an enjoyable and rewarding experience for participants and researchers alike.

APPLICATION ACTIVITY
ADDRESSING CHALLENGES AND ETHICAL DILEMMAS

Reflecting on QDM design considerations discussed throughout this chapter, use this worksheet to consider the design choices you will need to make in your own QDM project. These questions are intended to help you to effectively prepare your QDM study but also to help you structure and think about your rationale and justifications for your design choices when submitting to ethical review boards, discussing your project with supervisors/coauthors, and also writing up your QDM methodology. In completing this worksheet, we encourage you think about the potential limitations of each design choice but importantly how these align with your research question(s) and how your personal philosophical choices inform these decisions. (For a deeper treatment of issues of reflexivity in research design, see Cassell et al., 2020.)

Worksheet 1

1. Sampling considerations

- Who are your target participants and what is your target sample size?
- How and why will this sample enable you to address your research question(s)?
- How do your philosophical commitments/underpinnings inform your sample selection (e.g., to what extent are your participants "informants" or "coproducers" of knowledge)?
- Which sampling strategies are most appropriate and feasible for your research project and why (e.g., purposive, convenience sampling, a combination, etc.; include a consideration of contingency plans)?
- How will you recruit your participants (e.g., how, where, when, and why)?
- What information should you include in your advertisement/recruitment materials?
- Outline a plan for how you will maintain participant engagement and participation (e.g., contact maintenance, incentive measures, participant dropout).

2. Designing your diary: Aligning with your research questions

- Will your diary be interval, event, or signal contingent or a hybrid approach? And why?
- How frequently will participants be required to complete the diary? And why?
- Will your diary be semi-structured or unstructured? And why?
- Will you be combining QDMs with other methods? And why (e.g., the diary interview method; how will the different methods be combined/integrated? will data collection be sequential or concurrent)?

3. Ethical considerations

- How do you plan to navigate participant reflexivity (e.g., participant information sheet, debrief sheet, post-diary interview, or debrief meeting)?
- How will participant privacy and confidentiality be maintained (e.g., consider the risks of participants diaries being read by third parties and/or lost)?
- Does the design of your diary have any potential inadvertent negative impacts on participants (e.g., consider issues of sustained participation; continued reflection on subject matter, unreasonable time commitments)? How can you minimize these potentially negative impacts?
- How will you provide closure to the researcher–researched relationship (e.g., is a follow-up interview/debrief meeting appropriate; are there any risks of doing so)?

FURTHER READING

Batty, E. (2020). Sorry to say goodbye: The dilemmas of letting go in longitudinal research. *Qualitative Research, 20*(6), 784–799.

Bolger, N., Davis, A., & Rafaeli, E. (2003). Diary methods: Capturing life as it is lived. *Annual Review of Psychology, 54*(1), 579–616.

Radcliffe, L. (2018). Capturing the complexity of daily workplace experiences using qualitative diaries. In C. Cassell, A. L. Cunliffe, & G. Grandy (Eds.), *The SAGE handbook of qualitative business and management research methods* (pp. 188–204). Sage.

Rose, H. (2020). Diaries and journals: Collecting insider perspectives in second language research. In J. McKinley & H. Rose (Eds.), *Routledge handbook of research methods in applied linguistics* (pp. 348–356). Routledge.

Saunders, M. N. K. (2012). Choosing research participants. In C. Cassell & G. Symon (Eds.), *The practice of qualitative organizational research: Core methods and current challenges* (pp. 37–55). Sage.

3 TRADITIONAL DIARY METHODS

This chapter will provide practical insights into some of the more traditional diary methods—namely, pen-and-paper diaries and audio diaries. We will consider the different reasons why you might employ each of these diary methods for particular research projects, as well as the benefits and challenges of using each of these approaches, including practical suggestions in terms of how to navigate challenges. Exemplar studies will also be included for each diary method to provide you with insight into a variety of existing published diary studies using different QDM designs. Here we will consider how specific research aims influence the choice of approach, examine how the diary study was implemented, and even include some of the materials used in the process of these diary studies to help you consider the kinds of materials you might create for your own QDM research project. By the end of this chapter, you should be able to make informed decisions about whether these particular diary methods are suitable for your own research projects, including an understanding of why this is the case, alongside important insights into different practical and ethical considerations when designing projects using traditional diary methods.

TRADITIONAL APPROACHES: AN INTRODUCTION

As we have discussed previously, QDMs come in many different forms, from physical pen-and-paper diaries to those using various forms of technology (e.g., emails, online notepads, blogs, text messages). They may also be solely text-based or include visual elements by incorporating photographs or videos into the diary study design. In this chapter, we will focus on what we consider to be the more traditional approaches to diary methods, pen-and-paper diaries and audio diaries. We consider these to be more traditional QDM approaches in the sense that they have been around for the longest period of time and, until more recent years, were the predominant form of QDM drawn upon when researchers did engage with QDMs for the purposes of data collection.

In particular, we can find examples of pen-and-paper or handwritten diaries dating back to the pre-1900s. For instance, as discussed in Chapter 1, early work included written diaries that captured social conditions and economic productivity (see Bauman et al., 2019). Since the 1930s and 1940s, health researchers in particular have often drawn upon the use of pen-and-paper diaries, or "journaling" (Bartlett, 2012), and since the introduction of the previously discussed diary-interview method (Zimmerman & Wieder, 1977), which traditionally involved participants keeping a handwritten diary, it has also been fairly common for ethnographic researchers to use solicited written diaries as part of their ethnographies (Denzin & Lincoln, 1998).

Audio diaries, while not dating back as far as pen-and-paper diaries and certainly being less prolific, since the advent of the voice recorder, have been considered a well-established component of the QDM toolkit. Indeed, since the early 1990s, audio diaries have been perceived as a viable alternative to the written diary, particularly when the physical act of writing may be problematic or more challenging to attain for the study population in question for a variety of reasons (e.g., Buchanan, 1991; Hislop et al., 2005; Papadopoulos & Scanlon, 2002).

Over subsequent years, as both these QDM modes have continued to be explored and developed, important distinctions between the data collected using these different diary mediums have been brought to the fore (e.g., Crozier & Cassell, 2016; Markham & Couldry, 2007), with the choice between the written and audio diary requiring careful consideration, as we will discuss throughout this chapter. Further, and as we will discuss in subsequent chapters, as the pace of technological change has increased rapidly, diverse approaches to QDMs have also arisen and grown in popularity (see Chapters 4 and 5 for a detailed discussion and comparison to more traditional QDMs). Despite this, we argue that the more traditional approaches focused upon in this chapter remain relevant and important as part of the QDM toolkit. It is therefore important to understand when and why our research studies would benefit from the use of one, or even both, of these approaches

PEN-AND-PAPER DIARIES

As discussed above, handwritten pen-and-paper diaries can be considered the original and therefore most established diary format. It is likely that when the word *diary* is mentioned, it is indeed the written form of diary, the physical pen-and-paper diary that most readily springs to mind. You may recall that this was one of the general benefits of QDMs discussed in Chapter 1, meaning that when potential participants are asked to complete a research diary, they will likely be somewhat aware of what this entails. This may, therefore, be particularly the case when we are referring to pen-and-paper diaries, which will often be the most familiar to the variety of people with whom you are likely to discuss your research, particularly your intended research population. However, as we have also frequently mentioned throughout this book already, QDMs now encapsulate a wide variety of approaches, so in this case, it is pertinent to consider when and why you might use the more traditional pen-and-paper format as part of your research design and some of the important benefits and challenges that should be considered (see Table 3.1).

At this point, hopefully you have already carefully considered whether QDMs more generally are appropriate for your particular research project and the research questions you are seeking to answer (see Chapter 1). As well as ensuring that your choice of methods is appropriate for answering your specific research questions, another key factor to consider is always who your target

TABLE 3.1 ■ Pen-and-Paper Diaries: Benefits and When and Why to Use Them

Why Use Pen-and-Paper Diaries?	Challenges?
• Traditional approach, ensures participant familiarity and understanding	• Potential data loss (e.g., losing, misplacing, or not returning the physical diaries)
• When it is more appropriate for your particular sample (e.g., they are less likely to use technology, they often write as part of their daily practice)	• Practicalities of collecting the physical diaries
• To avoid technical challenges	• Effective recording and the risk of limited data (e.g., retrospective completion and irrelevant or minimal data)
• The act of writing can be viewed as empowering	• Privacy issues (ethical considerations)
• Fewer cost implications	• Participant inconvenience (i.e., of being required to carry around a physical diary)

population or sample will be and the research methods that might be most appropriate for this particular sample. This is, of course, no different when it comes to choosing the type of QDM you wish to use.

Sample-method alignment is imperative when we consider participant comfort and ethics, as well as our desire as researchers to attain as much relevant data from our participants as possible to enable us to answer our research questions. Usually, we also hope to find something new and interesting that can positively influence future research and practice. Therefore, when thinking about diary mediums, particularly where pen-and-paper diaries might be most useful in terms of the particular sample you are hoping to recruit and keep engaged throughout the duration of the study, it is important to consider the extent to which the practice of writing is something that your participants will be comfortable with. For instance, as alluded to in the introduction to this chapter, there are certain populations where writing would evidently be more problematic, such as those with visual impairments (e.g., Papadopoulos & Scanlon, 2002) or other physical conditions that might make writing difficult (Bartlett, 2012; Välimäki et al., 2007). Alternatively, diary mediums other than those constituting pen and paper often rely on some form of technology (e.g., voice recorders, mobile technology) and may be less appropriate and/or accessible for certain participants. For instance, there may be generational differences in technological comfort levels and prevalence of use alongside the potential for associated anxiety for some (e.g., Culp-Roche et al., 2020; Hagan & Manktelow, 2021). In this sense, the act of keeping a pen-and-paper diary may sometimes be more usual and comfortable and therefore appropriate. More broadly, particularly if you are aiming to achieve detailed, in-depth written recordings of daily experiences, thoughts, feelings, and actions, it can be useful to consider the extent to which writing is largely unproblematic for your particular target sample.

As well as being a medium with which many potential participants may be familiar and therefore more comfortable with, thus reducing the complexity or learning required to engage with the research, written diaries have also been demonstrated to offer particular benefits for participants themselves (Filep et al., 2015; Keleher & Verrinder, 2003; O'Dwyer et al. 2013). Indeed, the physical act of writing has been suggested to be empowering (Bazerman, 2009), enabling the release of complex emotions and thought processes by identifying them and thereby being able to reflect upon them, enabling a more in-depth understanding of personal daily experiences (Meth, 2003; Ryan, 2006). While we would argue that all QDMs create time and space to reflect on experiences, arguably, written diaries, considering their capacity to more fully embrace the editor

(Ryan et al., 2009), afford more extensive time to think about what is expressed and how to express it. This can further empower participants to share their stories in a way that they are comfortable doing so, providing greater opportunity to reflect, as well as a greater degree of control over the process, using their own words and style (Day & Hudson, 2012; Ryan, 2006). Indeed, in discussing the written journals of people with dementia, Ryan et al. (2009) highlight the therapeutic and empowering nature of the process of writing, suggesting that the act of writing enables the writer to become a contributing partner in society in a way that is within their control, thus renewing a sense of status and empowerment, affirming their own past, present, and future identities. Similarly, Thomas (2007) found that the process of keeping a written diary was therapeutic, enhancing feelings of personal validity. In this sense, the opportunity to write has been demonstrated to be beneficial for people with early dementia who still retain language skills (Bartlett, 2012) and more generally as a mode that enhances voice, empowerment, and a sense of control. Practically speaking, from the perspective of the researcher, pen-and-paper diaries also involve very little cost, which can be important in ensuring that employing QDMs remains feasible in terms of being a viable method of data collection for many researchers across various circumstances and with differential access to funding. While technological options are arguably becoming more affordable in the sense that many participants are likely to have access to their own devices, which may be used for the purposes of data collection within research studies (e.g., the audio record function or inbuilt camera that now typifies most smartphones), at the very least, researchers themselves will be likely to require access to a research-specific (rather than personal) mobile device of their own for the purpose of the study (see Chapters 4 and 5). Depending on ethical implications and requirements of particular ethics committees, researchers may also be required to provide distinct, nonpersonal devices to study participants (as we will discuss further in Chapter 5).

Potential Challenges

While we have above highlighted the benefits of written diaries in terms of allowing time and space for private reflection alongside the potential convenience and ease of use for some participants, these benefits are concurrently intertwined with some of the predominant challenges of working with pen-and-paper diaries. Here we must consider that, while written diaries are generally intended to be private, without ensuring that participants are always able to store their diary in a safe and secure place, while concurrently being readily at hand when they wish to record an entry, there is a risk that others may purposefully or inadvertently gain access to their contents. Without the technologically mediated password or biometric security that we are increasingly becoming accustomed to in terms of protecting our privacy, when relying on traditional QDM approaches, this can risk leaving data somewhat vulnerable to others within their local environments. It may therefore be pertinent to consider the extent to which the topic of focus in your research is particularly private, confidential, or potentially embarrassing or puts your participants at risk should others come across their written diary entries. For example, in the context of Leighann's doctoral project (Spencer, 2019; Spencer et al., 2021), which explored experiences of mistreatment at work, physical paper diaries were deemed inappropriate and potentially harmful to participants due to the risk of a physical diary being found by others at work (e.g., coworkers or even the perpetrator(s) of the mistreatment) or at home (e.g., by spouses), inadvertently exposing their sensitive and often secret experiences (see Chapter 5 for further discussion of alternative options for highly sensitive research).

Relatedly, while the familiar completion of a written diary might be convenient for participants in some cases, carrying around a written diary may be less convenient depending on where participants are likely to be required to complete entries. For instance, if they are likely to need to do this "on the move" or within their place of work, or indeed across multiple different locations, carrying around a pen-and-paper diary might easily become cumbersome, with the potential to also draw unwanted attention to their activities. Here as researchers, it is important for us to think carefully about the environments that our participants will be occupying while participating in our study and to subsequently design diaries that are inconspicuous or easily blend in with what could be considered "usual" or "normal" within their local environment. For instance, if diaries are to be completed within a workspace, a notebook similar to those used in such a space may attract less attention. This is also something important to discuss with your participants during a pre-interview or pre-diary communication to enable them to be part of the decision-making process as far as possible. Perhaps one of the most critical and frequently discussed challenges when using QDMs, particularly pen-and-paper diaries, is the potential for data loss due to participants forgetting to record entries, possibly leading to retrospective completion. As discussed in Chapter 2, when considering the general challenges related to using QDMs, given the ongoing commitment required from participants over a period of time, forgetfulness, lapses in participant motivation, and external constraints, maintaining engagement with a QDM research study can be challenging (Radcliffe, 2013, 2018; Stone et al., 2002). This may be exacerbated by utilization of pen-and-paper diaries wherein, as discussed above, this is likely to be something additional that participants are required to remember to have with them ready for completion at the appropriate time. Further, given the physical nature of the pen-and-paper diary, should the diary be misplaced, there is unlikely to be further entries completed until (and if) it is found. The possible challenges associated with a requirement to have a physical pen-and-paper diary on your person and the risk of even momentarily misplacing the diary make it more likely that diary entries will be completed in a degree of retrospect that is not ideal for the project, potentially undermining one of the key benefits of using QDMs. This is often referred to as "backfilling" (Piasecki et al., 2007), describing the varying degrees to which such retrospective completion might occur. While some degree of retrospective completion is often planned and anticipated for practical reasons, such as participants completing diaries a number of hours after a particular event or, in the case of interval-contingent designs, at the end of each day, more extensive retrospective completion can be more problematic. For instance, where participants resort to recording numerous diary entries on the final day of the diary study before quickly returning the diary to the researcher, it is likely to limit the way in which you are able to capture the details of "in-the-moment" experiences afforded by reduced retrospection or any changes that might occur over time, which you are likely seeking when using QDMs. This again further highlights the importance of maintaining ongoing contact with participants throughout the period of diary completion (Bolger et al., 2003) to ensure any challenges or issues are reported and addressed as they occur rather than being picked up only at the end of the study, when it may be too late to respond to problems raised (Radcliffe, 2013).

Another useful strategy particularly pertinent when using pen-and-paper diaries is the possibility of agreeing with participants' specific suitable times and places when diaries entries might be safely recorded. Such discussions should take into consideration what is practically feasible for participants. For instance, for event-based designs, in most cases, it is likely not reasonable to ask participants to report an incident in their diaries immediately after the event has occurred. This can be unrealistic and risks placing stress on participants, as well as putting them in potentially challenging situations depending on where they are and who they might be with when an event occurs, as well as potentially alienating them from the study. A more realistic approach is to allow participants to postpone recording their entries until a more opportune moment while also supporting completion as close to the event as possible (for event-contingent designs) or required interval (for interval-contingent designs) by considering with your participants what might work best for them personally. By engaging in discussions with participants in advance of diary completion, it is possible to take into account their individual circumstances and the places and times where they are likely to feel most comfortable recording their entries. For example, Symon (2004) suggests that one of her participants decided that regular completion of her diary on the train on the way home from work would be most practical and feasible, as this was a space she occupied daily that was relatively free from distractions and therefore easy for her to integrate diary completion into her daily routine. Another useful practice is to include a space for participants to record the date and time of each of their diary entries. For event-based designs, this could also be included alongside an approximate time of event occurrence (Radcliffe, 2018). While, of course, not preventing "back-filling," these practices are more likely to encourage an awareness of the importance of completing diary entries at specified time intervals or as close to the occurrence of relevant events as practically and safely possible while also providing the researcher with additional insights that can be advantageous when interpreting the findings.

A related challenge, and one that has also been discussed in Chapter 2 in relation to all QDMs, is the risk that participants will record limited relevant data, without the presence of the researcher to keep discussions on track and to ask relevant follow-up questions to encourage greater depth within their responses. While this is a consideration when designing most QDM studies, arguably it is especially pertinent when designing a pen-and-paper diary study as we will go on to discuss (cf. discussions around app diaries in Chapter 5), providing participants with much more personal space and free reign to record diary entries as they see fit. This, of course, has its advantages in terms of enabling a more participant-led research approach (e.g., Day & Hudson, 2012; Meth, 2003; Ryan, 2006), thus having the potential to gain important and potentially unexpected insights into personal challenges and experiences. This can be particularly beneficial to more inductive research approaches wherein researchers begin with a very broad research focus, with subsequent refinement being led almost entirely by the data.

However, it also brings with it challenges in terms of avoiding data loss or insufficiency. For example, there could be a tendency for participants to provide short answers to questions, as they might when filling out a survey, potentially leading to thin presentations of data on which to perform subsequent in-depth, qualitative data analysis, undermining the benefits of qualitative research. Alternatively, participants might write more but, treating the diary as a personal journal, write down all daily experiences, from what they had for breakfast to their evening sleeping routine. While such details may certainly be useful in some cases, in others, this can lead again to a thin presentation of usable data for a particular research project. Since pen-and-paper diaries are less easily shared with the researcher on a more regular basis than other formats (as we will discuss in Chapters 4 and 5), the study design needs to consider these potential risks to help mitigate them as far as possible. We will discuss some of the strategies you can put in place shortly when we discuss practical considerations for designing a pen-and-paper diary.

Before we do this, it is pertinent to consider a final challenge when using physical pen-and-paper diaries: the consideration of how these diaries will be returned to you for the purposes of data analysis, often conducted alongside the construction of follow-up interview questions based on diary content (see Chapter 2 on the diary-interview method; Zimmerman & Wieder, 1977). While this may seem like a minor detail in the broad scheme of research design considerations, it remains an important one. Given the importance of analyzing diary data before commencing follow-up interviews, diaries cannot simply be collected from participants at the point of these interviews. Further, given the time commitment already required for participants engaging in QDMs and the value of the energy- and time-intensive data incorporated within these diaries from the perspective of both the participants and the researcher, asking participants to engage in the additional task of physically posting diaries to the researcher may have limited appeal (even if stamped addressed envelopes are provided to support this) (Radcliffe, 2013). Of course, this might be an option but does rely on further time and commitment from participants, and therefore considering carefully other plans for collecting pen-and-paper diaries is advisable, in consultation with participants. For instance, locating a place from where researchers may easily be able to collect diaries on an agreed-upon date or, depending on the length of the diary study, at particular agreed-upon time points over the course of the diary study.

Practical Considerations

Keeping in mind some of the challenges particularly relevant to pen-and-paper qualitative diaries, as discussed above, and how we might best navigate these, we will now discuss design considerations when planning your pen-and-paper–based diary study.

First, as with all QDM studies and as discussed in Chapter 2, it is important to think carefully about the length of time you are requesting participants to keep their diary and how frequently you are asking them to record, balancing the data you need to answer your research questions with considerations of what is reasonable in terms of expectations placed on participants.

Another related consideration is whether your diary design will be event contingent, interval contingent, signal contingent, or a hybrid design incorporating more than one of these approaches concurrently (see Chapter 2). Once again, this decision will be dependent on your research questions. For instance, do your research questions require you to capture data every time a specific event occurs? This could be, for instance, a work–family conflict (see example in Case Study 3.1); a conversation with a particular individual, such as a line manager, child, teacher, or counselor; or engagement in a particular activity, such as eating a meal or attending a class. The focus on capturing data surrounding such specific events often requires an event-based design in which you ask participants to record a diary entry every time a specific event occurs. Alternatively, or in addition, your research questions might require you to capture more regular daily or weekly reflections, such as how participants have experienced a particular phenomenon over the course of a day or week, thus lending itself to an interval-based diary design (Bolger et al., 2003; see Chapter 2). When embedding any of these approaches within a pen-and-paper diary design, this will inevitably influence the written instructions provided, as well as the layout of your diary pages, particularly where diary designs are also semi-structured. For instance, as can be seen in the example diary instruction sheet and example diary page provided in Case Study 3.1, where an event-contingent design is adopted, it is pertinent to include a clear explanation of the triggering event(s), as well as carefully considering the different elements of, or related to, the particular events that you wish to capture—in this case, clarifying work–family conflicts as the triggering event while using the diary questions on each diary page to explore the decision-making process engaged in when work–family conflicts are experienced.

CASE STUDY 3.1.

PEN-AND-PAPER QDM EXAMPLE

Radcliffe, L. S. (2012). *An In-Depth, Longitudinal, Qualitative Study Exploring the Decision-Making Processes of Dual-Earner Couples in Incidents of Work-Family Conflict*. University of Manchester.

Couples' Decision-Making in Instances of Work–Family Conflict

Back in 2010, Laura and her coauthor began a study to investigate how dual-earner couples made decisions when they were faced with a conflict between their work and family roles. Prior studies investigating work–family conflict (WFC) had tended to measure the extent to which individuals perceived their

WFC as high or low rather than looking at work–family conflicts as discreet events. This meant we knew little about how an actual WFC was experienced and navigated. Research also often only investigated individual experience, while beginning to acknowledge that WFCs are often managed at the level of the couple, in many families. As a result, we were interested in understanding what happened when couples experienced fairly mundane, daily conflicts between work and family and the decision-making process they engaged in to navigate such conflicts.

As a result, our **research questions** were initially as follows:

1. How do couples negotiate work and family when they experience a conflict between the two?
2. Why do they negotiate work and family in this way?

We therefore decided it was important to capture "in-the-moment" decision-making processes that might be easily forgotten using more retrospective techniques and therefore that we would use qualitative diaries completed by both members of dual-earner couples. We also decided on the following when considering the study design:

DESIGN AND METHODOLOGY	
Design Aspect	Decision
Duration	4 weeks (to ensure a decent number of WFCs could be captured)
Diary type	Event contingent (record a diary entry whenever they experienced a WFC) and semi-structured, using pen-and-paper diaries
Other methods	The diary-interview method, including initial couple interviews using the critical incident technique and individual follow-up interviews after diary completion to explore diary content

Importantly, this study utilized pen-and-paper diaries following a pilot study trailing audio diaries utilizing audio recorders provided by the researchers alongside written diaries (see Radcliffe, 2013). It is also important to note that at this time, particularly within our sample, many participants did not use smartphones and were not accustomed to using such digital methods to record experiences "on the move."

So, why pen-and-paper diaries?

- Fewer "technology-based" options readily available at the time
- Sample—Participants struggled with audio diaries/tech during pilot, leading to discomfort and data loss
- Privacy important as two people keeping private diaries in one household (audio/video) could have been challenging

Diary Information Sheet

Understanding Work-Life Balance

The purpose of this research is to explore how couples make decisions when faced with conflicting work and family responsibilities.

Previous research has indicated that dual-earner couples often experience such incidents on a daily basis; therefore, I am keen to find out your own experiences using this day to day diary. However, some days you may find that you have less to report than on others so please do not feel that you have to write the same amount each day. Please try to fill in the diary as soon as possible after each incident occurs. It is important that the decision-making process is fresh in your mind so you can record this process as accurately as possible.

Please record as many details as possible each time you have to make a decision regarding conflicting work and family responsibilities. Please try to include the following details:

- The decision that you arrived at regarding the two competing activities.
- The factors that affected how you arrived at this decision.
- The outcome of the decision made and how you felt about it.
- Any other details that you think might be relevant.

Your experiences are valuable as this is the way in which future research can move forward and make a difference.

Anything that you write in this diary will be strictly confidential. If you have any queries at any time while completing the diary, please feel free to contact me via the contact details below. I will also contact you during this time to see how it is going.

Many thanks for your help with this research

E-mail: XXX

From L. S. Radcliffe, *An In-Depth, Longitudinal, Qualitative Study Exploring the Decision-Making Processes of Dual-Earner Couples in Incidents of Work-Family Conflict*, 2012, The University of Manchester (United Kingdom). Copyright 2012 by Laura Radcliffe. Reproduced with permission.

Example Semi-Structured Diary Page

Week 1
Day 1   Date: Monday _____ Time _____

Please record any decisions that you had to make today regarding how to deal with competing work and family responsibilities. Please include the decisions you made, how you arrived at these decisions, and how you felt about them afterwards, as well as any other details that you feel may be relevant.

   Please describe any decisions where you made a choice between work and family today.

What did you decide to do?
How did you arrive at this decision? Please describe in as much detail as you can the decision process that you went through and ALL the factors that had an impact on the decision you made.
What was the outcome of the decision that you made? Please explain how you felt about the decision and anything that occurred as a result of the decision.
Please use this space to add any other comments that you feel might be relevant

From L. S. Radcliffe, *An In-Depth, Longitudinal, Qualitative Study Exploring the Decision-Making Processes of Dual-Earner Couples in Incidents of Work-Family Conflict*, 2012, The University of Manchester (United Kingdom). Copyright 2012 by Laura Radcliffe. Reproduced with permission.

Example Diary Data

LUCY AND PAUL

Lucy	Paul
"I asked Paul if he would drop our youngest off at my dad's and I took the elder two to school so that I could get into work a bit earlier. I needed to take the food in to the day centre where I work early for their morning snack. I'm supposed to be managing the day care centre. Aarrgghh! But this made Paul late for work which means he will have to stay later today to make his time back up. My dad needs time to get back from school to drop his little boy off at school so won't be back in the house to take our son until 9:15 am!	"This morning we shared the responsibility for getting the children ready for school. The decision to jointly get the children ready ensures that the work is shared, and we can both interact with the children before school/nursery. I try to encourage the elder two to get ready themselves and hurry them along. Delays in the process of getting ready on time annoy me and it is a tight schedule between 7:40 am and 8:40 am. I would rather be involved in this process but I would prefer that our eldest at least gets herself ready.
I always feel like I'm loading on Paul and he can never build any extra time up at work but then I think 'hang on a minute, our kids are our joint responsibility and we are a team!' It really helps if one of you has a flexible working arrangement or works from home a bit. I don't know how we would manage otherwise. It would be a real struggle."	Lucy needed to get to work early for 9 am and took the elder two to school. I had a work experience student due at work for 9 am but I could only drop our youngest off at 9:15 am. I let my line manager know that I would get into work a little late and the student would have to be accommodated until I arrived. I chose to accommodate for the family before work as there was no other choice and there was cover

(Continued)

(Continued)

Lucy	Paul
	available at work. My manager is very experienced with introducing work experience students to our roles and team responsibilities.
	I had discussed the situation with Lucy before work and her priorities were more important as there was no cover at her workplace. I felt no guilt as I had to take charge of the work experience student for over 3 hours while the cover I was requesting was for a very short time. This meant Lucy was able to get to work on time."

SARAH AND ADAM

Sarah	Adam
"Hard work getting out of the house this morning! My eldest was taking no notice of anything I asked him to do! Sheer exasperation! Time was running out. I hate shouting at them like that because by that point I have lost the plot and feel really angry. But I did get to work on time."	"No issues today."
"Stressful picking the kids up after work. Both were tired and horribly grumpy and uncooperative . . . the little one was just bawling for the sake of things . . . I just flipped! They had just pushed me too far. I pick them up and am pleased to see them after being at work and neither of them even want to say hello . . . it makes me feel like not wanting to come home from work but obviously I have to. I shouted at both of them, drove home like a maniac . . . didn't want them near me. It felt horrible . . . I just feel drained and tired now. Sometimes I wonder if it's worth going to work and making life harder for myself but then I think I escape to work for my sanity."	

Again, as discussed in Chapter 2, preparation of the diary instructions sheet for those taking part in your study is an important element of designing any QDM diary. For pen-and-paper diaries, this instruction sheet can, where appropriate, form the front cover of a physical diary. This means that the specific instructions or points of reflection that participants need to remember to record will be easily accessible to refer back to whenever they are completing a diary entry. This is especially important for pen-and-paper diaries, wherein the technological means to readily communicate with researchers or sense check regarding diary entries by sharing on a more regular basis is reduced. The creation of a clear diary instruction sheet can help to mitigate some of these challenges and is therefore one of the main ways in which the researcher can stay "present," to some extent, throughout the duration of the diary study. An example of a diary instruction sheet from a research project using a written QDM design can be seen in Case Study 3.1.

Another important consideration when designing pen-and-paper diaries is the layout, in particular whether you will follow a semi-structured or unstructured diary design, as discussed in Chapter 2. If you are taking a semi-structured approach, you will need to consider carefully the diary questions you wish to include for participants on each day of entry and how these will be laid out on each of your diary pages (see Case Study 3.1 for an example diary page) so as to be accessible for your participants, to ensure enough space to record a detailed answer to each question, and indeed to indicate the level of detail you are seeking. Structured logs, with reduced space, can be highly effective in terms of obtaining brief responses in an open-ended questionnaire style (Sherliker & Steptoe, 2000) but will inevitably limit the depth of responses and data to be analyzed. When using pen-and-paper diaries, there is limited opportunity to update or amend questions asked during the process of the study, and therefore, such considerations require especially careful reflection before initiating data collection. See Table 3.2 for a list of pertinent considerations.

TABLE 3.2 ■ Pen-and-Paper Diary Checklist

Diary Study Design Question	Y/N
Have I prepared my **diary instruction sheet**, particularly including details about what should be recorded in each entry and the level of detail desired?	
Have I designed each of my **written diary pages**, including clear diary questions and date/time stamps as applicable and carefully considering writing space provided?	

(Continued)

TABLE 3.2 ■ Pen-and-Paper Diary Checklist *(Continued)*	
Diary Study Design Question	**Y/N**
Have I considered carefully the **appearance of the written diary**, its alignment with participants' local environments, and the likelihood it will draw the attention of others?	
Have I considered participant **convenience and privacy** and made any relevant detail changes as well as plans to discuss diary storage and completion location with participants where relevant?	
Have I considered how I might **maintain contact** with participants during the study, as well as **how I will retrieve written diary entries**? And have I planned to discuss this with my participants?	

Despite the many benefits of the traditional pen-and-paper diary, it is certainly not the best choice for all QDM studies or might make more sense integrated alongside other QDM modes. We will now go on to discuss another popular form of QDM, the audio diary.

AUDIO DIARIES

Audio diaries involve the audio recording of participants' experiences, thoughts, emotions, and reflections over a period of time (Buchanan, 1991). As discussed at the beginning of this chapter, while written diaries were certainly the original form of qualitative diary, since the advent of the voice recorder, audio diaries have also become a popular form of QDM. Such interest in audio diaries has grown rapidly not only due to technological advancements. permitting ease of audio recording with declining expense, but also due to critiques of the predominance of written diaries and the way in which this may be exclusionary to multiple social groups (e.g., Savage, 2007), as we will discuss below.

As alluded to in Table 3.3, if participants are less comfortable writing or less able to write for a multitude of reasons, offering only a written diary option will exclude the insights of important social groups, which is particularly pertinent to consider in terms of your target sample. Might some, or the majority, of your sample be less practiced at, less comfortable with, or potentially less physically able to complete a written qualitative diary? Subsequently, audio diaries have been used when studying groups who may have difficulty writing (Harvey, 2011; O'Reilly et al., 2022), including older people with potential eyesight difficulties (Koopman-Boyden & Richardson, 2013) and, more generally, those with visual impairments (Hislop et al., 2005), including young people (Worth, 2009). Rabinovich (2023) highlights the utility of employing audio diaries in

TABLE 3.3 ■ Audio Diaries: Benefits and When and Why to Use Them

Why Use Audio Diaries?	Challenges?
• When your sample is likely to be more comfortable speaking than writing and is comfortable using an audio recording device (e.g., those with visual impairments; those who haven't written in some time)	• Technical challenges and data loss (e.g., when participants may be less comfortable with technology or are required to use a researcher-provided device that they are not accustomed to)
• When your sample is likely to be busy and potentially time-poor (e.g., managers, front-line workers, working parents)	• Cost implications if audio recorders are required
• When capturing events "in the moment" with a great deal of depth is particularly important	• Potential for a reduction in structure of diary entries
• When voice intonation, emotion, and "naturalness" or authenticity are important	• Privacy issues during diary completion (e.g., Is this a particular sensitive topic? Are participants able to regularly record in a private space without being overheard by others?)

low-income, low-resource, low-literary settings. They used audio diaries to explore the financial lives of low-income women in Kenya during the COVID-19 pandemic and reported that the use of audio diaries in this context enabled rich, personal, and informative entries.

Beyond the consideration of the capacity or comfort of particular samples when engaging with the process of writing, other researchers have considered compatibility with the subject being researched and participant ease in terms of capturing particular topics. For instance, Williamson et al. (2012) used audio diaries to conduct research on new mothers' experiences of breastfeeding, enabling women to more readily record entries while breastfeeding their child, thereby allowing intimate access to the experience. The convenience of audio diaries has also been discussed in relation to being quicker and easier for busy participants more generally (e.g., Balogun et al., 2003), therefore potentially resulting in higher completion rates as compared to written QDMs due to relative convenience (Hislop et al., 2005; Markham & Couldry, 2007). This brings us to some of the particular benefits of using audio diaries more generally, specifically in relation to how they are considered to encourage ease of completion for participants (Markham & Couldry, 2007). For instance, in their study of managers within an organizational context, Balogun et al. (2003) reported that participants found it easier to dictate comments soon after a relevant event occurred, more readily being able to do so between other responsibilities, as something is recalled, or when an insight occurs. Greater ease of reporting, as suggested here, could therefore further encourage reporting closer to the occurrence of events within event-based designs, reducing the likelihood of heavily retrospective completion and allowing the researcher to capture phenomena as they unfold via increasing immediacy (Monrouxe, 2009). Of course, this must be considered carefully alongside the focus of your study in terms of degrees of sensitivity and the likely locations participants are likely to find themselves in when events occur. Considerations of participant comfort and safety in recording audio entries "in the moment" are key to ethical audio QDM study design.

Considering the relative ease of maintaining an audio diary as compared to a written diary, the length of the diary study might also play a role in decision-making surrounding the diary medium. Where QDM studies are required to be particularly longitudinal in nature (e.g., spanning more than 4–6 weeks), an audio diary might be more feasible when considering participant time commitment and also the cumulative risk of losing a physical pen-and-paper diary. Of course, audio recorders can also be lost, particularly when QDM studies are relatively long, but as is increasingly the case (e.g., Kaufmann, 2019; Williamson et al., 2015), if participants are using their own personal devices to complete audio diaries, this is less likely. In such cases, it is also more likely that any audio recordings made will be automatically uploaded to their personal storage system, and therefore, even if the device is lost, the data themselves are less likely to be.

Researchers who have compared the data produced via audio diaries to that obtained via written diaries have also suggested that "diaries spoken into voice recorders tended to be less structured but often saw the diarist reflect on his or her relation to a particular issue in great depth" (Markham & Couldry, 2007, p. 684). The audio format is therefore suggested to be more likely to encourage greater openness and directness, capturing more in-depth, natural narratives with greater self-expression and generally tending to include longer entries than those that were written (Hislop et al., 2005; Monrouxe, 2009) while allowing for more emotive observations (Balogun et al., 2003). While writing has historically been suggested to encourage a more linear record of experiences and events, imposing a linear temporality to some degree (Alaszewski, 2006), audio diaries are suggested to be less likely to entail a cohesive narrative but rather include different elements of events or experiences as they recall them (Monrouxe, 2009).

It is this relative fluidity in speech that enables not only increased immediacy of response but also more direct access to thought processes and sensemaking as they occur, via more natural speech patterns and with less opportunity for self-editing. Words are spoken with greater immediacy than they are written (e.g., Sargeant & Gross, 2011), with minimal cognitive processing suggested to take place before recording (e.g., Crozier & Cassell, 2016) and without the opportunity, or usually the inclination, to formulate sentences and ideas in a more formal manner (Alaszewski, 2006)—for instance, capturing more colloquialisms, thoughtful pauses, changes in thought direction mid-sentence, and unedited emotional expressions (e.g., Cottingham & Erickson, 2020; Fitt, 2018; Monrouxe, 2009). Crozier and Cassell (2016) argue that audio diaries may lend themselves to capturing cognitive processing—in their case, in terms of making sense of stress experiences. They draw upon Hayes and Flower's (1986, 2016) three-step process involved in writing and cognition, where planning forms the first stage, followed by translating the plans into text, before a final stage of editing and reviewing. Here, Crozier and Cassell (2016) suggest that audio diaries omit the third stage of this process and therefore allow the researcher access to the unfiltered accounts more readily than a written diary. One of our research students, Jo Gregory-Chialton (coauthor of Chapter 5 of this book), found further evidence of the reduced self-editing that takes place when participants audio record their diaries as opposed to using text-based approaches. In her study, 13 participants were asked to complete a 2-week diary (focusing upon work–family conflict experiences during the COVID-19 pandemic) using different functions within WhatsApp (see Chapter 5). Her focus was upon comparing the kinds of responses garnered when participants employed different QDM modes. In this study, participants explicitly discussed the more extensive thought processes and self-editing engaged in when writing diaries, for instance, explaining how they could "make sure I was using the correct words" or how they would

> over think a little bit which resulted in doubting things and not putting them into the diary . . . [I would] sit and think about it all first or write something and think, what are you on about? So, I'd delete it.

Alternatively, when directly comparing how they approached the recording of their written and audio diaries, they explained, for instance, how they would be "less likely to swear in writing than I am when I'm talking" or how talking enabled more free/spontaneous recording:

> If I had written it, there would be no . . .spontaneity, that I had via voice. "Oh yeah, I forgot about that." Or just reflecting. Like, there's no way you'd write that kind of stuff down. I'm going to do audio just because it's easier for me to, for me to think freely.

Jo further notes how those who used the audio mode expressed no desire to listen back to their entries, therefore reducing the likelihood of self-editing, which was also supported by the choice of language used in the diary entries. For instance, participants used expletives and emotive language when recording audio entries. Such direct comparisons between the experiences of employing different modes to complete diary entries by participants themselves further highlight the different kinds of processing that different modes may encourage or instigate, which is something that should be taken into consideration when designing QDM studies, and further when analyzing and interpreting the data (see Chapter 6).

We have also previously discussed the potential therapeutic nature of engaging in QDM studies in Chapter 2, and above we considered how written QDMs have the potential to be empowering, enabling the release of complex emotions and thought processes (Meth, 2003; Ryan, 2006). This is particularly related to their capacity to more fully embrace the editor (Ryan et al., 2009) and afford more extensive time to think and greater opportunity to reflect. Considering the reduced cognitive processing likely involved in sharing daily experiences verbally as opposed to in writing, it may be that employing audio diaries can reduce the opportunity for participants to act as editor of their own expressed thoughts and ideas in quite the same way as might occur during the completion of written diaries. There are clear benefits of this, as discussed above, in terms of ease for participants and researcher to access more natural, spontaneous, and unedited reflections. However, arguably it could reduce the cognitive processes engaged in by participants and therefore reduce reflexivity compared to that which is likely embroiled within the process of completing a written diary.

However, it is pertinent to note that this is relative and that engaging via any medium with a particular topic over time is likely to lead to increased participant reflexivity (Cassell et al., 2020). Further, audio diaries have also been discussed as beneficial for participants. For example, Hardy (2006) suggests that audio diaries within the area of stress research have benefits for participants similar to that obtained via "self-talk," which often takes the form of overt and external verbal dialogue and is considered an important cognitive coping strategy for managing stress, enabling individuals to make sense of their affective responses to stress exposure. In this sense, different QDM modes may instigate different kinds of engagement from participants and with different implications and potential for therapeutic effects. However, across modes, existing research suggests that QDMs can be a useful tool for participants and researchers alike and in a variety of ways.

Case Study 3.2, drawn from Crozier and Cassell's (2016) research, illustrates many of the aforementioned points in action.

CASE STUDY 3.2.
AUDIO QDM EXAMPLE

Crozier, S. E., & Cassell, C. M. (2016). Methodological considerations in the use of audio diaries in work psychology: Adding to the qualitative toolkit. *Journal of Occupational and Organizational Psychology, 89*(2), 396–419.

Diary Information Sheet

Thank you for agreeing to complete a Work Diary about your experiences as a temporary worker.

You will find enclosed in this pack the following documents:
- A Work Diary
- A tape recorder and blank tape
- A prompt sheet

How to complete the diary study:
- You are required to tape record your thoughts about your current work situation twice a week, for a period of three months.
- Please can you use the written diary to complete information about yourself and your job. In addition, the written diary gives you the opportunity to note any information that happens over the course of a week that you may want to elaborate on during your tape recordings. It is not compulsory to fill in this every week.
- Rather, this is an opportunity for you to make any notes about anything.
- The prompt sheets can be used to give you some content cues during the tape recording. For each tape recording, please work your way through the prompts on this. Some of the issues may be more relevant to you than others. You can talk in more detail about the issues which are more relevant to you.
- Tips on the tape recording:
- You will carry out tape recordings on a Wednesday and a Friday each week, after you have finished work for the day. You will be sent a text message to remind you that the tape recording should be carried out on that day.

Prompt Sheet

Each time you carry out a tape recording, please comment on the issues below. Please work through them in order.

You can talk in as much or as little detail as you would like. Some of the issues below may be of more relevance to you than others; therefore, you might spend more time on some prompts than on others.

- How satisfied you are with your career circumstances
- How accepted you feel by your manager and co-workers
- Whether you have experienced any discrimination
- Your opportunities for training and learning
- How much support you get from those around you
- How easily you have fitted into your role
- How you feel about your future employment situation
- Whether or not you feel stressed (and why/why not)
- Your workload
- Any other issues you would like to talk about

Example Data

This is crucial to me, this! What I will talk about now . . . basically I do not know how long this work will last, everyone is being secretive, managers included. There are Chinese whispers about when X (permanent employee) will be returning—today someone said I was next week . . . which will leave me in the lurch.

This isn't going to look good on my CV, it doesn't add anything . . . it has no relevance. I feel I am getting further and further away from getting a permanent role in law firm . . . at least it is only for a week

Today I was a bit bothered with it all to be honest. I didn't know how to enter data in a different system to the one I've used so far . . . and it was expected by the end! That was shocking . . . because I've not been trained! It was so hard. I had to ask someone who was snowed under, and they were a bit annoyed I think . . . I felt a bit worried.

Participant Reflections on Keeping Audio Diaries

I can be doing whatever at home and this at the same time . . . I don't have to take time out or plan around it . . . only ten minutes of my evening.

You don't have to plan I can just speak as it comes to mind . . . which is helpful I suppose. I don't have to spend time before; I can just go with it.

The kit worked well . . . I would have been a bit stumped without that . . . it was like a ticking off of all the things I could mention so it made the process seem simpler than if I just had to speak about me in general.

From "Methodological Considerations in the Use of Audio Diaries in Work Psychology: Adding to the Qualitative Toolkit" by S. E. Crozier & C. M. Cassell, 2016, *Journal of Occupational and Organizational Psychology, 89*(2), 396–419. Copyright 2015 by S. E. Crozier & C. M. Cassell. Reproduced with permission.

Potential Challenges

As with all methods, and indeed also with all types of QDM, there are challenges or limitations to consider. While problems related to technical challenges and data loss can be minimized by carefully considering the applicability to, and comfort of, your particular sample with technology, the risk of technical challenges and data loss remains to some extent (Radcliffe, 2013). For instance, even in cases where your sample includes frequent users of technology within their daily lives, especially where new, study-specific devices are used such as Dictaphones, errors can occur. Pre-diary briefings or, at the very least, detailed user guides or instructions and regular communication opportunities to field questions are usually required if participants are being asked to use devices that they are not already familiar with. This is important in reducing further the risk of errors in recording, accidental deletion, or simply participants becoming disengaged from the study because working the equipment is not straightforward.

Again, where study-specific Dictaphones are issued to participants, data loss can also occur even when all diary entries have been effectively recorded on the device, but participants subsequently lose the device or fail to return it. Indeed, Worth (2009) reported that the main challenge of the audio diary method was getting the diaries back, with many participants taking numerous months to physically return the diaries via mail, claiming that they were too busy. In this example, the researcher called the participants after 2 weeks if they had not received their diaries and gently encouraged them to return the device by letting them know that other participants were waiting to use the recorders. Despite this personal contact generally being effective, one recorder was never returned, with this participant suggesting that they had completed the diary but could no longer find it. In this case, just as is the case with physical written diaries, considering the process for returning the diary and making this as easy as possible for participants is important.

In addition to the above challenges, there are also cost implications if audio recorders are required, which may or may not be feasible depending on your budget. While audio recorders are now usually relatively inexpensive, depending on the audio quality you are looking for, when considering the ability for the recordings to be saved to the cloud (a real benefit considering the mitigation it provides against potential data loss) and the number of participants who will require such devices, this may be restrictive if access to funding is limited or is certainly an additional cost to build into study planning.

Finally, a particularly pertinent issue to consider if you are planning to use audio diaries within your QDM study is that of participant privacy (e.g., Jay, 2022). While we have already discussed privacy issues in relation to QDMs more generally and in relation to written diaries above, when employing audio diaries, this concern extends beyond the need to think about data storage for participants to the need to carefully consider where, when, and how the actual diary recording might take place. For instance, in Laura's study outlined earlier in this chapter, wherein couples within the same household were completing private diaries about their daily work–family experiences and decisions, using an audio diary would have been potentially highly problematic, given the close proximity of participants and their partners when recordings would often likely be made.

However, this should be a consideration not only for studies where both members of a couple occupying the same household are taking part in the research project but, more generally, if topics are sensitive, are highly personal, or have the potential to instigate conflict with others in their local environment should they be overheard. Researchers have the responsibility to think carefully about whether audio diaries are appropriate. For these reasons, Leighann also decided that audio diaries would be inappropriate when investigating participants' experiences of mistreatment in the workplace. Evidently, if participants wanted to report an incident during working hours, doing so via audio and within the workplace would engender real risks for participants. However, even if it were to be agreed that entries would only be recorded in the home at the end of the day, many participants had partners who were not aware of the difficult experiences they were facing within the workplace, and therefore finding a safe space in which they could record audio diary entries on such a sensitive topic and without risk of their privacy being breached was limited. Of course, there may have been spaces where certain participants would have felt safe to record audio entries, but to offer only this option would have been problematic. Similarly, in their study exploring the stigma surrounding HIV and AIDS, Thomas (2007) highlighted that, while talking about illness in a general context was not tabooed, the stigma surrounding HIV/AIDS meant that openly discussing personal experiences of illness risked upsetting, offending, and stigmatizing the ill person. Therefore, taking into consideration the well-being and safety of the participants, they opted to use written diaries to enable expression of thoughts and emotions privately. Evidently, striving to ensure that your research does not risk causing harm to your participants is of paramount importance, and the careful consideration of choice of QDM mode is no exception.

Practical Considerations

As is the case with all QDMs, one of the first practical considerations is the design of the diary information sheet, as well as considering how this will be introduced to, and discussed with, participants to ensure their understanding of the focus of the study and what they are being asked to do. While diary information sheets, including study prompts and/or open-ended questions (if employing a semi-structured diary design), can form the front cover (or inside cover as appropriate, considering participant privacy) of written diaries as a reminder of the study focus and questions to reflect on, this is more challenging when employing audio diaries. When using audio diaries, researchers have less control over whether participants will have diary instructions available when recording audio diary entries. As alluded to earlier when discussing some of the benefits of audio diaries, there is a tendency for audio diary entries to be less structured and more erratic in terms of flow and narrative, and the way in which diary information sheets are engaged with during audio diary research may further contribute to a less structured approach, with participants potentially less inclined to follow daily diary questions or prompts. For instance, Monrouxe (2009) reported that the young people taking part in their audio diary study often began recording entries prompted by the audio diary guide, but over time, they tended to diverge further from the guide. A reduction in structure can engender evident benefits, particularly in terms of freedom of expression, capturing thoughts and feelings as they occur with reduced opportunity for self-editing and refinement of expression. This can be especially useful in more inductive, participant-led studies, as was the case with the study by Monrouxe (2009), enabling researchers to "follow the data" and perhaps even amend research questions to focus on that which is particularly important for participants.

However, a lack of structure can also engender challenges in terms of ensuring that participants feel comfortable and confident in making the requested diary recordings, while ensuring that data collected are helpful in answering your research questions (Crozier & Cassell, 2016). Boyd et al. (2004) suggest that building in some degree of structure within audio diary designs, which is clearly reflected within diary information sheets, is particularly important in enhancing participation within audio diary studies to ameliorate challenges related to feeling unsure of where to begin, exacerbated by the verbal mode in which they are being requested to record their experiences. In other words, having key prompts for reflection can be key to support participants to begin recording, or as Worth (2009) explains, it can be useful to provide a "list of questions to start them off" (p. 11 Further, Monrouxe (2009) noted a lack of consistency across participant responses when diary information sheets used for audio diaries lacked more specific prompts or questions. In this sense, arguably having a set of clear prompts may be particularly important for audio diary studies to counter, to some degree, the potential lack of structure in responses and therefore a lack of consistency in terms of the focus of recordings across participants. Limited structure, notwithstanding the benefits, could be particularly challenging for fairly novice researchers or those whose research projects are intertwined with particular expectations from others (such as funders or supervisors). In this sense, a careful consideration of the ways in which diary instructions are prepared and delivered is often particularly important in the context of audio diary research.

As well as (or in some cases potentially instead of) preparing a more formal written diary information sheet, another consideration may be the mode of the diary information itself. Without being attached to a written diary, there is an increased potential for such instructions to be lost or misplaced and, therefore, where appropriate and feasible, you might also consider sending an electronic copy of the diary information sheet via email or mobile device to more readily enable participants to locate instructions as and when they are required (Crozier & Cassell, 2016). Further, in some cases, there may also be the possibility of the researcher making an audio recording of the diary information sheet on the recording device itself to better ensure that this is easily accessible when participants are ready and able to record an entry. This latter suggestion may be particularly pertinent in cases where visual impairments or reduced literacy are the reasons for using audio diaries in the first place. For example, O'Reilly et al. (2022) employed audio diaries in their research exploring how stress was experienced among newly married, pregnant women in rural India due to inadequate water, sanitation, and hygiene. Their decision to use diaries in this context was due to the opportunity they provide to collect participants' practices, feelings, reflections, and interactions with their physical and social environment in real time, and their use of audio diaries specifically was led by an awareness that many women in this context are illiterate. In this case, they ensured that diary instructions were also provided in multiple formats, including in writing for those who were literate, and also recorded verbally on the recording device in the native language of the participants so that they could listen back to this at any time.

As with all QDM studies, and as already discussed in relation to written diaries above, establishing personal contact and rapport, as well as maintaining contact throughout, are both key to acquiring and retaining participants.

With regards to the aforementioned utility of initial interviews for establishing rapport and supporting participants in their understanding of what is required in subsequent diary recordings once the researcher is no longer present, when audio diaries using study-specific devices such as Dictaphones are to be employed, this initial meeting arguably gains further importance. Here this is an opportunity to ensure that participants not only understand study requirements and details of what to record but also are able to use recording equipment. In most cases, those conducting audio QDM studies therefore meet participants face-to-face even if an initial interview is not conducted, in order to deliver the recording equipment and to support them in learning how to use it (e.g., Cottingham et al., 2018; Crozier & Cassell, 2016). For example, O'Reilly et al. (2022) individually trained participants on how to use the recorders and then asked participants to practice using them in the presence of the team. They also advised being careful to select a simple, battery-operated, handheld recording device so that training does not need to be extensive and so that all participants are likely to be able to use them without difficulty. Further, they met with participants again midway through the diary-keeping period to reinforce their training with the prompts and the recorders and to ensure they had not encountered any technical difficulties, and they also used this as a way to download recordings made up until this point.

As is once again the case across different QDM studies, this also speaks to the importance of maintaining contact throughout the duration of the study and, wherever possible, building in a way to attain diary entries on an ongoing basis to minimize data loss. Noting the challenges discussed above in terms of getting the data back, and where physically returning to all participants is not feasible, considering other methods by which diary entries might be more regularly shared between participants and researchers is an important consideration, particularly in terms of the potential for data loss, as outlined above. Where appropriate for your sample (e.g., in terms of easy access to the Internet, electronic devices, and their personal comfort with technology) and where funding allows, devices that enable cloud-based or email-based sharing of audio entries would be useful here. Alternatively, you can consider the extent to which the argument for allowing participants to use the audio record function on their own smartphones would be appropriate for your sample, which can then be easily shared directly from their device. However, this also requires careful ethical considerations, for instance, regarding the extent to which co-opting participants' own devices for the purpose of research might be considered an invasion of personal space (Kaufmann & Peil, 2020). This will be discussed further in Chapter 5 when we consider the use of apps. However, there are certainly numerous reasons why, where participants are comfortable doing so, drawing on participants' comfort and familiarity with their own devices, the ability to easily save and even share entries as they are made, and the password-protected affordance of mobile phone technology could arguably also engender ethical benefits for participants (Radcliffe & Spencer, 2018).

A final, but important, point to carefully consider when designing your audio diary study is when and where you will require participants to complete their diary entry, particularly in relation to privacy considerations, which become especially important when using the audio mode. For instance, consider whether your research topic is reliant on recording events particularly close to their moment of occurrence, whether these events are most likely to occur in a public place, and the extent to which events to be reflected upon are likely to engender somewhat personal, private, or even sensitive reflections. If this is the case, you might need to carefully consider whether audio diaries are the most appropriate mode. This is somewhat counterintuitive in terms of the relative ease of audio diaries reported in numerous studies (e.g., Balogun et al., 2003; Hislop et al., 2005; Markham & Couldry, 2007; Williamson et al., 2015), which can indeed encourage recording closer to event occurrence, but ethical considerations, as always, need to remain a priority. This was also emphasized in Crozier and Cassell's (2016) study, in which participants concurrently discussed the convenience of simply recording their responses into an audio device alongside suggestions that audio diaries impinged on flexibility, due to their being a need to be alone to record a diary entry. As previously discussed, ensuring that safe diary recording is feasible for your participants is pertinent, and we would always recommend careful consideration of when and where participants will be able to comfortably make regular diary recordings. This should be considered and reflected on both at the point of study design and again with individual participants.

Relatedly, if you intend to rely upon an event-contingent or a signal-contingent design, audio diaries may be more challenging as participants may be less likely to be able to make an audio recording when an event occurs or, when contacted by the researcher, if they find themselves in a place where privacy is not possible at that time. Of course, this should not rule out the use of audio diaries altogether but rather should form a key part of diary design considerations to ensure that participant privacy is considered of paramount importance. This could be enabled by, for instance, the use of an interval-contingent diary design and/or a careful discussion with participants in pre-diary interviews (or briefings) regarding when and where may be most appropriate and comfortable for them to make a recording. Another option might be to provide participants with greater flexibility regarding diary modality so that audio diary recordings might be made wherever possible but where there remains the option to record a written diary entry should that be more appropriate or comfortable for participants at a particular moment (see also Chapter 5). Indeed, you may now be spotting a pattern regarding our recommendations and increasingly across multiple diary studies (e.g., Budworth, 2023; Gibson et al., 2013; Hayes et al., 2024; Kelland et al, 2025) for greater flexibility in diary modality wherever possible within QDM studies, a discussion that will continue throughout the remainder of this book. Table 3.4 summarizes many of these points.

TABLE 3.4 ■ Audio Diary Checklist

Diary Study Design Question	Y/N
Have I prepared my **diary information sheet** and considered the **appropriate modality** in which to present these instructions? Have I also incorporated instructions regarding **how to use audio recording devices** and the possibility of training (where appropriate)?	
Have I considered **whether I will use Dictaphones or other study-specific devices (and obtained these where relevant)** or whether participants will be asked to employ their own audio recording device? Have the implications of both options been carefully considered, alongside ethical guidelines?	
Have I considered **participant privacy** and whether, when, and where they may be able to safely audio record diary entries and **whether this is appropriate** given the nature of the topic and/or likely locality of my participants? Have I prepared to discuss this with them?	
Have I considered how I will **maintain contact** with participants during the study, as well as **how I will retrieve Dictaphones** where these will be used? And/or how I might retrieve diary entries on a more regular basis? And have I planned to discuss this with my participants?	
Have I considered the **feasibility of offering both audio and written options** to participants? If so, have I considered how to readily combine these modes for ease of use and how to discuss the use of each of these with participants? Is this clear within the diary information sheet?	

APPLICATION ACTIVITY
WHICH TRADITIONAL QDM APPROACH WOULD YOU USE?

In the exercise that follows, we ask you to consider three different research studies, each with a distinct research question and, drawing on insights attained in this book so far, consider which traditional diary approach you would choose if this was your research project. This exercise should help you to consider the practical application of learning about different QDM modes so far and also to think about how you would rationalize different choices in relation to QDM modality choices. (Note: You can find an outline for suggested answers in the Appendix.)

EXERCISE: CHOOSE AN APPROPRIATE QDM APPROACH

Project Brief	Approach & Rationale
RQ: How do parents experience and navigate living with teenagers diagnosed with obsessive-compulsive disorder (OCD)? • How do parents cope with the challenges on a daily basis? • How (if at all) do these coping strategies develop and change over time? Sample: Cohabiting mothers and fathers with one or more child with OCD	*What kind of traditional diary is appropriate for this research project, and why?*
RQ: How do police officers (POs) make sense of negative interactions with the public directly after their occurrence? • How do POs describe and narrate these experiences? • What emotions do these POs experience? • How do these experiences differ across different POs? Sample: Serving POs with public-facing roles	*What kind of traditional diary is appropriate for this research project, and why?*

Project Brief	Approach & Rationale
RQ: How do managers experience leading remote and office-based workers? • What daily challenges do they experience in each context? • What communication strategies do they use and why? Sample: Managers in organizations with remote and/or office-based working arrangements	*What kind of traditional diary is appropriate for this research project, and why?*

FURTHER READING

Crozier, S. E., & Cassell, C. M. (2016). Methodological considerations in the use of audio diaries in work psychology: Adding to the qualitative toolkit. *Journal of Occupational and Organizational Psychology, 89*(2), 396–419.

O'Reilly, K., Ramanaik, S., Story, W. T., Gnanaselvam, N. A., Baker, K. K., Cunningham, L. T., Mukherjee, A., & Pujar, A. (2022). Audio diaries: A novel method for water, sanitation, and hygiene-related maternal stress research. *International Journal of Qualitative Methods, 21*, 1–10.

Worth, N. (2009). Making use of audio diaries in research with young people: Examining narrative, participation and audience. *Sociological Research Online, 14*(4), 77–87.

4 INCORPORATING THE VISUAL
Photo and Video Diaries

This chapter will provide a practical insight into visual diary methods, namely photo diaries and video diaries. It will provide the rationale for incorporating the visual in research more broadly, and within diary studies in particular. It will take the reader through the different rationales for using each of these diary methods and provide clear guidance on managing the practicalities of each of these approaches, including a consideration of important issues such as ensuring responsible photography/videography, issues surrounding "participant as researcher," and considering alignment between research aims/questions and the particular diary method used. This chapter will also consider the benefits and challenges of each of these diary methods, including practical suggestions as to how to address these challenges. Exemplar studies will also be included for each diary method, allowing readers to see existing examples of published diary studies using each of these diary methods, how the research aims influenced the choice of approach, and the materials used to develop the diary study, as well as example data excerpts. By the end of this chapter, readers will be able to make informed decisions about when and why they might incorporate a visual element into their diary studies and the most suitable approach for their particular project. They will also have a good understanding of the different practical and ethical considerations to think about when designing projects using visual diary methods.

VISUAL APPROACHES: AN INTRODUCTION

While our visual experiences of the world have, of course, always been pertinently present, researchers have been arguing for some time now that contemporary society has seen an explosion in terms of the visual (Baudrillard, 1994; Bell & Davison, 2013), with our everyday lives increasingly permeated by photographs, television, video, and digital technology. In the context of QDMs, it is therefore important to consider how the use of text-based diaries alone privileges a particular ontology in terms of our understanding of daily reality or, in other words, a presumption that daily realities constitute only that which is describable in words alone. Of course, if we take even a minute to stop and think about how we experience our own daily realities, it is evident that the visual plays an important role far beyond that which we can capture using speech or text only. Indeed, researchers have highlighted how visual communication is different from that which is verbal or text-based (e.g., Rose, 2007, 2023). Therefore, considering such distinctions between text-based and visual experiences and realities, visual research has been increasingly argued to be a necessary antidote to an overreliance to text-based understandings of our social world (e.g., Bell & Davison, 2013; Strangleman, 2004). Visual methods include an extensive range of methods, employing images in a wide variety of ways, such as via (elicited and non-elicited) photography, drawings, or video, and are broadly well established in particular social sciences disciplines, such as anthropology and sociology (Warren, 2009). While it is beyond the scope of this chapter to cover the exciting array of visual methods that exist across the social sciences, for those interested in attaining a broader understanding of visual research methods, there are multiple excellent reviews and textbooks on this topic (e.g., Rose, 2007, 2022; see also Holliday, 2000; Pink, 2006). In this chapter, we focus on the visual particularly as it relates to QDMs, with a focus on photo and video diaries.

PHOTO DIARIES

Photographs are increasingly used within research studies across the social sciences, including where researchers take their own photographs or analyze preexisting photographs, such as those available online or in company documents (Cassell et al., 2016). All of these are interesting methodological approaches that can yield rich visual insights into a diverse range of research topics. However, when considering photo diaries, we are particularly interested in, first, photo-elicitation, where photographs are elicited by participants as part of a research study, and, second, photographs that are elicited across a particular period of time. When first starting out on our own photo diary research projects, we found it useful to draw on photo-elicitation research more broadly. Much of this research did not necessarily discuss or consider their photo-elicitation approach as a type of QDM but was nevertheless aligned with QDM research in that participants were asked to photographically record their experiences in the moment and over a defined period of time. Therefore, for the purposes of this chapter, we draw from our own experiences, as well as existing research on photo-elicitation research that aligns with a QDM approach, whether or not the researchers explicitly label it as such. As was the case in Chapter 3 when considering written and audio QDMs, we will next consider when and why you might use photo diaries as part of your research design, including some of the important benefits and challenges that should be considered (see Table 4.1) before turning to important practical considerations when engaging with photo-based QDMs.

As always, it is important to consider the diary and data modes alongside your specific research questions and study aims, to decide and clearly justify your methodological choices. Why is it important and appropriate to ask participants to collect photographic data for your particular study? It may seem somewhat obvious to suggest that photo diaries should be used when the visual is important, and indeed, this is certainly a key consideration when selecting your diary mode. While, arguably, the visual is always important, you might want to ask yourself whether you will be able to gain access to the understanding you need to answer your research questions without capturing the visual.

TABLE 4.1 ■ Photo Diaries: Benefits and When and Why to Use Them

Why Use Photo Diaries?	Challenges?
• When the visual is important to gain insights into your topic that may not be fully captured by text alone	• Challenges in terms of anonymity and privacy *(for participants themselves and those captured in photographs)*
• When this would make sense for your participants *(consider participant ease/ comfort/ enjoyment)*	• Practicalities around whether and how to ask for written discussions of photos in the moment
• To encourage participant reflexivity regarding a particular topic prior to discussion during a follow-up interview	• When the participant also acts as editor, awareness of what may (not) be represented and why should be carefully considered
• When seeking to empower the participant to take charge of the research, thereby having a positive impact on power dynamics *(e.g., participant as researcher/editor)*	• Challenges regarding how best to analyze visual data and being able to do all data modalities justice *(see also Chapter 6)*

Particularly apparent examples of studies in which a visual approach to QDMs would be important to consider are those in which the environment is pertinent or where an understanding of how participants interact with particular objects within this environment is required. For example, Platt and Rybarczyk (2021) used photo diaries to examine the dynamic relationships between the built environment and skateboard and scooter-riders in Los Angeles, California, with a focus on how they responded to urban features. In this case, it was important to capture participants' momentary physical interaction with the environment. While arguably, this study could have also used audio diaries to capture participants' immediate reactions during engagement with their environment, without the visual element, the researchers would miss a more aesthetic understanding of the environments they explicitly sought to understand.

Beyond a need to capture the physical environment and surroundings, it might also be relevant to consider the extent to which the topic you are investigating may be intangible or difficult to put into words. For instance, you could ask yourself how readily you expect your participants to be able to fully express their thoughts, ideas, and experiences in relation to your particular project verbally and what might be missed via words alone. One particular study relying on photo diaries as a means of "researching the intangible" is that by Bennett (2014), who was interested in understanding the everyday practices constitutive of a sense of belonging. She reflected on the challenges of gaining insight into such an intangible experience and one that is likely fluid, elusive, and often somewhat unconscious. Prior research in this area had attempted to interview participants about how they feel or where they feel comfortable. However, considering that sensing belonging is a heavily embodied experience, not often consciously considered, at least in terms of something one is able to verbalize, she argued that capturing participants' experiences of actually engaging with the world was essential in being able to answer her research questions. In this respect, the photos allowed her to "visit" the places that permeated participants' daily lives "in a subtle and non-intrusive manner," enabling a practical, physical, and embodied understanding of people's daily experiences from their subjective viewpoint. Indeed, in the broader visual literature, the visual is highlighted as having a particular capacity to capture the unspoken, ambiguous, elusive, unconscious, tacit, and more sensory, embodied aspects of social life (e.g., Bell & Davidson, 2013; Meyer et al., 2013).

Another related reason that it may be important to capture the visual is to ensure theory-method alignment, with some theoretical lenses suggesting, or requiring, a visual understanding (e.g., symbolic interactionism, wherein visual cues and nonverbal communication are key, or semiotics, focused on the study of signs, symbols, and their meanings). Laura and her coauthors (Ashman et al., 2022) drew upon photo diaries as part of a broader netnographic study investigating how working mothers' networks were reordered during the COVID-19 pandemic lockdown when usual networks broke down. Here they drew upon actor network theory (ANT) (e.g., Callon, 1986; Law, 1994), a sociological theory that examines how social networks of actors (both human and non-human objects) shape social actions and institutions. ANT is most often aligned with an ethnographic approach due to the crucial nature of the visualization of these networks and the disparate elements that constitute them, including objects, environments, materials and techniques, taxonomies, and symbolic systems, which are inextricably intertwined within practices. Indeed, the methodological guidance is to "follow the actor" (Latour, 2005), and Law (2004) further problematizes a reliance on text-based accounts alone when using ANT:

> The coherences of textuality make powerful realities, but they also lose something: the noncoherent, the non-textual. Realities enacted in other ways. And if we simply stick with the textual then we stop ourselves from "reading," from knowing, from appreciating, those realities. (Law, 2004, p. 97)

However, the context of the pandemic, alongside the disparate nature of the networks under study, made this "visualization" particularly challenging. In this case, the use of photo diaries enabled theory-method alignment in circumstances in which this would otherwise have been challenging, by creating "visual windows" (Ashman et al., 2022) into participants' daily lives, wherein participants captured photographs associated with work such as desks, technology, and documents but also images of untidy rooms, views from windows, and pictures of children within "home working" areas.

Beyond the need to capture the visual, as discussed in the previous two chapters, it is always important to consider sample-method alignment or that the choice of method is appropriate for your particular sample. As previously discussed, a key consideration is the comfort of your participants and the ease with which they are likely to be able to engage with your proposed method. Therefore, when thinking about employing photo diaries, many of the considerations discussed in Chapter 3 in relation to audio diaries also apply here.

For instance, you might consider the extent to which your participants will feel comfortable using whatever technological means you intend for them to use to capture the photographs, as well as how comfortable they are likely to be in providing you with visual access to their personal worlds. This, of course, will depend on not only your particular participant sample but also your topic of study and what you would be asking them to photograph. Ethical implications and considerations will be discussed later in this chapter, but in relation to participant comfort, any concerns they might have about handing over personal visual accounts of their lives should also be taken seriously. Having said this, most studies report that participants enjoy taking part in photo diaries, that it is easier to attain and retain participants when compared with text-based diaries, and that participants also find this an easier, more efficient way to capture daily experiences (Cassell et al., 2016, 2020; Pilcher et al., 2016).

This reported ease in terms of capturing experiences brings us to another potential benefit of photo diaries, their particular capacity to capture the everyday, often taken-for-granted aspects of daily lives and in a way that is arguably even more immediate, or "real time," than that which can be captured by written or even audio diaries (e.g., Ray & Smith, 2012; Rose, 2012; Stowell & Warren, 2018), providing a "visual window" (Ashman et al., 2022) into a particular moment. As Bennett (2014) highlights, mundane or usual elements of everyday life can be difficult to research because they are, by their very nature, often taken for granted or somewhat habitual and therefore infrequently considered or discussed. When engaging in routine activities, we may simply act, with limited thought or reflection, limiting the likelihood that we might verbally report such daily activities or certainly that we might be aware of why we engage with such activities in the way we do.

The use of photo diaries can encourage us to capture and think about routine practices in action as part of the data collection process, enabling access to mundane activities in a way that is unlikely to arise using other methods, facilitating the exploration of the everyday, taken for granted (Bennett, 2014; Cassell et al., 2016; Pilcher et al., 2016; Rose, 2012; Stowell & Warren, 2018). As Chaplin (2004) explains, "In the short term, a photographic diary may record a series of 'heightened' ordinary moments . . . over time, patterns of continuity— and even routine—may become apparent" (p. 35). Arguments from the field of psychology examining "visual cognition" give further weight to this argument, highlighting the way in which the visual holds a more powerful place in cognitive memory than words (e.g., Chater, 1999; Tversky, 1974), further enabling reflections on particular routines, objects, or events that may otherwise go unrecalled and thereby unexplored. As you will see in a later case study, in the field of the work–life interface, the use of photo diaries enabled Laura and her coauthors to capture and thereby discuss and analyze particularly mundane but important aspects of what constitutes people's daily experiences of work–life navigation, including shoes, dustbins, and washing piles!

Another benefit of photo diaries is their capacity to particularly encourage "participant reflexivity" (Cassell et al., 2020). As we have discussed in previous chapters, this is a benefit associated with all QDM modes, but in line with arguments above regarding the additional insights photo diaries can provide into the routine, habitual, and taken for granted, such participant reflexivity has been particularly linked to diaries that capture the visual. For example, in the photo diary study conducted by Laura and colleagues (see Case Study 4.1), the act of taking photographs over a period of time was found to encourage participants to engage in internal reflexive conversations with regard to the photographs they were taking, which subsequently raised self-awareness and provided them with the opportunity to observe their own lives from a different perspective. In some cases, this led to participants critiquing their own assumptions and routines that were previously taken for granted (Cassell et al., 2020; reproduced with permission), as can be seen from the two participant excerpts below:

> There was some awareness [previously] but in talking about them [the photographs] there were things that I thought "oh, I hadn't really thought about that before." . . . In talking about it, yeah, there were a couple of times when I thought about things perhaps a bit differently from how I normally would.

> It made me realize my own work-life balance . . . I realized having a glass of wine, that that is also part of work-life balance. Buying something for the kids, that is also part of work-life balance, you are able to buy expensive toys for them because you are working, and you are able to afford it. So, I had never thought of these things from that angle but after you asked me to do it, it made me think and I quite liked it actually, because it gives you a different angle to think of your work and life.

Such participant reflexivity triggered by the process of keeping photo diaries, and sometimes also in the subsequent recounting of these images when they returned to them later, was shared with the research team during follow-up, photo-elicitation interviews. Here the photographs are discussed in turn, capturing the particular meaning of each image for the participant, and the process of capturing the photographs was also reflected upon.

It is pertinent to note here that visual research more broadly also highlights how visual communication is fundamentally different from verbal communication due to the immediate, multisensory impact of viewing an image that combines rationality with emotionality (Spencer, 2011). In this way, photographs can act as a "conversational technology" (Gammack & Stephens, 1994, p. 76; see also Ashman et al., 2022; Cassell et al., 2020) or referred to as having a "can-opener-effect" (Walker & Weidel, 1985) to describe how combining visual and verbal accounts can enable researcher insights into participant reflexivity and thereby to new, unexpected data that provide alternative ways to talk about, reflect upon, and thus understand phenomena (Warren, 2002, 2008). A particularly pertinent example is a study by Slutskaya et al. (2012), who conducted photo-elicitation interviews with butchers, finding that the use of photographs encouraged working-class men, whose accounts and experiences are usually considered less accessible to researchers, and enabled them to talk in depth about their work, including detailed and expressive accounts of everyday experiences of physical labor.

Relatedly, the way in which photo diaries are usually very much led by the participant is often considered to have a positive impact on the researcher–participant power dynamic (Hayes et al., 2022; Neves, Colón Cabrera, et al., 2023; Rose, 2012). This might include the control that is given to participants in terms of what is captured, what is not captured, and subsequently what is (or is not) discussed during follow-up interviews and in what order. In this sense, research is conducted "with" rather than "on" participants (e.g., Neves, Colón Cabrera, et al., 2023), where the participant is acting, to some degree, as the researcher, collator, and editor; collecting, arranging, and analyzing data in the field; and choosing what is important about a given phenomenon from their perspective. Here, Rose (2012) points to a distinctive collaboration between the researcher and the researched that she describes as being different from that which occurs when using other methods. As a result of their acknowledged participant-led nature, photo-based QDMs are increasingly used when researching marginalized communities (e.g., Carlson et al., 2006). Interestingly, pictorial diaries, in which participants are asked to create drawings to describe their experiences, have also been used in settings in which there are low literacy levels (e.g., Wiseman et al., 2005), highlighting the exciting potential of visual diaries to help us gain greater insights into groups whose experiences may otherwise have remained silenced.

Challenges

As with all forms of QDMs discussed so far, the key benefits of particular diary modalities are often closely intertwined with associated challenges. Just as we have discussed in previous chapters, issues of anonymity and privacy remain a challenge within photo diary research, but here with additional ethical implications particularly associated with visual data. As is the case with all modes, protecting participant privacy during diary completion remains pertinent. However, where password-protected smartphones, or indeed more traditional cameras, are used, this arguably becomes less of a challenge as the opportunities for others in participants' local environments to gain inadvertent access to participant data collected are reduced. What becomes more of a challenge is the consideration of the anonymity and privacy of others who may purposefully, or accidentally, become part of these photographic data. Of course, while participants who have agreed to take part in a research study will have provided informed consent before doing so, the same cannot usually be said for other family members, work colleagues, or those simply passing by at the time of a photograph being taken. For instance, one participant in Laura and colleagues' study (i.e., Cassell et al., 2016, 2020) discussed how they would be extremely cautious about taking photographs of children. Other researchers also highlight challenges regarding how the inclusion of other potentially identifiable symbols (such as company logos) might risk jeopardizing anonymity and also risk contravening organizational confidentiality policies in some circumstances (e.g., Vince & Warren, 2012). In this sense, a key consideration in visual QDM modes is that other people captured by participants may not have given their consent and also that logos, images, or objects may risk lack of adherence to assured anonymity, with important ethical implications.

The careful consideration of others beyond your participant sample, and how they might enter the research frame in such studies, is therefore an important element of visual QDM study designs, which should be continually monitored by researchers throughout the course of the project. From the beginning of the study, this can be addressed by providing ethical guidance to participants within participant information sheets or potentially via the creation of a more detailed additional guidance document providing specific instructions for keeping photo diaries. Laura and colleagues have found the use of Vince and

Warren's (2012, p. 295) notion of "responsible photography" to be particularly helpful here:

> **EXAMPLE 4.1**
> **EXAMPLE BRIEF FOR PARTICIPANTS FOLLOWING RESPONSIBLE PHOTOGRAPHY**
>
> Taking pictures can be a personal thing—please ask any people who are the subjects of your photographs for permission to show them to us either before or after you take the picture). You might also need to take care not to photograph anything which invades another person's privacy or contravenes your organizations' confidentiality policy (for example, visible contents of documents or computer screens). Rest assured that we can digitally obscure any identifying features of people or the company (e.g.: faces, company logos etc) and you will be given full opportunity to have any of the pictures we discuss deleted. In fact, we will ask you for permission to use each individual picture in any articles or books resulting from the research during our 'interview' meeting, so you will be in full control at every stage.
>
> Other than these common-sense precautions, feel free to take the camera anywhere and everywhere for a few days to help you remember to use it. We hope you will enjoy taking part in the research and look forward seeing the pictures you take.
>
> Once again, we'd like to thank you for agreeing to help us with this important study, if you have any questions at all about the research at any stage, please do not hesitate to
>   Contact us on XXX
>
> ---
>
> From "Participatory Visual Methods" by R. Vince & S. Warren, 2012, in C. Cassell & G. Symon (Eds.) *Qualitative Organizational Research: Core Methods and Current Challenges* (pp. 275–295). Copyright 2012 by Sage Publications. Reproduced with permission.

The guidance here is important, highlighting key steps that researchers can take to address anonymity and confidentiality challenges associated with visual QDMs, in particular, providing detailed instructions for participants that ask them to seek permission from anyone who they wish to capture in their photographs and avoid capturing potentially identifying information such as company logos. Further, researchers can obscure any such information that inadvertently ends up appearing in photographic data. Researchers should also take care in the selection of photographs that eventually appear in any resulting publications or presentations to ensure that photographs that might risk the privacy or anonymity of anyone involved in the study, whether this be participants themselves or others indirectly involved via being part of the data collected, are not included. Just as we would anonymize the names or potentially identifiable features of those discussed by participants during verbal or text-based data collection (e.g., by using pseudonyms for people and organizations), this is also a pertinent consideration when looking to ensure that photographs are fully anonymized and, where this is not possible, that such data are not included in any subsequent output. As you will see in the example study provided later in Case Study 4.2, we also drew upon and adapted this guidance for use in our own participant instructions for taking photographs.

Another consideration when using photo-based QDMs, which may pose challenges, is whether or not to also ask participants to capture text-based data alongside the photographs. What might be missed in the moment if we have access only to the visual and not also participants' verbal interpretation at the time of taking the picture? It is often the case that text-based accounts are used alone, and we invariably miss something here, particularly considering the literature discussed above highlighting the ways in which the visual captures something that text cannot. Arguably, the same can also be true vice versa. Of course, photo-based QDMs or photo-elicitation studies more broadly are usually accompanied by an interview following completion of the photo-based element of the study (e.g., Harper, 2002), in which the photographs are discussed, thereby obtaining participants' verbal reflections on what is in the photograph, why they took it, and the personal meaning of the photograph to them. As discussed above, this is particularly useful in surfacing reflexivity and gaining more in-depth insights based on this reflexivity with regard to participants' broad position in relation to the study focus. Yet, returning again to the two key benefits of QDMs and the two primary reasons for employing QDMs (i.e., capturing details of events/experiences/thoughts/emotions "in the moment" or closer to the moment and/or capturing how these change [or remain the same] over time), it is an important reflection point to consider the extent to which it would be vital within your study to capture "in-the-moment" interpretations, thoughts, and reflections as participants are taking the photographs. This may be variably important alongside more retrospective verbal reflections after diary completion. An example can be seen in the study by Hayes et al. (2024) focused on the experiences of international students and their learning during the COVID-19 pandemic. In their study, participants could submit anything they chose as part of their diary, from photographs to paintings to other forms of artwork, but alongside these artifacts, they were always asked to also provide narratives explaining how these artifacts represented their experiences and orientation toward learning. This text-based, participant analysis of the visuals enabled them to capture how the students themselves interpreted the artifacts in the moment of creating and choosing to share them. In this particular project, they deemed this important in line with their focus on understanding how international students deploy their epistemological resources to learn the curriculum, as they are doing so. By capturing both artifact and verbal reflections in the moment, they were better able to meet the research aims of their study.

However, there is not one correct answer to this question, and as always, it will be dependent on the aims of your particular study, as well as your views in relation to the way in which visuals should be interpreted and analyzed (see Chapter 6 for further discussions around this). If you do decide that you would like to capture text-based reflections alongside photographs taken, this raises the more practical issue of how to achieve this in a way that is as easy and straightforward as possible for participants. For instance, if you plan to provide participants with disposable cameras (or similar), this will then require an additional piece of diary equipment for participants to carry around, as well as them becoming accustomed to completing two separate kinds of diary entries. It may be that for your participant sample, the use of mobile app-based diaries (or the use of other technological-based means such as online blogs) that more readily permit multimodality within one specific online space may be suitable (see Chapter 5).

While we have discussed above the benefits of photo diaries being led by the participant in a way that gives them control in terms of what is and is not captured and highlighted the "participant as researcher" phenomenon that often comes from engaging with QDMs, it is also important to consider the implications of this for the data that are presented back to the researcher. Paradoxically, we may consider here the potentially performative, less "naturalistic" nature of photo diaries (Latham, 2004; Pilcher et al., 2016), for instance, when compared to audio diaries in which, as we discussed in Chapter 3, there may be reduced time for reflection or participant editing as they talk. In contrast, when using photo diaries, participants may be more likely to think carefully about what they do (and do not) take photographs of, as well as the overall image they wish to create and present.

This was apparent in Laura and colleagues' study on work–life balance (Cassell et al., 2016, 2020), wherein they included questions within follow-up interviews specifically to capture the thought processes of participants when taking their photographs. For instance, participants discussed making a conscious effort to ensure they included photographs that represented different elements of their lives, explaining that they sought to capture family time or walks in nature as signifiers of "balance." As an example, one participant explained,

> I don't know whether to take my desk, but I don't know if that would be such a good story...just that it's where I sit all day for like a big part. Just to illustrate my life. . . . But I thought I'd choose some things to illustrate that my life isn't all about work. (Cassell et al., 2020; reproduced with permission)

Here we can see how studies that encourage "participant as editor," while enabling a participant-led, more empowering approach, may also be likely to engender a more performative, carefully considered, as opposed to more naturalistic, data presentation, with time taken to think about how they might tell "a good story" or, in the context of this particular study, to try to present themselves as having well-rounded, balanced lives to highlight that their "life isn't all about work." As part of the decision-making process about which photographs to submit, participants considered how their photographs would be interpreted by the researcher and the impression of themselves that the photographs would convey. Therefore, in choosing their photographs, they were creating their own narrative of their work–life balance. In the context of this study, these insights were helpful, as we sought to understand this performative element of work–life balance and the connotations of such terminology in participants' ordinary lives, and therefore, a portion of our follow-up interview questions was designed in a way to specifically capture and understand participants' considerations when choosing which photos to take. Similarly, in a study by Hayes et al. (2024, p. 8), when discussing a photograph of one of the students' desks that was presented to the researcher within their multimodal diary entries, the research team reflected that "there was a clear attempt here by the student to curate and construct the image. The perspective in the picture excludes anything 'ugly' and foregrounds the 'pretty' elements which are lined up."

However, rather than suggesting that this process, which they refer to as "staging," compromises its authenticity, they instead highlight how it reflects the students' agency as socially constructed, demonstrating that their ability to exert control over their life is influenced and shaped by the context in which they exist (here both the U.K. pandemic-instigated lockdowns and the British education system). Therefore, in a similar way to our own study, an understanding of the performativity engaged in when the participant becomes both researcher and editor can add important insights to studies where researchers are interested in considering the ways in which social norms and cultural contexts might shape participants' daily experiences, lives, and the way in which they (seek to) live them. However, the potential for photo diaries to engender a performative element is something to be carefully considered when designing your own QDM study. Indeed, we would certainly recommend building questions into follow-up, post-diary interviews that permit insights into these processes to ensure such an understanding can be used to inform your analysis and the conclusions you draw (see also Cassell et al., 2020).

A final consideration that can engender further complexities for QDM researchers is how to analyze photographic data, usually alongside text-based data, whether this has been collected as part of the diary itself and/or during follow-up interviews. Indeed, more broadly, Shortt and Warren (2019) highlight how "analytical protocols for the investigation of still, field-study photographs remain underdeveloped" (p. 539). Specific analytical approaches that might be used to analyze photo diaries will be discussed in Chapter 6, but here it is pertinent to note that this will usually involve decisions surrounding whether and how to follow a "dialogic" approach where the focus is on analyzing the text-based data produced by participants when reflecting on the photographs produced, or an "archaeological" approach, where the data for analysis are viewed as being contained within the image itself (see Meyer et al., 2013). Alternatively, you may wish to consider both elements as part of your analytical process (e.g., Shortt & Warren, 2019). Either way, in order to do justice to the multimodal data collected during photo-based QDM studies, there are important additional decisions to make when it comes to analyzing your data.

Practical Considerations

As with all QDM study designs, regardless of modality, considerations of diary length are pertinent (see Chapter 2), and in relation to photo-based diaries, such considerations are also likely to include whether diaries will consist of photographs alone or whether they will include a text-based/multimodal component.

While capturing experiences via photographs alone may be less time-consuming for participants, if there is also a need for them to record text-based momentary reflections, time investment required will inevitably increase. As always, alongside considerations of feasibility and participant comfort, the time period decided upon will also depend heavily on your research questions and aims. For example, as you will see in Case Study 4.1, we decided that 2 weeks was a sufficient time period to enable participants to capture a range of regular experiences of work–life "balance" and "conflict" as they occur, and are experienced, in their daily lives.

In terms of diary design and whether this will be event contingent, interval contingent, signal contingent, or a hybrid design, when referring to photo diaries specifically, this is most likely to constitute a particular form of event-based design in that researchers are usually asking participants to take pictures of a particular event or their experience or understanding of a particular phenomenon. As with other types of event-based design, this will often require clarity in terms of what you are seeking participants to capture, even where you may be seeking participant interpretations of particular experiences expressed visually. For instance, while in other studies, we have been able to provide the particularities of what we are seeking them to capture in the photographs, such as asking participants to take photographs of daily work and family tasks, within the study captured in Case Study 4.1, we were seeking participants' interpretations with regard to how they experienced work–life balance and conflict during their daily lives and therefore purposefully avoided being prescriptive in terms of what should be included within their photographs. However, it was still important for us to be clear about the particular experiences we were looking to capture (i.e., daily experiences of a sense of work–life conflict and/or work–life balance) (see also Latham, 2004). In our experience, participants are likely to request further details and seek more specific guidance, with a fear of "doing it wrong." We received numerous queries from participants in which they were seeking further clarification regarding exactly what we wished them to capture. However, in this case, given the aims of the study were to understand their individual personal understanding of these concepts, it was important to strike a balance between providing clear instructions but without leading participants in a particular direction. Reassuring them that they could not do this "wrong" was important here. The instructions provided should once again be informed by study research aims and must often strike a fine balance between being adequately informative, without leading participants in a particular direction.

CASE STUDY 4.1.
PHOTO-BASED QDM EXAMPLE
Cassell, C., Malik, F., & Radcliffe, L. S. (2016). Using Photo-Elicitation to Understand Experiences of Work–Life Balance. In *Handbook of Qualitative Research Methods on Human Resource Management* (pp. 146–152). Edward Elgar Publishing.

Investigating Experiences and Interpretations of "Work–Life Conflict" and "Work–Life Balance" in People's Daily Lives

Laura and her coauthors began a study to investigate how work–life balance (WLB) and work–life conflict (WLC) are interpreted and experienced in people's daily lives and the complex relationship between the two. Existing work–life literature considering the interactions between work and life highlights wide-ranging explanations regarding how one influences the other (e.g., Minnotte, 2011; Voyandoff, 2005) but at the time of the commencement of our study there had been increasing concern about the term 'work–life balance' and what this actually means or looks like in people's daily lives and an acknowledgement of the subjective nature of this concept. We, therefore, wanted to capture moments of WLB & WLC for a diverse range of participants (with and without children, male and female, of different ages) to understand the complex relationship between balance and conflict.

As a result, our **research questions** were initially as follows:

1. How do people conceptualize and understand work–life 'balance' & 'conflict' in their daily lives?
2. How do the two relate to one another in daily practice?

We therefore decided it was important to capture 'momentary experiences' considered by participants to represent work–life balance & work–life conflict. Given our interest in the more mundane, momentary experience, we considered that these might be easily forgotten using retrospective techniques, and even that describing a momentary sense of 'balance' or 'conflict' might be difficult to immediately put into words, or to represent only via text. We, therefore, decided to use photo diaries with a diverse range of participants. We also decided on the following when considering the study design:

DESIGN AND METHODOLOGY	
Design Aspect	**Decision**
Duration	2 weeks (deemed adequate time to capture a range of daily experiences without being burdensome)
Diary type	Event contingent (take a photograph whenever they experienced something that represented, for them, WLB or WLC) using their own mobile devices. Accompanying text-based accounts not requested in the moment.
Other Methods	Photo-elicitation follow-up interviews after diary completion to explore participant interpretations of WLB & WLC captured in the photographs provided.

Importantly, this study drew upon Vince and Warren's (2012) notion of 'responsible photography' to underpin the instructions for the research participants to ensure ethical practice.

So, why photo diaries?

- Desire to capture 'Episodic Snapshots' and the mundane
- To gain deeper understanding of the *holistic nature* of people's experiences of the work–life relationship—strong participant-led approach
- Ease of use for participants to enable access to diverse sample.
- Photos could be easily taken on most smart phones.

Diary Information Sheet

Instructions for Photo-Elicitation and Interview

Over the next two weeks, please take some photographs that illustrate your daily experiences of work–life conflict or work–life balance.

Taking pictures can be a personal thing—please ask any people who are subjects of your photographs for permission to show them to us (either before or after you take the picture).

You might also need to take care not to photograph anything that invades another person's privacy or contravenes your organization's confidentiality policy (for example, the visible contents of documents or computer screens). Rest assured that we can digitally obscure any identifying features of people or the company (i.e., faces, company logos, etc.), and you will be given full opportunity to have any of the pictures you send us omitted.

Other than these common-sense precautions, feel free to take pictures of whatever you feel illustrates your work–life balance or conflict. We hope you will enjoy taking part in this part of the research, and we look forward to seeing the pictures you take.

At the end of the two-week period, please come and one of the researchers (two of the researchers will come if that works best) and we will ask you some questions about how you went about taking your photographs and ask you some other questions about your experiences of work–life balance and conflict.

Once again, we'd like to thank you for agreeing to participate in this research study. If you have any questions at all about the research, then don't hesitate to contact any of us at XXXXX.

Instructions For Photo Elicitation and Interview from "Using Photo-Elicitation to Understand Experiences of Work–Life Balance" by C. Cassell, F. Malik, & L. S. Radcliffe, 2016, in *Handbook of Qualitative Research Methods on Human Resource Management* (pp. 146–152). Copyright 2016 by Edward Elgar Publishing. Reproduced with permission. Adapted from Vince, R., & Warren, S. (2012). Participatory Visual Methods. In *Qualitative Organizational Research: Core Methods and Current Challenges* (pp. 275–295).

Example Data

FIGURE 4.1 ■ A 2 x 2 Grid of Photos: (A) Trainers Under Desk, (B) Dustbin, (C) Shoe Drawer, and (D) Washing Piles

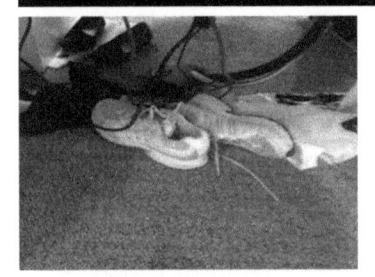

Participant Reflections on Keeping Photo Diaries

We learned that when employing such interesting methods, there is likely to be something methodological to learn too (as you will see from our resultant publications below, which, so far are both methodological in focus).

On reflection, in the future, I would go beyond text-based analysis of participant interpretations of the photos alone, to also incorporate an analysis of the photos themselves (e.g., see Shortt & Warren, 2020, for an interesting analytical approach).

Resulting publications

Cassell, C., Malik, F., & Radcliffe, L. S. (2016). Using photo-elicitation to understand experiences of work–life balance. In *Handbook of qualitative research methods on human resource management*. Edward Elgar Publishing.

Cassell, C., Radcliffe, L., & Malik, F. (2020). Participant reflexivity in organizational research design. *Organizational Research Methods, 23*(4), 750–773.

Given the previously discussed important considerations in terms of diary instructions and the balancing act frequently involved, the design of the participant diary instruction sheet is another important step in the design of your photo-based QDM study (see Table 4.2 for this and other important design considerations). If also seeking to incorporate text-based entries alongside photographs with diaries, clarity in terms of what you are seeking to capture in written or audio form will also form a key part of this information sheet (see Chapter 3) as well as clarity with regard to whether and how the two connect. For instance, it may often be the case that you are seeking immediate reflections on images captured, including why they decided to capture this particular image and what it means to them. However, there may be additional questions that you wish them to think about in relation to your research aims that are less directly related to the image. Here it might be helpful to separate out guidance on what to capture via photographs and guiding questions for text-based reflections. As highlighted in the discussion of ethical challenges above the preparation of the diary instruction sheet, for QDM studies that incorporate a visual element, researchers will also need to include guidance relating to the privacy of others. In relation to photo-based studies in particular, and as can be seen in Case Studies 4.1 and 4.2, we find drawing on Vince and Warren's (2012) notion of responsible photography particularly useful. As with all QDM studies, and as discussed in Chapter 3, establishing personal contact and rapport, as well as maintaining

TABLE 4.2 ■ Photo Diary Checklist

Diary Study Design Question	Y/N
Have I prepared my photo **diary instruction sheet**, particularly including guidance on the kinds of photos they should (not) capture, "responsible photography," and clarity around the extent to which researchers can/will edit photographs for purposes of anonymity?	
Have I considered how **photographs should be taken** (i.e., using which kind of device), **acquired appropriate devices where necessary**, and made sure that participants have access and are comfortable using this device?	
Have I considered whether or not I will seek **text or audio data alongside the photo diary**, and if so, how this will be captured (i.e., using what formats/materials)?	
Have I considered how I might **maintain contact** with participants during the study, as well as **how I will retrieve photo diaries**? And have I planned how to discuss this with my participants?	
Have I considered **how I will analyze photographic data** and whether this will focus upon a dialogic approach, archaeological approach, or some combination of the two (see also Chapter 6)?	

contact throughout, are also important, and photo diaries are no exception. Once again, initial interviews or short briefing sessions are one way to establish rapport and aid understanding regarding what is required in subsequent diary recording (e.g., Bartlett, 2012; Latham, 2004), including ethical considerations as outlined above. Such pre-diary face-to-face contact time may limit queries and anxieties later but also requires additional time commitments both for you and your participants. Whether or not to engage in pre-diary interviews is therefore an individual decision based on your participant sample and the nature of your research aims, but equally, the equipment you are asking participants to use to capture their photographs may also form a part of this consideration.

Where photo diaries involve specialized equipment that participants are not accustomed to using (e.g., Latham, 2004; Shortt & Warren, 2019), pre-diary interviews or briefings are important to ensure comfort in using the equipment. However, modern studies are more frequently relying on participants' personal devices (e.g., Cassell et al., 2020; Plowman & Stevenson, 2012), which are often more convenient for those already accustomed to doing so and are more readily "digitally returned" to the researcher. However, for some, this could be experienced as invasive in terms of infiltrating the personal space of their smartphone

(Plowman & Stevenson, 2012; see also Chapter 5), and therefore using a separate device, such as a disposable camera, may be preferable. While it is our personal experience that participants have been happy to or even preferred using their own devices rather than being required to carry a separate device with them for the purposes of the study, once again, being flexible in terms of participant preferences is important (Bartlett, 2012; Budworth, 2023; Hayes et al., 2024).

VIDEO DIARIES

Videos have been used for research purposes across the social sciences for quite some time, often as part of ethnographic methodologies wherein cameras are positioned by the researcher as a form of observation, something that particularly proliferated as camera equipment became easier and cheaper to obtain (see Erickson, 2011). However, video diaries are a comparatively recent addition to the QDM toolkit. Here, we are interested in video diaries specifically in the sense that the camera is in the hands of the participant (rather than the researcher), who, with various levels of guidance depending on the specific research project, uses these cameras to capture their daily lives and experiences from their perspective. Video diaries have proliferated in recent years due to rapid technological advances, leading to video cameras becoming a standard feature of personal smartphone devices and people becoming more accustomed to recording their own videos. This, in turn, makes it easier for researchers to ask participants to capture such recordings as part of research projects and for them to potentially be more comfortable in doing so (Zundel et al., 2018).

As a result, existing video diary studies have been used to capture a multitude of phenomena, from examinations of everyday technology use (e.g., Iivari et al., 2014; Kaur et al., 2018), including that which is used to move or "switch" between paid employment and the rest of life (e.g., Chamakiotis et al., 2014; Whiting et al., 2018), to experiences of living with a variety of health conditions (e.g., Bates, 2013; Gibson et al., 2016) or engaging with different training programs (e.g., Nash & Moore, 2018; Roberts, 2011). Those using video-based QDMs may be particularly interested in "making the body visibly, audibly and viscerally presents" (Bates, 2013), capturing emotions, bodily expressions, and personal gestures, therefore asking participants to use an "inward-facing" approach, in which participants record themselves, almost in the manner of a confessional (e.g., White, 2012; Zundel et al., 2018), with some researchers even purposefully setting up a "big brother–style" video diary room for this purpose (e.g., Larkin & Jorgensen, 2016; Nind et al., 2012). Alternatively, although perhaps less frequently, other researchers have adopted video diary methods for the purpose of capturing participants' surroundings and the various spaces that they occupy and move through, thereby using an "outward-facing" design (e.g., Chamakiotis et al., 2014; Nash & Moore, 2018; Whiting et al., 2018), although at times it was noted that participants still elected to turn the video on themselves, demonstrating the participant-led nature of video diaries (Whiting et al., 2018). Across these studies, it is evident that video diaries are used not only to capture the visual but also to enable a broader multimodal understanding of the topic under study, as we will outline in greater detail over the remainder of this chapter. We will begin by considering when and why you might use video diaries, including some of the important benefits and challenges of adopting this method (as summarized in Table 4.3), before providing useful practical considerations when engaging with video-based QDMs.

TABLE 4.3 ■ Video Diaries: Benefits and When and Why to Use Them

Why Use Video Diaries?	Challenges?
• When "in-the-moment" multimodality would be particularly suited to answering research questions—When access to participants' wider worlds is important	• Participant discomfort/reluctance
• When access to participant emotion, body language, and physicality is important	• Participant anonymity and privacy issues during recording
• When it is appropriate for your participants (e.g., they are likely to be comfortable video recording themselves or elements of their daily lives)	• Recording devices, technical challenges, data storage, and data loss (e.g., deleting or not properly recording entries)
• When seeking to empower the participant to take charge of the research, thereby having a positive impact on power dynamics (e.g., participant as researcher/editor)	• When the participant also acts as editor: awareness of what may (not) be represented and the burden on participants
• To stimulate and capture participant reflexivity *both* in the moment and in retrospect	• Practicalities of data analysis (see also Chapter 6)

One of the integral benefits of using this type of QDM is the capacity to capture "in-the-moment" multimodal data. While photo diaries provide static visual windows into participants' lives, video diaries provide active, audiovisual insights, or "audio-visual glimpses into the wider world of participants" (Zundel et al., 2018, p. 387). Therefore, when deciding whether or not to use video diaries within your own research, you might ask yourself to what extent this is required to enable you to fully answer your research questions, alongside a consideration of other pertinent issues such as participant comfort and appropriateness, as we will discuss.

The first key consideration is whether access to participants' physical wider world is important to capture in order to answer your research questions (e.g., Brown et al., 2008; Muir & Mason 2012). For example, the Digital Brain Switch project (e.g., Chamakiotis et al., 2014; Whiting et al., 2018) aimed to explore how daily work–life boundaries are negotiated in a digital world, including seeking to understand how contemporary technologies influence our ability to switch between different roles and identities. They noted that such "switches" could be rapid, almost instantaneous, and regular across our daily lives. In this sense, they sought to capture often fleeting experiences to enable them to understand how participants experienced and navigated these momentary "switches." The use of video diaries enabled them to do this in a way that was enriched by verbal reflections in the moment regarding how participants were internally navigating such identity transitions, alongside gaining momentary access to contextual cues and actions engaged in during such transitions. This highlights a potential benefit over and above photo-based QDMs, wherein audio accounts easily and naturally accompany the visual, where the visual is narrated by the participant, providing momentary reflections.

While Zundel et al. (2018) took a more "inward-facing" approach to the design of their video diary study exploring distributed sensemaking processes in relation to strategic decisions, they also highlight the benefits of observing each diarist in multiple role contexts, including in their office, in their home, and even in airport lounges. They noted how this enabled them to capture additional visual clues that supported them in answering their research questions regarding sensemaking processes, here in relation to physical context. For instance, they observed the use of props (e.g., showing an academic paper, flicking through it, tossing it aside), the ways participants dressed in different situations, and how they furnished their environment. They also gained insights into intentionally recorded elements alongside unintentional ones, providing a greater sense of various and sometimes conflicting roles being enacted as part of the sensemaking process. They, therefore, concluded that video diaries are particularly suited to recording sensemaking processes over time and across geographical locations and therefore particularly relevant for studying practices in situ. Similarly, Noyes (2004), in exploring student learning dispositions, highlights how video diaries enable participants' momentary thoughts, feelings, and reflections to be grounded in the physical context in which they are made, enabling important insights into how physical context matters. For instance, it was noted that students talked differently about their feelings toward mathematics when in their home space. This was particularly important in meeting the aims of this study, which sought to understand the influence of wider sociocultural climates on learning dispositions.

Another related point of consideration is whether attaining access to momentary bodily expressions, emotions, and physicality is required to answer your research questions. Increasing interest in studying the body has led to social scientists paying greater attention to the concept of embodiment (Bates, 2013), including, for instance, studies demonstrating that bodily expressions, including gestures and facial cues, play a crucial role in communication (e.g., LeBaron & Jones, 2002; Manusov & Trees, 2002). Further, researchers across the social sciences have emphasized the significance of bodily expressions and physicality in terms of studying, for instance, cultural rituals or the context-specific ways in which people interact with one another. In this sense, bodily expressions function as potent instruments for the embodiment of particular identities (e.g., Bates, 2013; Bell & King, 2010; Cherrington & Watson, 2010; LeBaron & Jones, 2002; Pink, 2009). However, methods adept at studying the body remain more of a challenge (Bates, 2013), and when considering the other types of diaries discussed so far within this book, it is evident that all other approaches may fall somewhat short of capturing such bodily experiences. It is here that video diaries can offer particular insights.

For example, Bates (2013) used video diaries to document daily experiences of individuals with various long-term physical health conditions, including capturing heaving asthmatic lungs and aching arthritic shoulders, walks, gym sessions, bike rides, and even moments of injecting insulin. In terms of the latter, in physically capturing the needle piercing through her flesh, this purposefully lays bare, beyond that which might be captured by words, spoken or written, the reality of living with Type 1 diabetes, challenging viewers to confront something they might typically avoid. Here, Bates argues that the methodological strength of video lies in its ability to vividly communicate the physicality of embodied experiences, transforming the body from elusive to tangible and knowable in the flesh and, in doing so, offering a more comprehensive understanding of the subject's lived experience. In terms of capturing emotions, Zundel et al. (2018) similarly noted the limitations of text alone in conveying depth of emotive expression, highlighting how video diary data were instrumental in capturing less guarded emotions mediated through participants' own expressions—transitory phenomena beyond that which a participant is readily able to put into words.

Other researchers have used video diaries to garner insights into identity construction and development through the lens of performativity, in which identity is not conceived as fixed or inherent but rather something that individuals actively perform in their everyday actions and interactions. For instance, Holliday (2004), in researching how individuals make and remake their identities according to the spaces they occupy, particularly focused upon queer identities during work, rest, and play to chart the similarities and differences in identity performances. Video diaries were used in this study to capture participants' embodied performances in different locations, including, for instance, capturing different comportments, demeanors, and behaviors, alongside personal reflections. Similarly, Nind et al. (2012), in their study focused upon inclusive education, found that video diaries offered significant potential for individuals to "play" with identity through interactions with the camera, allowing participants to actively engage with and shape their own narratives. In this sense, video diaries have a great deal to offer in terms of capturing a more comprehensive view of embodied experiences, emotions, and identities and the multifaceted nature and physicality of human interaction. However, as is always the case, the potential benefits of employing the approach must be weighed against participant comfort and preference. Here, once again, we turn to considerations of the extent to which video diaries might be appropriate for your sample. Monrouxe's (2009) point discussed previously, in relation to the use of audio diaries, similarly applies here in terms of both audio and video diaries capitalizing on young people's familiarity with technology and their pop culture understanding of solicited diaries, with the potential to be perceived as novel and fun as well as something participants feel they can use with confidence.

Other researchers have highlighted how video diaries may be a particularly useful and appropriate method of data collection when participants are children and young people, helping to overcome lowered verbal and written skills in terms of self-expression, become a conversational partner (Buchwald et al., 2009), and generally support their comfort and engagement with the research process (Larkin & Jorgensen, 2014; Nind et al., 2012; Rodd et al., 2014). Indeed, Iivari et al. (2014), described how children enthusiastically embraced the task of recording video diary entries, producing these in the style of news anchors, stage performers, or more personal confessionals. This is not to suggest, of course, that video diaries are only appropriate in studies with children, with numerous other successful video diary studies conducted with adults (e.g., Zundel et al., 2018). However, undoubtedly capturing video diaries requires confidence with technology (Cherrington & Watson, 2010) and participant comfort in both recording their personal worlds, as well as being recorded themselves.

As an example, one of Laura's PhD students also originally sought to use video diaries to capture senior managers' sensemaking processes, but each manager engaged with the project expressed discomfort and reluctance in doing so and opted to use audio diaries instead. This is something that should again be carefully considered for not only the broader sample of participants you are aiming to engage in your project but also ideally for each individual participant, keeping in mind the importance of ensuring participant comfort. Another often noted benefit of all qualitative diaries, but arguably particularly relevant when it comes to video diaries, is the way in which this method empowers participants, requiring them to take charge of the data collection process. Just as we discussed earlier in this chapter in relation to photo diaries, when using video diaries, control is given to participants in terms of what is captured and not captured, thereby making this a highly participant-led approach, empowering participants and shifting the researcher–participant power dynamics (Brown et al., 2010; Holliday, 2004; Rodd et al., 2014; Whiting et al., 2018). Video diaries involve participants overseeing, narrating, and sharing their own videos, resembling the practices of visual anthropologists (Gubrium et al., 2014; Iedema et al., 2006; Muir & Mason, 2012). As Whiting et al. (2018) highlight, video diaries in particular, therefore, offer the potential to move beyond researcher-led theorizing by empowering participants to control the video camera and, in doing so, control the process of rendering their experiences visible, through their own eyes (Jewitt, 2012). While the same can also be said of photo diaries to some extent, when using video diaries, this control extends not only to the visual images captured in the moment but also to participants' momentary narratives, thought processes, and reflections as they create and attribute meaning to their worlds, simultaneously empowering their own verbal understanding as it relates to the context to which they are directing attention (Cherrington & Watson, 2010; Pink, 2007).

This leads us to the final benefit of using video diaries: their capacity to stimulate and capture participant reflexivity both in the moment and in retrospect (Iedema et al., 2006; Pink, 2001; Roberts, 2011). As a result, researchers employing video diaries frequently highlight that they capture particularly rich data (Roberts, 2011), thereby enabling movement to more in-depth conversations during interviews (Danielsson & Berge, 2020). While we have discussed the important ways in which QDMs are generally acknowledged as a method particularly conducive to participant reflexivity (Cassell et al., 2020), video diaries somewhat uniquely provide access to audiovisual momentary reflections as well as reflections on prior personal reflections overtime, lending themselves particularly well to capturing both "being" and "becoming" harnessed by the immediacy of events and reflections recorded while also providing opportunities for replay and reflection (Roberts, 2011). The latter can be particularly harnessed in post-diary interviews, where researchers may replay participants' video clips to enable them to look back and retrospectively reflect on their own video diary entries, referred to by Whiting et al. (2018) as "video-elicitation interviews." Toraldo et al. (2018) similarly highlight videos as "reflective artifacts" (p. 13), fostering sensemaking as participants reflect on their on-screen activities during interviews.

Just as we have previously discussed the potential for QDMs and the way in which they trigger participant reflexivity to have the potential to also be therapeutic for participants, Iedema et al. (2006) point out how, in recording video diary entries, participants engage with issues not only for the benefit of researchers but also as an integral aspect of their own explorative and reflective process, allowing them to act out and later reflect on existing challenges. An example of this can be seen in the study by Whiting et al. (2018), in which engaging with the process of editing and reviewing their own entries discussing work–life balance led to some participants experimenting with ideas for improvements in this element of their lives. Taylor et al. (2019) similarly highlighted how participants used the camcorder as a confidante, a sounding board, and even a motivator in a way that participants experienced as therapeutic.

Challenges

Evidently, there are numerous exciting benefits of engaging with video diaries, but they also bring with them some particularly complex challenges to be carefully considered.

Once again, participant comfort with the technology and the process of completing a video diary should be given thought. Offering video diaries as the only method by which to record entries can be an initial barrier to participant recruitment (e.g., Zundel et al., 2018), and as we described earlier for one of

Laura's PhD students, it can be useful to be prepared to switch to a different QDM approach where necessary. When compared to other types of QDM, getting to grips with the required technology used for video diaries may be especially challenging, particularly where researcher-provided camcorders are to be used, with researchers consistently highlighting the importance of fairly detailed participant training before data collection (e.g., Nash & Moore, 2018; Owens et al., 2019; Whiting et al., 2018).

Other researchers further highlight the challenges and labor involved for participants engaging with video diaries (e.g., Muir & Mason, 2012; White, 2012). While video diaries may have the potential to be particularly empowering for participants as a strongly participant-led approach, in this "participant as researcher" context, the burden of data collection and even data curation and editing can be passed onto the participant (Muir, 2008; Muir & Mason, 2012). While all QDMs have the potential to be more burdensome than cross-sectional research, arguably video diaries require additional participant engagement, exposure, and potentially the need for extensive training, depending on your sample. It is, therefore, also worth considering that not all participants may want to take charge or be in control of the research process in this way (Jones et al., 2015; Muir, 2008).

Holliday (2007) also points out that video diaries can act as one-way conversations in which participants are unable to engage in immediate dialogue regardless of whether they are discussing topics they find challenging or where such revelations would usually engender empathy. While, again, noting previous discussions regarding the often-cited benefits of participant reflexivity (Cassell et al., 2020; Taylor et al., 2019), researchers should also consider participant burden and ethics carefully when deciding whether to engage with video diaries, including assessing the ways in which engaging in the completion of video diaries will impact (both positively and/or negatively) participants (White, 2012).

Potential reluctance and discomfort can often be related to two further challenges when using video diary methods: challenges regarding anonymity, as well as technical issues and associated risks of data loss. When it comes to video diaries, there are additional challenges and ethical implications to consider, even beyond those already discussed earlier in this chapter in relation to photo diaries, where still images can be more carefully planned and edited than the moving visuals inherent in video diaries. As White (2012) concludes, the use of videos makes traditional approaches to anonymity, such as the removal of names, almost impossible. Different concerns in this area may depend on the predominant focus of the video diary, in particular whether the request or intention is for participants to use video diaries in an inward- or outward-facing manner, or both. Importantly, the participant-led nature of QDMs means that researchers have limited control regarding what participants will actually choose to capture in practice.

For instance, if the focus is on the inward-facing video diary, a pertinent challenge here is whether or how to ensure the anonymity of participants themselves. Zundel et al. (2018) highlighted how anonymity was difficult to maintain, noting significant ethical considerations heightened by the exposing, personal, and revelatory nature of some of the data, alongside the visual animations, therefore, particularly personal representations of participants. If you might wish to include actual snippets of video data in online appendices upon publication or even still images of video data, careful consideration of whether or how participants can actually be anonymized, given that their personal selves will likely constitute much of these data, is integral. Facial blurring can be used in presenting video diary snippets or the use of replacement avatars during actual video recordings if participants were more comfortable with this. However, this prevents the capturing of data such as facial expressions; therefore, the extent to which such data are pertinent to your research project, and indeed a potential reason for using inward-facing video diaries in the first place, would need to be considered. Further options regarding anonymity in video diary studies will be discussed in the below section on practical considerations.

In those studies where outward-facing designs are used or simply where participants are likely to record entries in public contexts due to the focus of the research topic, the anonymity and privacy of others who may become part of video diary entries also require careful thought. For instance, Wiggins et al. (2014) describe how some video entries were recorded in public places and contained other people in the background, as well as discussions with others featured within the diary entries themselves. Such capturing of others poses more complex challenges than those captured within photo diaries, wherein nonparticipants can often be edited out of images fairly easily early on in the data storage process and certainly prior to use in publications. However, for video diaries, again depending on the way in which you intend to use these data during dissemination, the process of removing nonconsenting others is likely to be much more complicated, raising particular ethical challenges and also posing restrictions on usable or presentable data. For instance, should a participant engage in such conversations with others during video entries, where this other person has not provided informed consent to be part of the project, it may be that the content of this conversation, however illuminating, will not be able to be used as data.

A related consideration is the availability of private spaces for participants to record entries. Similar challenges arise here to those discussed previously in relation to recording audio diary entries, with researchers noting challenges reported in terms of locating such private spaces to record more personal entries (e.g., Holliday, 2004), including participants resorting to using toilets to record entries, raising further questions about participant comfort (Nash & Moore, 2018). Here, the sensitivity of the topic of focus should be considered when designing your QDM study, as well as the likely availability of safe, private spaces in which to record. Of course, for other studies, capturing public contexts is key to the study aims, and while problems associated with disclosing sensitive topics may be less relevant, participant comfort levels surrounding being observed by others while recording should be contemplated, alongside potential guidance regarding how to maintain adherence to ethical protocols in a context in which exchanges with others may be highly likely.

Intertwined with each of the challenges discussed so far are challenges associated with technical difficulties, data storage, and the risk of data loss, with researchers often reporting that a lack of technical skills compromised the quality of the data in some cases (e.g., Nash & Moore, 2018; Owens et al., 2019). Owens et al. (2019), who trialed the use of video diaries with older people to study "aging in place," noted that while video diaries can be an effective way to capture interesting data, the older people in their study expressed a need for more in-depth training. They reported that video diary entries commonly exhibited issues that compromised video quality, including with regard to framing, such as whether participants' faces were fully visible when talking into the camera, whether they were fully capturing what they were intending to capture, or whether participants could actually be heard properly in the entries. Zundel et al. (2018), who used private YouTube channels as online spaces in which video diary data could be uploaded by participants, also highlighted practical challenges in terms of participants both creating and also uploading diary entries. This included failed entries and the possibility of not only losing important data but also eroding participant commitment over time, as failed entries were reported as frustrating. For example, one participant recorded an entry explaining,

> Right, this is the third time I've uploaded this, hopefully. The first time, it crashed but I hadn't got that far. The second time I [pause]

I was about 12 minutes into it, so that is really, really fucking annoying. (p. 407)

This highlights the potential challenges faced by those undertaking video diary research and the importance of researchers considering the extent to which this is the most appropriate mode for your particular sample but also building in a relevant degree of training that keeps in mind the likely needs of your sample. It also highlights the importance of thinking through the most appropriate technology to use for your particular sample—what will they be most comfortable with or accustomed to using?—alongside the most appropriate way to transfer data securely between participants and the research team, again, in a way that will limit additional challenges for participants. While other electronic diary modes may be more easily transferred via secure emails, video diary data are often too large to do so. This is, therefore, something that should be discussed with your local ethics committee early on in the design of your research project to establish agreed-upon secure data transfer and storage arrangements for large data.

In addition to some of these more practical challenges, other researchers employing video diaries have pointed to the performative nature of video entries as challenging the idea that video diaries necessarily offer a direct insight or "window" into events captured (Buckingham, 2009; Gibson, 2005; Jones et al., 2015; Zundel et al., 2018). Gibson (2005), for instance, draws our attention to video diaries as meaning-making devices involving participants engaging in identity work to present a particular kind of self. However, arguably, more "naturalistic" data are likely to be captured in video diaries compared to those using photo diaries since, in a similar way to audio diaries, there may be less time to think through or momentarily edit what is said and presented. While participant surroundings can certainly be curated, and in the context of "participants as researchers," they will to some extent select what is and what is not shown on camera, there is greater potential for unpredictability and for things (e.g., people, noises, pets) to creep in, albeit with the potential opportunity for participant editing prior to sharing content with the researcher.

Just as others have argued, in relation to photo diary data, rather than suggesting that such curation and performativity compromise the authenticity of the data, attaining an understanding of the performativity and reflexivity engaged in when using video diaries can add important insights regarding the ways in which social norms and cultural contexts might shape participants' daily experiences and associated identity work (e.g., Holliday, 2000; Pink, 2001). Once again, this is something to be considered in the design, analysis, and presentation of your research. Zundel et al. (2018, p. 387) suggest considering video diaries as "translating rather than transmitting" phenomena, thereby maintaining an awareness that the process of selecting, deleting, editing, and reproducing video diary entries can make certain things (and not others) visible or meaningful primarily by virtue of being recorded and reproduced, with a heavy reliance on what the diarist chooses to reveal.

A final important consideration is how to analyze video diary data, which can be particularly complex given the rich multimodal, shifting data captured within videos. Depending on your research questions and rationale for selecting video diaries in the first place, this is likely to involve analysis of phenomena including tone of voice, facial expressions, body language, gestures, visual subjects, props, artifacts, symbols, camera angles, and framing, also including a consideration of what is not shown or remains hidden (Knoblauch et al., 2006; Vettini & Bartlett, 2022), alongside more usual text-based data analysis. Undoubtedly, this takes time, with researchers often suggesting the use of project-specific data logs to capture pertinent elements of visual data alongside related text-based data (Noyes, 2004; Wilkinson et al., 2020). Given time sensitivity and the extensive nature of these rich multimodal data, some researchers advocate a focus on "critical events" or moments in line with particular research questions (Noyes, 2004; Vettini & Bartlett, 2022). Studies that have analyzed video data are discussed in Chapter 6, but here it is important to begin thinking about how you could ensure, within your research design and specified project budget and time frame, an ability to do justice to the rich, multimodal data collected.

Practical Considerations

Considering both the benefits alongside some of the complex challenges discussed above, we next turn to look at specific design considerations when planning a video diary study. Researchers using video diaries recommend piloting the use of video diaries specifically with the research population with whom you intend to focus (e.g., Vettini & Bartlett, 2022; Whiting et al., 2018). This might involve the use of different means by which to record video entries or the kinds of instructions that are most useful to locate the most suitable and appropriate video diary design for your sample and project needs. Alternatively, noting that video diaries may not work for everyone, this is also valuable to learn ahead of the key phase of data collection and can mean that alternative or backup diary options can be made available and integrated into the overall project design.

CASE STUDY 4.2.
VIDEO QDM STUDY EXAMPLE

Whiting, R., Symon, G., Roby, H., & Chamakiotis, P. (2018). Who's Behind the Lens? A Reflexive Analysis of Roles in Participatory Video Research. *Organizational Research Methods, 21*(2), 316–340.

Project Summary

Project Aims:

- To contribute to a critical understanding of how switches between roles are managed, and the role played in this by modern communication technologies.
- To develop new tools that will allow people to better manage how they switch between work–life roles.

Diary Design: 1 week, event-contingent, outward facing design.

Diary Information Sheet

What do I need to do?
What we would like you to do is to record and narrate "a week in your life" using a digital video camcorder. This will mean you take the camcorder and use it to show us what you do over a week and in a range of locations (including your home, your workplace and other places that you may visit).

What sorts of things should I focus on?
We'd like you to focus on the different roles that you have across a range of settings (both physical such as home or office and digital such as online communities). These could include:

- Working as a colleague, manager, team member or mentor etc.
- Working as a digital colleague, manager, team member or mentor etc.
- Looking up to a leader, chief member of team/player etc.
- Communicating via email, digital communication methods etc.

Think about how you manage these different roles. This might be:

- Physically e.g. through the way your workspace looks
- Digitally e.g. through using technology such as mobile phone, computer, netbook, iPad etc.
- Through an established routine, new or interesting

What should I film?

What we would particularly like you to film are:

- Transitions between different roles, in particular how you do this physically e.g. moving between locations, and digitally e.g. using technology to adopt different identities. Showing us what you see when you transition (you might want to narrate occasionally).
- Situations where it is difficult to switch between these different roles—is this coupled with physical distance or can it be managed at the end of the working day or working week.
- Commentary on these transitions—we don't need a commentary on everything you would usually do; please keep your usual routine with any ongoing narration to a minimum, but we would like to hear your thoughts as you switch roles—any kind of notable commentary would be welcome.

This is a general approach, it's up to you to record what you feel, but what you are interested in is seeing what it is like to manage different roles. Additionally, we are also particularly interested in seeing your interaction with different technologies.

However, feel free to say what you like, and to record for as long as you like. You can record in long or short takes or simply record what is happening in front of you. Feel free to be creative - there's no one 'right' way to approach this. The exercise should be interesting and fun, not a chore.

To summarize: please film as it is happening

- transitions between roles, both physical and digital
- situations where it is difficult to switch between roles
- And include your commentary on these

What about confidentiality?

All video data collected will be treated in strict confidence in accordance with the Data Protection Act. Therefore please:

- Do not film inside a confidential, sensitive or highly personal nature including such material at your own home or workplace.
- Do not film children unless they are your own children and both parents give their consent to their inclusion on the film.
- Be aware of your surroundings and ensure that other people might reasonably expect to be filmed.

What equipment will I be given?

We will give you a video camcorder with a memory card so that you can upload it when you get the chance (we will also include a spare battery). The camera will be charged and ready to use, so we will arrange to show you how it works. The equipment will be yours to use for two weeks, and then we will collect it from you.

What should I do with the data I record?
Please upload the data on the memory card so that we can upload it when we get the chance (we will also include a spare battery). The camera will be charged and ready to use, so we will arrange to show you how it works. The equipment will be yours to use for two weeks, and then we will collect it from you.

What happens at the end of the visit?
We will arrange for the collection of the equipment from you at a mutually convenient time. You will also be invited to an interview when we will watch some of the footage together. You will also be given the opportunity to reflect on the experience and provide feedback on your QDM study, whether you think this would be a useful technique to explore in more detail.

What if I have other questions?
Thank you for participating in our project. If you have any questions please contact the research team on xxx

---

Digital Information Sheet from The Digital Brain Switch Project by H. Roby, R. Whiting, G. Symon, & P. Chamakiotis (http://www.scc.lancs.ac.uk/research/projects/DBS/outputs-media/participant-documents/). Copyright 2013 by The Digital Brain Switch Project. Reproduced with permission. The research project was funded by EPSRC (EP/K025201/1).

In previous chapters, we have also considered the use of QDMs alongside other methods of data collection, particularly with regard to the diary-interview method (Zimmerman & Wieder, 1977), and we have discussed how pre- and post-diary interviews may be more or less appropriate for a variety of reasons. When it comes to video diaries in particular, most researchers would agree that an initial interview, or at least a pre-diary briefing session, is highly recommended. For example, in Case Study 4.2, Whiting et al. (2018) conducted a detailed pre-diary briefing session that included a PowerPoint presentation talking participants through all elements of diary completion, including how to use the camcorders provided and guidance on recording responsibly. As well as the practicalities of being able to explain the complexities of the video diary recording process, researchers also point out the importance of establishing trust and rapport (Bates, 2020; Noyes, 2004; Zundel et al., 2018). This is something that is again pertinent to all QDMs, but in the case of video diaries, in which participants are being asked to share their private lives in a more wholistic and intimate way than when using other methods, establishing trust becomes ever more integral to a successful project. In this case, it can be particularly important to build additional time into the project design before commencement of the diary element of the study, as well as build a shared set of expectations and agreed-upon boundaries, which are revisited over the duration of the study. For instance, Noyes (2004) spent a great deal of time with the young people who were to participate in their video diary study ensuring they had plenty of time to ask questions, to understand what participating required, and also to play a key role themselves in defining how they would take part and how privacy and anonymity should be managed.

Post-diary interviews also often form part of video diary designs, providing an important opportunity for participants to share their experiences of taking part. As has been discussed in previous chapters, when participants have invested a great deal in a research project themselves, providing an opportunity for them to debrief in a safe space can be useful (Cassell et al., 2020). In relation to video diary projects in particular, some researchers have also used follow-up interviews to rewatch particular video clips with participants to attain their retrospective reflections upon their momentary reflections within the video (e.g., Gibson, 2005; Noyes, 2004; Whiting et al., 2018), offering researchers another interpretive layer to their analysis while also further enabling a participant-led research design in which participants here also become part of the data analysis process. Of course, the ethics of asking participants to relive particularly sensitive video clips must be carefully considered here, choosing any clips to be watched alongside participants (or indeed used for dissemination purposes more generally) with great care, keeping in mind, for instance, the degree of personal intrusion or emotive nature of the particular clip (e.g., Muir & Mason, 2012). Alongside the importance of preparing a carefully thought-through pre-diary briefing, considering that it is unlikely that all information given in such a session will be readily retained by participants, the diary instruction sheet remains essential. While the design of a diary instruction sheet is again important in all QDM studies in which the researcher cannot be physically present during completion, the design of information sheets for video diary studies will need an additional level of careful deliberation and detail. This will include information on what you are hoping participants will capture within their video diaries, how to use recording equipment, how to share recordings with the researcher(s), and how to record and share such information responsibly and according to ethical principles. As can be seen in Case Study 4.2, video diary instruction sheets may, therefore, be somewhat longer and more detailed than those associated with other types of QDM.

In line with the usual challenge of walking the fine line between being overly prescriptive and ensuring that participants understand what they are being asked to do, researchers employing video diaries have discussed the practicalities of the desire to remain participant-led while simultaneously providing adequate instructions. For instance, Jones et al. (2015) discussed how they were particularly struck by the students' additional requests for more specific guidance and prompting, commenting that "without such structure, quite simply, very few video diaries would have been produced" (p. 404). Here they noted not only the requirement to provide more detailed instructions than they had originally intended but also a need to keep in touch with them more regularly during the project than they had originally anticipated. The initial discomfort with commencing video recording often reported, including discomfort not only in terms of recording their own voices but also their whole selves and/or their private lives, may particularly require additional prompts beyond those required when using other diary formats. Bates (2020), in their study of bodies, health, and illness, describes how associated uncertainty regarding how to begin can prevent action, therefore suggesting the inclusion of initial hooks, prompts, or activities to help get them started. In this particular study, she found asking participants for a video tour of their home and neighborhood a useful initial starting point to help move past initial discomfort.

Another essential element of video diary instruction sheets, and indeed all participant-facing project information (e.g., consent forms), is clear information regarding anonymity and confidentiality, which, as we have discussed above, is particularly complex when considering video diary data. As discussed, video diaries raise particular challenges in terms of adhering to more traditional ethical principles and guidelines, particularly in relation to confidentiality and anonymity. Indeed, Noyes (2004) questions what anonymity means in the context of video diary research, highlighting how simply removing participants' names would not render them anonymous and that this type of data is, by its very nature, capable of identifying participants. Instead, he adopted a general principle in which video footage would not be reproduced or made available to others, stressing the importance of responsible consideration of the extent to which such data are used in publications and research dissemination, particularly in the context of carrying out research with children, as was the case in this study. Instead of ensuring anonymity and confidentiality, other researchers have selected to be clear in participant information sheets and consent forms that such anonymity cannot be ensured, attaining informed consent for visual data distribution from the outset (e.g., Bates, 2013, 2020; Taylor et al., 2019). Bates (2013, 2020) described working within an "ethics of recognition," referring to an adaptation of the approach taken to anonymity for each individual participant to provide them control over the extent to which they desired anonymity, highlighting that the assumption of automatic anonymity for all participants prevents opportunities to think of more novel ways to gather research data and also to think in a different way about participant control and authorship. In practice, this meant being explicit in participant information sheets and consent forms that participants were able to choose whether to reveal or conceal themselves through the way they were comfortable using the video camera. Such differential desires and comfort levels with anonymity versus recognition are highlighted across multiple studies. For instance, while Bates (2020) describes one participant who elected to write down her personal reflections, presenting these on the camera almost in the form of subtitles to conceal her voice and further protect her anonymity, Whiting et al. (2018) described how some participants in their study came to seek explicit association with project and the data they had themselves collected. For instance, one participant in their study explained,

> I gave time, I found [the project] interesting, and I hope the learning that is developed from it, is owned by the people who co-produced it. So, I am part of the team. I am not a subject. That is a very key thing for me. (p. 329)

Such reflections highlight how, particularly within participatory research designs engendering "participants as researchers," participants are progressively directly contributing to the project in ways more aligned with being part of the project team. Therefore, acknowledgment for such in-depth engagement may be desired or even expected (see also Hayes et al., 2024, regarding participants considered research assistants, thereby part of the research team). In this sense, providing participants with the choice as to whether or not, and to what extent, they would like to maintain anonymity or be explicitly tied to the data they have collected seems to be arguably more ethical. However, in practical terms, this does make the task of developing instruction sheets for participants more complex and further emphasizes the importance of a pre-diary briefing to answer any questions and discuss these options in depth with participants.

A further area of guidance that is useful to include in video diary information sheets includes "how to" reminders regarding equipment use. As well as how to use the particular device selected, some researchers also recommend discussing lighting, framing, and audio to ensure usable data and avoid data loss (e.g., Taylor, 2015). In contrast, others suggest the importance of weighing up the specificity of such instructions with the potential risk of more "staged" approaches to filming as opposed to more free, less considered recording (e.g., Zundel et al., 2018). As always, the degree of specificity provided in the information sheet must be considered in line with way in which this influences the data produced—another reason why piloting QDMs, including different versions of instructions that might be used, is generally recommended.

Thinking about technology is a key element of video diary project design. Most studies use funding to purchase project-specific video cameras, suggesting that without the use of such cameras, how and where to store video data, as well as how best to safely share these data, can be difficult (e.g., Whiting et al., 2018). However, this is certainly not where the decision-making ends. For instance, Bates (2020) describes considerations around the type of camcorder to choose, including it being ultracompact and light so that it would be easier for participants to use and less obtrusive while going about their daily activities. However, even despite such well-thought-through choices, they had not anticipated that such cameras would be difficult to rest on surfaces, meaning that hands-free filming was not possible. Here, they importantly note that it is imperative to consider the way in which the choice of technology and the affordance of this technology shape the filming and data capture that take place. It also highlights the importance of consideration regarding your participants' requirements and the needs of your project in terms of what you want them to be able to readily record and how this will work in daily practice.

As an alternative to selecting a project-specific device, Nash and Moore (2018) asked participants to use their own cameras, which led to participants using a range of devices, from smartphone cameras to high-quality SLR cameras. Importantly, this meant that participants were more familiar with how this technology works, with the potential to reduce the need for extensive training prior to diary completion and to reduce the risk of data loss due to technical errors. Zundel et al. (2018) took a similar approach in which participants used cameras within their own phones or tablets, which they highlighted as also being beneficial within an organizational context where using specialist equipment may have required consent from other organizational actors. In terms of addressing the challenges related to storing and transferring data when personal devices are used, Zundel et al. (2018) asked participants to upload video diary entries at least weekly using a private YouTube channel where the researchers could immediately gain access to the data. Such regular access to data also has the benefit of enabling data check-ins, ongoing analysis, and iterative instructions based on recent diary entries as described above. Further, it may also work to minimize previously mentioned issues around one-way conversations, risking feelings of isolation, as well as removing the need to find a way to collect a physical camcorder from participants.

In considering practicalities of video diary completion for your participants, it is important to think about when and where entries will be recorded and what is safe and feasible for participants. This will likely be influenced by whether the diary design is interval or event contingent. For those employing an interval-contingent design, discussing a safe place in which participants feel comfortable recording their regular (i.e., daily or weekly) entries can be useful (e.g., Zundel et al., 2018). Alternatively, if your study requires participants to capture an event or activity as it happens (i.e., event contingent), this requires further thought. In the Whiting et al. (2018) study (Case Study 4.2), their focus was on understanding the act of transitioning between roles, therefore requiring participants to capture such events in the moment. Considering the particular focus of your study, what you are asking participants, and the likely locations in which they will be situated while doing so is important to think about ahead of commencement of the study, and it is important to discuss with participants themselves to assess comfort levels and feasibility.

As with all QDM studies, the length of time during which participants are being asked to complete video diaries is also a key practical consideration. Generally, although with some exceptions (e.g., Zundel et al., 2018), it is more usual for video diary studies to be shorter in length, with around 1 week of diary completion being fairly usual (e.g., Bates, 2013, 2020; Symon & Whiting, 2019; Whiting et al., 2018), keeping in mind not only the particular burden on participants associated with regularly capturing their lives on camera but also the extent of the resultant data for analysis and how much data can feasibly be managed and analyzed. Bates (2020) also points out that it is important to provide flexibility to participants and, even if you are seeking 1 week's worth of diary data, this may take participants longer to capture as recording every day or capturing every instance in a particular day may not always be possible for a variety of reasons. It is therefore advisable to build in a degree of temporal flexibility when planning your study. (This and many of the preceding factors have been summarized in Table 4.4.)

TABLE 4.4 ■ Video Diary Checklist

Diary Study Design Question	Y/N
Have I **piloted the use of video diaries with members of my intended participant sample** (potentially trailing different equipment and instructions) and made any design alterations as appropriate?	
Have I designed a clear and detailed **diary information sheet** and an informative **diary briefing session** (which may involve a presentation), incorporating guidance regarding what (not) to record as well as details about using required technology and how to obtain support should technical challenges arise?	
Have I considered participant **privacy and anonymity** (and the privacy of others), as well as **potential "participant as researcher" burden**, and been transparent about this in participant-facing information, including consent forms, and providing participants the opportunity to ask questions and express comfort levels?	
Have I developed a clear **data storage and transfer plan for large data** that is in line with local ethical protocols? And have I planned to discuss this with my participants?	
Have I designed a clear **analytical protocol** or project-specific data log that will allow me to capture all pertinent elements of visual data alongside related text-based data as relevant to my research question(s)?	

Indeed, building flexibility in line with individual participant needs and potentially shifting requirements and circumstances over the course of diary completion is always something that we advocate, as we will discuss further in the next chapter. With regard to video diary studies specifically, what is evident here is the importance of building in additional time in both the planning and data collection phases to ensure project success. Such additional time required also extends to the data analysis phase, which we have touched upon in this chapter but will be considered in further detail in Chapter 6.

APPLICATION ACTIVITY
WHICH ETHICAL ISSUES WOULD YOU CONSIDER?

In the exercise that follows, we ask you to consider two different research studies, each with a distinct research question, and, drawing on insights attained in this book so far, consider the potential ethical issues, challenges, and benefits that it would be pertinent to address. (Note: You can find an outline for suggested answers in the Appendix.)

EXERCISE: IDENTIFY PERTINENT ETHICAL CONSIDERATIONS

Project Brief	Ethical, Privacy, and Other Considerations
RQ: How do people with food allergies experience and navigate eating outside their homes? • What are the daily eating patterns of these individuals? • What do their meals consist of? • How do they make meal choices in the moment? Sample: Individuals with moderate to severe food allergies Diary design: Photo and text based diaries; event contingent—participants instructed to take a photo of meals and/or snack they consume outside of their homes e.g., in restaurants, at work etc.	*If you were carrying out this project, what ethical, privacy, and other issues would you need to consider?*
RQ: How do new parents, recently returned from parental leave, experience daily transitions between their work and home roles? • What are the regular transitions between work and home that new parents make? • How are these transitions between work and family roles experienced? • Are there any gender differences in the type of transitions and the experience thereof? Sample: Working parents (mothers and fathers) who have recently returned to work following parental leave Diary design: Video diaries. Participants instructed to record and verbally explain daily transitions between home and work roles (e.g., daily commute between home and place of work)	*If you were carrying out this project, what ethical, privacy, and other issues would you need to consider?*

FURTHER READING

Bates, C. (2013). Video diaries: Audio-visual research methods and the elusive body. *Visual Studies*, *28*(1), 29–37.

Bennett, J. (2014). Researching the intangible: A qualitative phenomenological study of the everyday practices of belonging. *Sociological Research Online*, *19*(1), 67–77.

Whiting, R., Symon, G., Roby, H., & Chamakiotis, P. (2018). Who's behind the lens? A reflexive analysis of roles in participatory video research. *Organizational Research Methods*, *21*(2), 316–340.

Zundel, M., MacIntosh, R., & Mackay, D. (2018). The utility of video diaries for organizational research. *Organizational Research Methods*, *21*(2), 386–411.

5 THERE'S AN APP FOR THAT! INTRODUCING MOBILE "APP" DIARIES

(Coauthored With Joanna Gregory-Chialton)

This chapter will provide a practical insight into app-based diary methods, including the rationale for choosing app-based diaries, including considerations and the rationale for repurposing existing apps or potentially developing bespoke diary apps. In line with the preceding chapters, we will consider the benefits and challenges of using app-based diaries and review existing studies that have used app-based diaries. As a result, in this chapter, you will gain insight into how apps (both existing and bespoke) may be used in QDM research in practice. We also discuss guidance on managing the practicalities of app-based QDMs, including a consideration of important issues such as accessibility and data privacy and protection. By the end of this chapter, readers will be able to make informed decisions about when and why they might choose to use app-based diaries and the most suitable approach for their particular project. They will also have a good understanding of the different practical and ethical considerations to think about when designing projects using app-based diary methods.

MOBILE "APP" DIARIES: AN INTRODUCTION

With the proliferation of smartphones and the increase in digital research methods in the social sciences (e.g., Paulus & Lester, 2021; Whiting & Pritchard, 2020), it is perhaps unsurprising that qualitative researchers have added app-based collection methods to their toolkits. Indeed, given the wealth of smartphone apps (upward of 1.8 million on the iOS Appstore alone[1]), many researchers have opted to draw on and/or adapt existing apps for qualitative research purposes. For example, the digital turn has made it increasingly popular to collect data from social media apps such as Instagram (e.g., Brown et al., 2020; Rohn et al., 2022), Facebook/Facebook messenger (e.g., Biedermann, 2018; Robards & Lincoln, 2017), X (formerly Twitter) (e.g., Hays & Daker-White, 2015), Reddit (e.g., Baleige et al., 2022; Ritwick & Koljonen, 2023), WeChat (e.g., Chen et al., 2022), TikTok (e.g., Rodgers & Lloyd-Evans, 2021; Zhao, 2024), and of course, WhatsApp (Colom, 2022; Kaufmann & Peil, 2020; Kelland et al., 2025). An in-depth discussion of social media–based research can be found in Quan-Haase and Sloan (2022); here, however, we focus on how mobile apps may be and have been used in a way that aligns with QDM research (i.e., participants were asked to record experiences in the moment, over a defined period of time).

Due to our own interests in using apps for diary data collection, app-based qualitative research first came to our attention in the mid-2010s, when there were relatively few examples of studies employing apps (e.g., Do & Yamagata-Lynch, 2017; Garcia et al., 2016). However, with the increase of QMDs generally, but also arguably as a result of the COVID-19 pandemic (Kauffmann et al., 2021; see also Chapter 1), there has been a significant increase in studies drawing on app-based diaries ("app diaries" hereinafter), illustrating their potential and affordances as both remote, pandemic-friendly diaries but equally as multi-modal and accessible methods. Thus, as we have done previously in Chapters 3 and 4, in this chapter, we will delve into when and why you might use app-based diaries as part of your research design, including some of the important benefits and challenges that should be considered before providing important practical considerations when engaging with app-based QDMs.

APP DIARIES: BENEFITS AND WHEN AND WHY TO USE THEM

Arguably, the overarching benefit of app diaries is that they offer a versatile and multimodal tool that enables researchers to collect textual, visual, audio, video, and/or geolocation data using a single device (Colom, 2022; Welford et al., 2022). As such, depending on the functionality of the app you use to collect diaries, many of the benefits and associated challenges, as well as design considerations discussed in depth in the preceding chapters (in particular, Chapters 3 and 4), endure when considering the use of app diaries. As such, it is imperative that you consult Chapters 2 to 4 to develop an understanding of the specific benefits, challenges, and design considerations for each modality (i.e., text, audio, photo, and video diaries) prior to this chapter. Thus, rather than discussing the rationale and virtues of the different kinds of data you may collect using app diaries, as we have done previously, here we focus on the specific benefits and challenges associated with using apps to collect these data.

However, before doing so, it is important to acknowledge that there are important distinctions in the *types* of apps that may be used for research, which we will refer to throughout this chapter:

1. Existing apps—apps that have been created for another purpose that are readily in use for non-research purposes (e.g., WhatsApp, Evernote, Instagram) that researchers can adapt for research purposes
2. Fit-for-research (FFR) apps—platform-based apps that offer free or subscription-based services that enable researchers to tailor an app to their research needs (e.g., Indeemo, Epicollect5, EthosApp)
3. Bespoke apps—apps that have been created for a specific research project and purpose (e.g., De-Re-Bord app, Frąckowiak et al., 2023; WIM diary, Spencer, 2019)

These three categories of apps will feature throughout the discussion of the main benefits and challenges of using app diaries, as often they have contrasting benefits/challenges (see, e.g., section on cost). However, for the purposes of reviewing existing studies, FFR and bespoke apps will be discussed together. For now, however, let's consider when and why you should use an app diary, as summarized in Table 5.1.

As a result of the technological capabilities of most modern smartphones, as noted, the overarching benefit of app diaries is that they offer researchers multimodal data collection, thereby a "one-stop shop" (Garcia et al., 2016, p. 521) wherein researchers can collect different kinds of data (e.g., photos, text, videos, audio) and do so using a singular device (Bartlett & Milligan, 2015; Colom, 2022; Karadzhov, 2021; Welford et al., 2022). This, in turn, means that researchers can easily and efficiently collect multimodal data at the same time (e.g., photos along with text entries; e.g., Pinilla et al., 2023) and offer participants autonomy and flexibility in how they record their entries (see Chapter 2), for example, enabling those who prefer to audio record rather than create text entries to do so, but equally enabling participants to switch between modalities depending on their given situation in a particular moment. Using apps also offers researchers and participants the ability to add "emotional textures" to text-based entries, through the use of emojis as is typical of how people use messaging applications. For example, in their WhatsApp focus groups, Colom (2022) notes emoji usage among their participants in that they were used "to show agreement ('The idea is ok and support it 💯💯'), to tone down potentially uncomfortable statements, or to show disapproval: 'Its hard as an African Woman to

TABLE 5.1 ■ App-Based Diaries: Benefits and When and Why to Use Them	
Why Use App-Based Diaries?	**Challenges?**
• When multimodal data collection is required/important to gain insights into your topic/research question	• Challenges regarding how best to analyze different types of data and being able to do all data modalities justice (see also Chapter 6)
• When offering flexibility and convenience is important to your sample	• Challenges in terms of privacy and intrusion (e.g., using apps that are part of participants' private spheres)
• When this would make sense for your participants (consider participant capabilities/ease/comfort enjoyment)	• Challenges in terms of technical capabilities and affordability (e.g., does your sample have access to smartphones, the app you wish to use, data/WIFI)
• When you are seeking to recruit participants across dispersed and remote locations (e.g., international projects, hard-to-reach populations)	• Challenges in terms of providing adequate instructions and training to participants

Actively engage in Community activities because of perception that you will be seen by other Men😂😂'" (Colom, 2022, p. 459). In this way, emojis can help to overcome the lack of nonverbal cues (e.g., facial expressions) in textual format, by adding emotional cues and conveying and/or clarifying meanings (see also Bai et al., 2019; Kauffmann et al., 2021). In the context of diaries, this therefore enables participants to convey and clarify their emotions and feelings when making an entry that may be difficult when using pen-and-paper diaries or more formal digital entries such as word document and/or email-based diaries. App diaries therefore have the potential to be significantly beneficial to both researchers and participants, owing to their versatility.

In addition to the ability to offer participants choice and flexibility in how they complete their diaries (see Chapter 2), there are several reasons why app diaries have been argued and shown to enhance participant engagement and retention in diary studies. The first of these is the "familiarity" of smartphones and (some) apps. As smartphones are already deeply embedded into people's lives, (most) participants are likely to be familiar with using these devices to take photos, record videos, create text, and record audio. And as they are so embedded and portable (i.e., we carry them everywhere), the ability to record events, experiences, perceptions, and emotions in situ and in real time is arguably made easier because the smartphone is likely to be readily accessible (Colom, 2022; Gibson, 2022). This means that app diaries arguably significantly improve the convenience of keeping a diary for participants (Gregory-Chialton, 2020; Kaufmann & Peil, 2020) but are also argued to be less obtrusive and more discrete than using separate equipment such as diary booklets, cameras, and/or Dictaphones (Garcia et al., 2016; Karadzhov, 2021). For example, in their study of the everyday lives of homeless adults with serious mental illness, Karadzhov (2021) argued that smartphones were a more naturalistic approach relative to providing participants with disposable cameras that may have attracted unwanted attention and put participants at risk. This rationale was also reflected in Leighann's research exploring mistreatment at work, wherein the use of an app-based diary was deemed more appropriate than providing participants with diary booklets because it would be "normal" for participants to be on their phones and people would be less likely to question what they were doing relative to completing a pen-and-paper diary. Accordingly, app-based diaries are a familiar tool that offers both convenience and discretion, which in turn may help overcome some of the issues with participant retention but equally ensure your research design is participant-led, as we discussed in Chapter 2.

However, while providing participants with a familiar, convenient, and discrete means to complete their entries is likely to help with participant retention and engagement (Garcia et al., 2016), in line with the recommendations outlined in Chapter 2 regarding the importance of maintaining contact with participants (see also Bolger et al., 2003; Plowman, 2010), app diaries arguably offer expedient ways in which to do so but equally unique affordances in terms of notifying/reminding participants and "keeping track" of participation. First, in relation to notifying participants, a key affordance of app diaries is the ability to send participants notifications to either signal them to complete an entry that is particularly useful for signal-contingent designs (see Chapter 2) but equally to politely remind participants to complete their entries in interval-contingent designs. This ability to remind participants using the notification capabilities of most, if not all, apps can therefore help to ensure timely completion of the entries and thereby overcome issues of retrospective completion or backfilling. Indeed, researchers have also found that receiving a reminder to complete their diaries (i.e., a notification) on the same device that participants use to record their entries (e.g., such as a mobile phone) increases response rates (Lev-On & Lowenstein-Barkai, 2019) and increases the speed with which they respond (Frąckowiak et al., 2023). In this way, app-based diaries may be particularly useful for signal-contingent designs by helping to ensure the validity of your design (i.e., participants may be more likely to report when they are required/requested to do so if notified) (Lev-On & Lowenstein-Barkai, 2019; see also Mehrotra et al., 2016) but equally help to ensure data sufficiency in interval designs by reminding participants to complete their entries according to the desired interval.

Second, many apps offer the capability to monitor participants' "presence" in diary studies by providing "social information," such as when they are online, whether and when they have read a message, and when they are typing (e.g., Colom, 2022; Kaufmann & Peil, 2021). This, in turn, means that researchers can identify when a participant has potentially disengaged from the study and thereby initiate contact with the participant to discuss any issues or potentially formalize their withdrawal. Equally, because the data are often instantaneously available to researchers when using app diaries, be it through direct access such as in the case of WhatsApp or indirect backend/server (e.g., cloud storage) access through FFR/bespoke apps, this means that researchers can monitor participation or lack thereof in real time (Garcia et al., 2016). In addition to helping to track participation progress, the immediacy of the data being available to the researcher is a highly significant benefit for QDM-based research. As outlined across Chapters 3 and 4, retrieving the diaries and/or devices can be a significant challenge in that it may delay data analysis or potentially result in data loss. Indeed, across most app-based QDM studies, this was a consistently cited benefit (e.g., Frąckowiak et al., 2023; Garcia et al., 2016; Welford et al., 2022).

Third, many apps offer two-way interaction/dialogical capabilities between researchers and participants. This means that researchers can maintain communication with participants for engagement purposes (e.g., reminders, identification of issues/problems) but equally, as evident in some studies, enabling researchers to pose follow-up questions on particular entries and/or ask for elaborations on content (e.g., King & Dickinson, 2023; Mendoza et al., 2021). This may also go some way to mitigate concerns surrounding the way in which diaries might feel like one-way conversations, lacking in empathy (Holliday, 2007). While these affordances can undoubtedly enhance engagement and retention, it is important to consider how they may inadvertently impose on, burden, or perhaps even alienate participants (see discussion of challenges below).

In addition to these benefits, app diaries also offer significant benefits in terms of being able to recruit participants. Interestingly, this has been found to manifest, somewhat paradoxically, as a result of the both the familiarity and novelty of apps. Indeed, researchers who have developed bespoke apps report that the novelty of their app (and approach) may have aided recruitment of participants. For example, Welford et al. (2022) note how the novelty associated with apps may mean that they offer something new to potential participants, thereby enhancing recruitment and retention. This was similarly the case for Leighann's doctoral research (discussed in the section on bespoke apps that follows) wherein the "Work Interactions and Mood" (WIM) diary developed to collect data was a key draw in securing access to members of various trade unions to recruit participants through buy-in from senior members, aided by the tangibility and novelty of having developed an app. In contrast, others have lauded the value of the familiarity of apps in recruiting participants and, in particular, participants who are hard to research (e.g., Karadzhov, 2021; Pinilla et al., 2023; Welford et al., 2022) and/or geographically dispersed (Colom, 2022; Garcia et al., 2016; Keedle et al., 2018; Mendoza et al., 2021). Exemplary of this is the study of Mavhandu-Mudzusi et al. (2022), who used WhatsApp to study members of the LGBTIQ+ community in South Africa and Zimbabwe during the COVID-19 pandemic, thereby illustrating its advantage in accessing geographically remote and vulnerable populations. The authors do, however, note that their sample may have been limited to those participants who had smartphones and could afford mobile data to run the app. In this way, it draws our attention to the suitability of apps in populations with low socioeconomic status and, in particular, how app-based diaries may inadvertently exclude these populations. Contrastingly, Colom (2022) notes that their use of WhatsApp to conduct focus groups with activists in Kenya was a practical and inclusive option but still cautions researchers to be mindful of digital inequalities. A key consideration when using app-based diaries is therefore to consider the feasibility of using apps, such as WhatsApp in relation to your study population—for example, whether your population has access to smartphones and whether the infrastructure (e.g., mobile networks and availability of WIFI) is conducive to participation, but equally whether these devices and app are appropriate and accessible for your participants. However, it is noteworthy that mobile phones and messaging apps such as WhatsApp are widely used in developing countries (e.g., World Bank Group, 2016), and thus (Western) researchers should not impose a perception of a "digital divide" where there might not be one. In addition, as researchers arguably have a responsibility to cover the costs of participation (e.g., cover any data costs for participants) (e.g., Mendoza et al., 2021) or alternatively consider incentivizing participation more generally (e.g., Seide et al., 2023), both may encourage participation but also reduce the risk of excluding participants on the basis of cost to participate. In addition to the potential of excluding participants on the basis of cost, other significant challenges are necessary to consider when seeking to use app-based diaries, which we discuss below.

Challenges

Potential Digital Divides

While it is important that as researchers, we do not impose a perception of a digital divide on our participants and thereby do not assume that particular participants or populations may not have access to or be proficient in smartphone-based technologies, it is still important that we consider the potentiality of a digital divide when designing app diaries. For example, as briefly discussed above, is it possible that your desired population may not own smartphones and/or have access to mobile networks or WIFI or have the financial means to support their participation. Indeed, is it ethical to expect participants to use their own financial means to participate (e.g., purchase mobile data) or, alternatively, to incentivize participation (for discussion, see Head, 2009). Even in cases where the research team is covering the costs of using the mobile device or indeed providing the mobile devices to participants (e.g., Karadzhov, 2021; Sonck & Fernee, 2013), it is imperative that the ethics of these decisions is considered.

Beyond the significance of whether it is financially and/or technologically feasible to employ app-based diaries for a given population, as with all diary designs (see Chapters 2, 3, and 4), it is equally important to consider how accessible and user-friendly an app-based diary is for your desired sample. For example, do your participants have the skills and technological know-how to effectively use an app to record their diary entries? It is important that researchers consider how accessible and comfortable using an app, and all its functionalities to complete their entries, will be for their participants. While not an exhaustive list, factors you may need to consider, in addition to financial and infrastructure concerns, may include how accessible an app may be for your population and thereby whether your participants have any physical and/or cognitive limitations that may make completing their diaries on an app difficult or burdensome. In addition, is the technology itself suited to your population—for example, are there potential generational differences or preferences in your sample that may make using an app-based diary and different functions more or less desirable?

However, while numerous studies emphasizing how digital methods, such as app-based diaries, are particularly suited to studying young(er) populations (e.g., Colom, 2022; Wilkinson, 2016), it is arguably the case that given the proliferation of smartphones and the ubiquity of communication apps, such as WhatsApp, they are equally suited to older populations. Indeed, research has suggested that older populations (65+) are increasingly technologically adept (Caliandro et al., 2021; Hunsaker & Hargittai, 2018; Rosales & Fernández-Ardèvol, 2019), and as was the case for many of us, the COVID-19 lockdowns were a catalyst to increased technology usage and proficiency in older populations (Sixsmith et al., 2022). Further, in their comparison of pen-and-paper diaries and app-based diaries, Lev-On and Lowenstein-Barkai (2019) found no generational differences when comparing participants aged 18 to 37 with those aged 38 to 85. In this way, while we may have the impulse to consider app-based diaries more suitable to younger populations, it is important that we avoid imposing erroneous ageist assumptions on our (prospective) participants.

As such, it is important that when seeking to adopt app-based diaries, we avoid assuming particular populations and participants' technological capabilities and instead enable these decisions to be participant driven, allowing them to decide what medium is most suitable. As we have noted in previous chapters, offering participants choice and flexibility in terms of the diary mode (e.g., pen and paper, audio, text, and now app based) is a key means through which to help participant engagement and retainment (see also Budworth, 2023). This is equally the case for app-based diary studies, but arguably unique to app-based studies is that "choice" can manifest both within apps and outside of them. Specifically, owing to the multimodality of smartphones, many apps have the capabilities to record text, audio, photo, and video entries and do so interchangeably; thereby, app-based diaries are often inherently flexible. However, as some app-based diary studies have illustrated, while apps provide the capability to record in different ways, including text-based entries, some participants still prefer more traditional modes of recording, particularly handwritten entries. For example, Seide et al. (2023) developed a website on the WordPress platform, which enabled participants to record diaries on their smartphones and enabled participants to do so using typed text, images, and audio recordings, but equally handwritten text that participants could photograph and upload. In this way, participants were able to handwrite their entries if they chose to, and many did. Equally, in Frąckowiak et al.'s (2023) study, wherein they developed a bespoke app, despite owning a smartphone, some participants still requested to use a paper diary rather than the app because they did not use their smartphone frequently. Therefore, when deciding whether app-based diaries are appropriate for your study, it remains imperative that participants are given the choice of how to report their diaries both within apps but equally to consider offering participants more traditional diary options, such as pen and paper (see Chapter 3). In addition, it is equally important that we do not presume or assume particular populations and/or participants will be more comfortable with a particular type or mode of diary, particularly when it comes to sociodemographic factors such as age, socioeconomic status, and physical dis/abilities. Instead, as with all research methods, these considerations should be participant-led. As we have noted in previous chapters, interviews and/or pre-diary meetings/training are an opportune time to discuss these preferences with participants and, in the context of apps, particularly important to help ensure your participants are technically versed in how to complete their diaries.

Technical Issues

The second challenge related to the use of app-based diaries is related to the technology and related functionality, which manifest in two main ways: first, the need to ensure that participants understand and are confident in using the app and, second, the potential for participants to experience technological malfunctions.

As discussed in previous chapters, ensuring that participants have clear instructions on how to complete their diaries is important for all types of diary studies, regardless of medium. However, in the context of app-based diaries, particularly where you have created a new app (e.g., FFR app or bespoke), it is imperative that participants know how to use the app to create and submit their entries. To do so, many studies report running dedicated training workshops for participants prior to diary completion. For example, Welford et al. (2022) ran an interactive face-to-face training workshop for all participants to provide information about the study and support participants downloading and subsequently using the app, as they note:

> The research team used a live demo of the app and provided a training task participants could complete on their own smartphones; this provided an opportunity for participants to familiarise themselves with responding to different question types and answering questions using different media. A large amount of preparation went into the workshop and four of the research team attended to support participants. (Welford et al., 2022, p. 198)

Training sessions are therefore important to ensure that participants have confidence in completing their diaries, but equally, when researchers have developed an app (e.g., FFR or bespoke), it is often necessary to help participants download, sign up, and access the app (see also Garcia et al., 2016; Mendoza et al., 2021). Where training events such as workshops are not possible (e.g., it would not be ethical, appropriate, and/or feasible for participants to attend a training session together), initial interviews or individual briefing sessions should ideally be conducted with participants instead (Garcia et al., 2016). However, this is not always practical or desirable, for example, when there are large sample sizes or where anonymous participation is desired/required. In these instances, creating detailed information packs and potential accompanying videos in lieu of a brief/workshop should help participants to understand and use the app. For examples of each, see Mendoza et al. (2021) and Keedle et al. (2018), as well as our discussion of practical considerations later in this chapter.

While information and training go a long way in ensuring that participants are informed and proficient in how to use the app and thereby complete diaries, there is still significant potential for participants to experience technical difficulties. For example, if the app is unfamiliar to participants (e.g., FFR or bespoke apps), participants may be initially proficient but then over time become less confident or even forget how to use some functions. Equally, if the app functionality has a degree of complexity or is perceived as such, participants may lose confidence in completing their entries using the app. It is therefore important that, in addition to the initial training discussed above, participants are provided a detailed information pack and/or accompanying video that they can consult over the course of their participation, but equally, this once more highlights the importance of maintaining contact with your participants. Here, in the context of app-based diaries, this is especially important to ensure that participants remain confident in using the app and are therefore completing the diary as intended but also as a key opportunity for participants to report if they are experiencing any software/technical issues.

The emergence of technical/software issues in app-based diaries is particularly prominent in FFR apps and bespoke apps. Indeed, numerous studies that developed bespoke apps report the emergence of software/technical issues as a significant challenge. Indeed, as will be discussed later, when developing an app, numerous rounds of testing and piloting are required before launch, and yet many studies still report participants experiencing technical difficulties. For example, both Garcia et al. (2016) and Welford et al. (2022) report how despite piloting and testing the app on different devices, participants still experienced malfunctions, such as the app not loading correctly on particular screen sizes. Participants subsequently reported data loss or being unable to update the app to solve such problems and in turn withdrew from the study. This was similarly experienced in the app developed as part of Leighann's PhD project, wherein a bug in the app led to excessive notifications, with some participants being unable to download the "patch" update to correct this fault and instead withdrawing due to frustration with the app. It is also notable that when smartphone operating services (e.g., IOS and Android) publish software updates, this can in itself lead to the app malfunctioning and the need to update the app. In this way, while piloting and testing should help to iron out major functionality issues, the emergence of unexpected technical difficulties is commonplace in app-based diaries, particularly when those apps have been developed by researchers. Accordingly, it is important that contact is maintained with participants to identify any issues but equally that the app itself is maintained to avoid the emergence of significant technical faults. Failing to do so can undermine a significant benefit of app-based diaries: that they can be accessible and easy to use. If the app becomes troublesome, it therefore increases the risk that participants will withdraw.

Privacy and Personal Boundaries

A further consideration in app-based diaries is the notion of privacy and personal boundaries. While an exhaustive discussion of the specifics of data protection and privacy is beyond the scope of this text[2] and indeed our expertise, as these are governed by country-specific laws (e.g., The General Data Protection Regulation (GDPR) in the United Kingdom and European Union) and particular institutional requirements, specific points of consideration are complex and can become challenging when it comes to using app-based diaries. Specifically, while we as researchers are likely aware of the importance of protected data storage (e.g., university encrypted servers) when handling participants' data as well as the need for informed consent and confidentiality, it is important to note that when using app diaries, you are essentially introducing a third party into this dynamic. It is therefore *very* important that whatever app you decide to use, whether it be an existing app (e.g., WhatsApp), an FFR platform app (e.g., Indeemo), or a bespoke app, is compliant with the legal and ethical requirements that are specific to your national and institutional context. It is likely that most platform-based apps and professional app developers will be compliant, but those within the United Kingdom and European Union need to pay particular attention to how and where these companies encrypt and store participant data, as well as how these data are protected in transmission, and to ensure that this is GDPR compliant and that there is a data process agreement in place.[3] Due diligence in relation to how the particular developer or app platform manages and processes data is particularly important. For example, while an organization or individual may sometimes be based in a country that is legally bound to laws such as GDPR in the European Union, this does not guarantee that all of their operations are in-house, and some of their work may be outsourced (e.g., to non-GDPR-compliant countries). Given the complexity of GDPR, we strongly recommend that if you are seeking to use app-based diaries, you do so with the guidance of your institution and, in particular, legal and research ethics departments that will also help to ensure that you are protected in terms of intellectual property and ownership. Of utmost importance is that this is done *prior* to any subscription agreements or contracts being put into place with developers or app platform subscription services. It is also important that all participant-facing materials (e.g., information packs, consent forms) are clear and accessible to participants in explaining how your project and app (regardless of type) are compliant and that participants have clear understanding of how their data will be processed, stored, and shared when securing informed consent.

Beyond the need to ensure that your study and app usage is legally and institutionally compliant, a further challenge pertaining to participant privacy is the risk that using apps may impinge on personal boundaries. In particular, while participants may have consented to the study and to using an existing/new app for research purposes, it is important to consider whether this may be inadvertently encroaching on your participants' personal "spheres." Here, researchers need to be mindful of how app functions such as notifications may start to feel bothersome for participants but equally how the potential to monitor participants' presence and engagement may inadvertently be perceived as surveillance. A potential means to overcome this in messenger-based apps is to consider switching off "social information" capabilities. For example, in WhatsApp, information such as online status and whether a message has been read by participants can be disabled. While this may hinder researchers' ability to monitor participant engagement, it is important that the needs of the researcher are balanced with the ethical commitments to participants, here providing them with a sense of privacy and hopefully reducing the potential for participation to feel like surveillance.

In addition, when using apps that are readily used in daily practice, such as WhatsApp, while this everyday use can be beneficial, it is important that researchers consider that participants may not be comfortable introducing researchers into these social, yet usually private, spaces. Equally, it is important to consider this from the perspective of the researcher if using their own device to maintain contact with participants on a given app (e.g., WhatsApp), which may similarly blur boundaries and harm researchers' well-being, for example, through always being accessible to participants (Kaufmann et al., 2021). We therefore recommend that researchers use a separate device for research purposes and refrain from using private personal devices. We also recommend that researchers agree on a clear communication schedule and window with participants. For example, you may stipulate particular days and hours that you are available to be contacted through the app, being clear upfront that you will not be checking the app outside of these hours. Equally, it should be collectively agreed on when you will contact participants and how you will do so during initial interviews or briefing sessions, and it is important that you then adhere to this. For further guidance in relation to maintaining contact with participants, please see Chapter 2.

The Paradox of "Cost-Effectiveness" in App Diaries

As noted, we have categorized apps that can be used for research as "existing apps," "FFR apps," and "bespoke apps," which broadly reflect the level of adaptability and customization involved in the design of the apps, with existing apps (e.g., WhatsApp) reflecting the highest level of required adaptability and the lowest level of customization and bespoke apps reflecting limited required adaptability but high levels of customization. But these apps also reflect significant differences in terms of their costs, with the costs associated with app-based diaries paradoxically being noted as both a benefit and a challenge in the literature. For example, researchers adapting existing apps for research, most notably WhatsApp, often cite the cost-effectiveness of the app (e.g., it is free to download and use) as a significant benefit for both researchers and participants (e.g., Colom, 2022; Kaufmann et al., 2021; Kelland et al., 2025). In contrast, those apps that have opted to tailor FFR apps or create bespoke apps have done so on a pro bono basis (e.g., Pinilla et al., 2023) or reflected how the use of apps incurred significant and at times unexpected costs (e.g., Garcia et al., 2016; Welford et al., 2022). For example, researchers discussing the cost of developing apps for research note:

> With app-based research, there are costs associated with development, the design, the testing, the ongoing maintenance, the cost of the devices (if users do not have their own) and the costs associated with time; this is a time intensive methodology on the part of the researcher which should not be underestimated. (Hadfield-Hill & Zara, 2018, p. 155)

It is therefore important that researchers are aware that developing an app can be very costly but equally that your budget will determine the functionality of the app (i.e., the more functions, the more costly) and that these costs are ongoing (e.g., updates, maintenance, server host costs, and technical support). In addition, as Hadfield and Zara (2018) highlight above, it is important to consider costs associated with time—apps require *significant* time to design and develop, and they involve several iterations of testing before being ready for use by participants (see also Patel et al., 2013; Welford et al., 2022). Accordingly, it is important to factor this, alongside likely delays, into your project timeline.

Equally, you might consider whether it is feasible to develop a bespoke app if your project has a short or fixed time frame (e.g., PhD projects). A further point of consideration is whether the research design warrants the cost of developing a bespoke app. For example, if your intended diary-keeping period is relatively short and/or if your desired or actual sample size is likely to be small, then it is important to reflect on whether the potentially significant cost and time it takes to develop an app is justifiable and whether relying on existing apps or FFR subscription platform-based apps is more sensible. Indeed, as discussed in Garcia et al. (2016), when considering that their app was only used by 14 participants, they note that the project was very costly when calculated per participant. Equally, as discussed earlier, even when researchers have opted to develop an app, some participants still request non-app formats (e.g., Frąckowiak et al., 2023; Garcia et al., 2016). In this way, the paradoxical nature of cost in app-based diaries is a key factor and, in particular, the decision whether to use an existing app, tailor an FFR app, or develop a bespoke app, thereby whether to *adapt, tailor,* or *create*. To explore this in more depth, we now turn to the practical considerations of designing app diaries.

DESIGNING APP DIARIES: PRACTICAL CONSIDERATIONS

In discussing the practical considerations in designing app diaries, we now discuss exemplar studies and our own experiences across the three categories of apps we introduced in the initial sections of this chapter. To briefly recap, these are as follows:

1. Existing apps—apps created for another purpose that are readily in use for non-research purposes (e.g., WhatsApp, Evernote, Instagram) that researchers can adapt for research purposes

2. Fit-for-research (FFR) apps—platform-based apps that offer free or subscription-based services that enable researchers to tailor an app to their research needs (e.g., Indeemo, Epicollect5, EthosApp)

3. Bespoke apps—apps that have been created for a specific research project and purpose (e.g., De-Re-Bord app, Frąckowiak et al., 2023; WIM diary, Spencer, 2019)

It is important to note that the practicalities of designing diary studies using different formats discussed in Chapters 2 to 4 are relevant to app-based diaries depending on the design. For example, if your diary is going to include photo-elicitation, then the guidance provided for conducting photo diaries in Chapter 4 is important to consult. Accordingly, the below discussions focus specifically on the considerations specific to apps, and readers are encouraged to consult Chapters 2 to 4 for the finer details of designing diaries with different modalities. For parsimony and owing to the overlap in considerations when tailoring and creating an app, these are discussed together.

Adapting an App

As should be evident from the discussion thus far in this chapter, WhatsApp is an increasingly popular app to use for research purposes and is arguably the app that is most suited to diary studies owing to its familiarity and inherent multi-modality (i.e., users can text, take and send photos and videos, add voice notes, and attach documents). Accordingly, a key consideration when designing diaries using WhatsApp is what functions participants should use to create their entries. As discussed throughout this book, deciding on what kinds of data your diary will collect should be driven by your research questions in the first instance but equally your participants' preferences. In line with this, as part of her PhD project, supervised by Laura, Jo Gregory-Chialton used WhatsApp diaries in her research exploring how same-sex couples negotiate and challenge heteronormative assumptions of the family when making decisions about their career advancement and parenting roles. Participants in Jo's study were required to complete their entries using WhatsApp at least once a day for 2 weeks, thereby following an interval-contingent design (see Chapter 2), and were offered the choice of diary format according to their preference and what was convenient in a given moment. For example, participants could take a photo of something to act as a reminder to complete an entry later, complete a voice note to record something immediately after it happened, or choose to write their entries if they were in a situation where they could not talk. In this way, Jo's use of WhatsApp illustrates the utility of using WhatsApp to collect rich multimodal data but equally enabling participants to choose how to record and use different modes of reporting that best suited a given moment. Therefore, when using WhatsApp for diaries, it is once again important that participants have clear instructions and understand how and what to record, which can be aided by including diary questions and prompt sheets within WhatsApp. As an illustration, Laura and colleagues relied on WhatsApp diaries for their study of employed parents during the COVID-19 pandemic (see Kelland et al., 2025). Here they were interested in how employed parents experienced prolonged blending of work and family roles (i.e., as a result of lockdowns), how work–family decision-making processes and routines shifted in this context, and how gender influenced this experience. Multimodal diaries (i.e., text, audio, and photos) were therefore kept by dual-earner couples with children who were working from home during lockdown once a day for a period of 2 weeks following an interval-contingent design. Thus, as illustrated in Figure 5.1, each day Laura would send participants a brief prompt question followed by a more detailed prompt sheet (which was also originally shared with them at the start of the study) to remind participants of what to include in their entries. This approach therefore capitalizes on the dialogical nature of WhatsApp, wherein the two-way conversation enables the researcher to prompt participants with reminders of diary questions or things to consider when recording their entries.

It is, however, important to consider how you will manage this and that how you will do so is clearly communicated and agreed on with your participants upfront. As noted earlier in this chapter, it is important that clear protocols are in place to manage how and when you will communicate with your participants when using apps, particularly those that are used by participants for non-research purposes and therefore part of their private spheres (see Kaufmann & Peil, 2020). This is to avoid encroaching on your participants but equally to ensure that this does not become overwhelming for you as a researcher. As previously mentioned, it is also advisable that researchers use a separate device to run their WhatsApp QDM studies rather than their personal device. Doing so is practical in terms of managing communications with your sample and enabling the researcher to more effectively keep track of participation (cf. difficulties in having numerous research participants intermingled with your personal conversations) but also important in creating a clear boundary between your research (work) and nonwork lives, therefore enabling you as the researcher a degree of privacy. This is particularly important in terms minimizing risks to researchers.

A final consideration when using WhatsApp diaries is how you will retrieve and organize participants' data. In contrast to FFR and bespoke apps wherein data are typically available through a (secure) backend/cloud storage system, here you will have access to participants' data in the form of direct messages. Thus, retrieving participants' data will require you to do so manually. However, this process is relatively straightforward in WhatsApp as you can easily export the entire chat content, including media, from within the app. As will be

144 Qualitative Diary Methods

FIGURE 5.1 ■ Screenshot of WhatsApp Diary

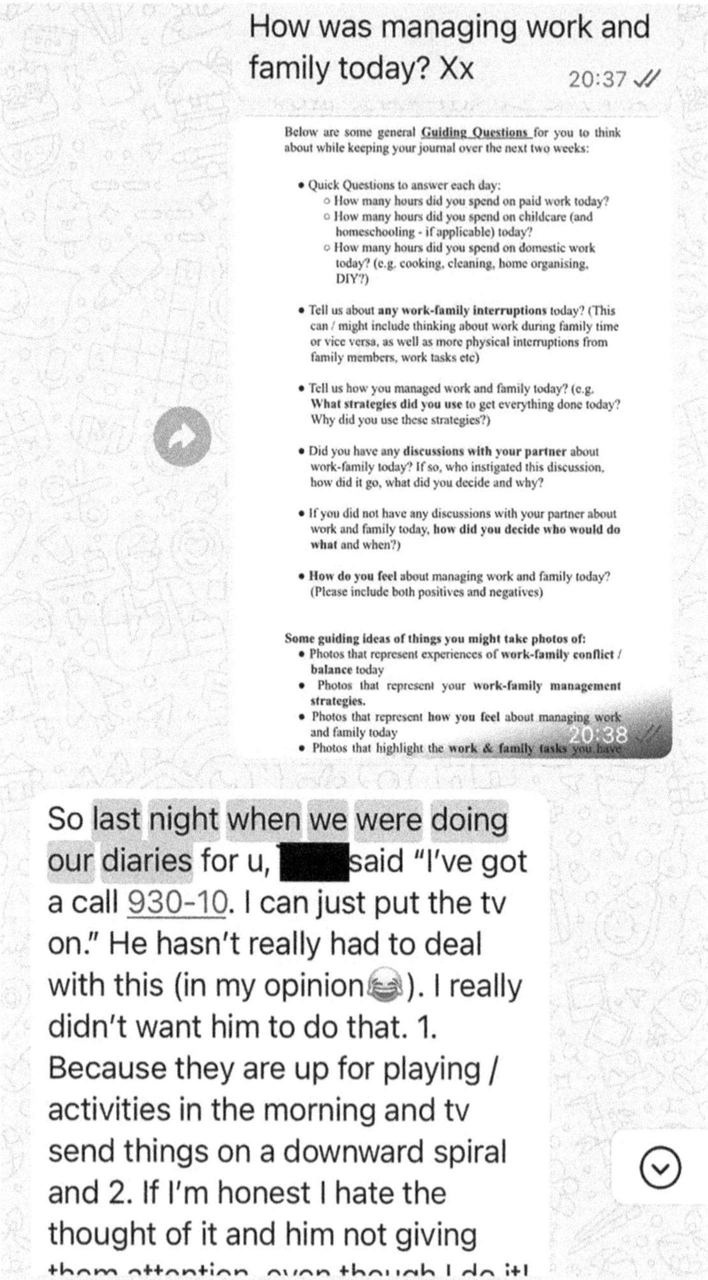

> How was managing work and family today? Xx 20:37
>
> Below are some general <u>Guiding Questions</u> for you to think about while keeping your journal over the next two weeks:
>
> - Quick Questions to answer each day:
>   - How many hours did you spend on paid work today?
>   - How many hours did you spend on childcare (and homeschooling - if applicable) today?
>   - How many hours did you spend on domestic work today? (e.g. cooking, cleaning, home organising, DIY?)
> - Tell us about any **work-family interruptions** today? (This can / might include thinking about work during family time or vice versa, as well as more physical interruptions from family members, work tasks etc)
> - Tell us how you managed work and family today? (e.g. **What strategies did you use** to get everything done today? Why did you use these strategies?)
> - Did you have any **discussions with your partner** about work-family today? If so, who instigated this discussion, how did it go, what did you decide and why?
> - If you did not have any discussions with your partner about work and family today, **how did you decide who would do what** and when?)
> - **How do you feel** about managing work and family today? (Please include both positives and negatives)
>
> Some guiding ideas of things you might take photos of:
> - Photos that represent experiences of **work-family conflict / balance** today
> - Photos that represent your **work-family management strategies.**
> - Photos that represent how you feel about managing work and family today
> - Photos that highlight the **work & family tasks** you have
>
> 20:38
>
> So last night when we were doing our diaries for u, ▓▓▓ said "I've got a call 930-10. I can just put the tv on." He hasn't really had to deal with this (in my opinion 😂). I really didn't want him to do that. 1. Because they are up for playing / activities in the morning and tv send things on a downward spiral and 2. If I'm honest I hate the thought of it and him not giving them attention, even though I do it!

discussed in Chapter 6, it is important that you export and transfer participants' data regularly and consistently during data collection rather than waiting until the end to enable a robust data management system but, most importantly, avoid data loss.

Tailoring or Creating an App

As discussed in relation to the cost of app-based diaries, there are substantial costs associated with both FFR subscription-based and bespoke apps. These costs are therefore a significant consideration in terms of feasibility (e.g., can you secure funding to develop or tailor an app) but equally have significant influence on the functionality and usability of your app. As noted previously, typically the more functionality and complexity that is built into your app, the more expensive it is. In this way, an important consideration is how you will balance your budget with the design features required to gather the data needed to address your research questions. This includes which smartphone capabilities (e.g., photos, videos, text, audio recording) you will incorporate in your app but also, if aiming to use a subscription platform-based app service (e.g., Indeemo, EthosApp), what features these platforms support.

In deciding what features your app will have, it is therefore important that you first determine this in line with your research questions, for example, if the visual is important to address your research questions (see Chapter 4), then your app will need to incorporate the smartphone visual capabilities. However, as we have argued throughout, providing participants flexibility in how they report is key to encouraging participation and ensuring that your design is participant-led (see Chapter 2), and it is therefore important that you consider providing participants flexibility in your app by including multiple ways to complete their entries. Doing so, however, will necessitate that your app includes multiple functions, and therefore likely increase the cost of your app. As a result, the difficulty here is determining *which* features are important to include for your sample but equally those that address your research aims and questions. This is important to ensure that your app does not include redundant features. For example, in Leighann's PhD project, the Work, Interaction, and Mood (WIM) diary app was developed with multimodal capabilities; participants could enter text, record audio, and add photographs to their entries, but other than one or two audio entries, participants completed their entries using the text option, thereby rendering the other completion options largely redundant.

It is therefore important that you pilot your app design either through the app development process (e.g., through beta round testing) or, if using a subscription service, through different iterations of what the platform service offers. However, doing so will still necessitate that you have some kind of financial agreement in place (e.g., you will have already agreed on a contract with a developer/servicer to get to the point that you are testing different versions). Alternatively, a potentially cost-effective way to determine what capabilities might be most appropriate for your sample is to draw on an existing app (e.g., WhatsApp) to determine what features your indicative sample may or may not use and why. In this way, your desired sample will have direct input into how you design your diary. Of course, it is important that your pilot sample is representative of your wider study sample.

A more inclusive, yet intensive, way to include your participants in your app and study design is to conduct a participatory research study, where participants are explicitly co-designers of the app and research more broadly (see also Welford et al., 2022). A detailed example of this can be found in Hadfield-Hill and Zara (2018), who discuss their study aimed at investigating the everyday experience of urban transformation in India and to understand the impacts of urban development on the lives of diverse groups of young people. In their approach, young people were heavily involved and therefore had a significant stake in the design of the app (form and function), its implementation, and the analysis of the data. In relation to the design of the app, the authors describe, for example, how in Stage 1 they conducted workshops initially with UK young people to get input into the design, layout, process, and form of the app, but then in Stage 2, further workshops were held with Indian participants to adapt the content of the app to further suit their specific cultural context. For example, they note the following:

> Workshops addressed: (i) the design and layout of the app and cultural appropriateness of the logos; (ii) the language of the app content ensuring age relevance and cultural specificity; (iii) translation into the local language, Marathi; (iv) the design and implementation of an app related consent form for young people and their guardians. (Hadfield-Hill & Zara, 2018, p. 151)

The authors discuss how this gave the young people agency (Hadfield-Hill & Zara, 2018) but also note that it is important to manage participants' expectations when they are included in the design of apps, particularly in relation to the capabilities of the app and associated costs. Including participants in the design of your app is therefore a means through which you can ensure that the app design and resultant functionality is participant-led, which in turn may reduce the risk of redundant or missing features but also help to enhance participant engagement.

Once you have decided the main functions of the app (e.g., text, photos, videos, and/or audio), considerations then turn to the aesthetics of the app and its usability. A core consideration in designing app-based diaries when developing or tailoring an app is how your diary questions will translate on an app interface. Typically, when working with a developer, you will be required to create a screen-by-screen interface. In Leighann's project, for example, we did so on paper before proving this markup to the developer, who then mirrored this design in the app. Part of this translation process is to consider how appealing the interface will be to participants but equally whether it is easy to use; if participants find the app cumbersome, it is likely they will withdraw. While ease of use is something that will be refined through the piloting and testing process, if your budget is conducive to doing so, you may consider including gamification or tracking elements within the app. For example, if your diaries are aimed at understanding the experience of a phenomenon that is likely to induce fluctuating emotions (e.g., experience of mistreatment at work, work–family conflicts), then including a tracking element in the app related to these emotions may help the app to be perceived as having utility to participants as a reflective tool (i.e., being able to track their own emotions over time). In line with this, in Leighann's app (WIM diary), to help usability of the app and provide participants with a tracking element, when entering a diary entry, participants were able to swipe up or down to select a "face" that best described their emotions at the time of entering before progressing to the text entries, where they were required to describe their emotions and answer the diary questions (here Question 1 out of 4; see Figure 5.2). While the app did not include sophisticated analytical capabilities to transform participants' daily emotion "ratings" into graphical representations, if your budget allows, this is a feasible means with which to enhance participants' perceptions of the app's utility and benefits to them, in turn hopefully enhancing participation.

Finally, in addition to these important functionality and usability considerations, there are important considerations related to the process of securing a developer or platform. First, as noted earlier in this chapter, when using app-based diaries, there are additional and, at times, complex requirements related to ensuring that your use of an app is GDPR (or your specific country's data privacy laws) and institutional ethics board[4] compliant but also that you have a

148 Qualitative Diary Methods

FIGURE 5.2 ■ Screenshots of the WIM Diary App

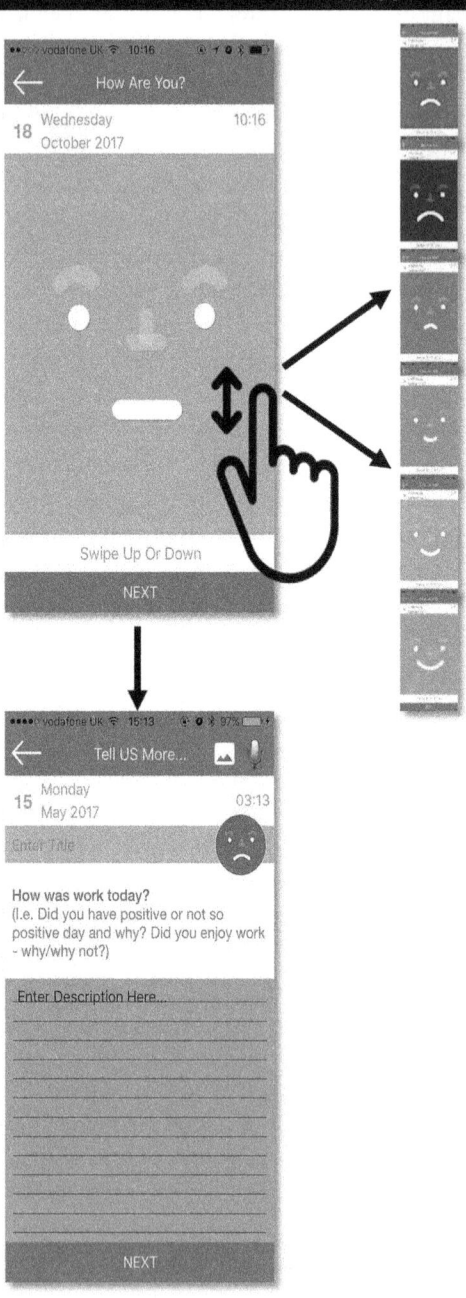

clear intellectual property agreement with the developer. Given the complexity of these laws, we strongly advise that you seek advice and guidance from your institution *before* you meet with prospective developers or platform services. Second, because of the significant costs involved in developing an app, it is advisable that you "shop around" and ensure that the quotes you receive are comprehensive and clear in terms of what you are paying for and for how long. In particular, it is important that you have an understanding of the ongoing costs involved for app maintenance, technical support, and server costs. Where feasible, it is worth investigating whether you can secure a discounted rate or even a pro bono agreement (e.g., Mendoza et al., 2021). Many organizations are likely to have a prosocial interest in supporting research, particularly if it aligns with their values; alternatively, they may see the opportunity as a means to promote their organization. Equally, it is important to note that there are more cost-effective services through which you can create an app. For example, Seide et al. (2023) used the website platform "WordPress," which participants were able to use on their smartphones and could submit different forms of data (i.e., audio, text, photos). While WordPress is still a subscription-based service, it is significantly cheaper than many "pay-to-play" app services that are specifically for collecting data (e.g., Indeemo and EthosApp) and, as demonstrated by Seide et al. (2023), highly effective for multimodal diary research. Alternatively, there are some free services that may be suitable; for example, "EpiCollect5" is a mobile data-gathering platform that could be reasonably used for diary-based research. Indeed, the platform enables users to collect text entries as well as photos, videos, audio, and geolocation data and has been used in a wealth of projects that can be explored on their website.[5] It is also feasible that Google Forms could be used for text-based diaries. However, with these free-to-use services, you are limited in terms of customization and will be restricted to whatever functions the service offers.

TO ADAPT, TAILOR, OR CREATE AN APP

As should be evident, there are significant practical considerations when it comes to designing app-based diaries, and these are strongly influenced by the type of app and thereby whether you decide to use/adapt an existing app, such as WhatsApp, or opt to tailor (using a FFR subscription service) or go the bespoke route and create your own app. This is arguably the overarching question when it comes to using app-based diaries, and while this is something that will be determined by your individual project and its budget, there are reflection points that are helpful when making this decision. To aid this process, Table 5.2 compares the main considerations we have discussed in this chapter across the three types of app diaries that you might consider:

TABLE 5.2 ■ Comparing Different App-Based Diaries: Benefits and Challenges

Benefits/ Challenges	Adapt/Adopt an Existing App	Tailor an App (FFR Apps)	Develop an App (Bespoke App)
Cost	Typically low. Many apps are free to download and use (e.g., WhatsApp). Still need to consider the costs to participants in terms of devices and/or mobile data charges.	Potentially high. Subscription costs vary but are typically dependent on the features and capabilities that researchers opt to include. Need to consider whether the cost of tailoring the app using a subscription service is warranted for your sample size and length of study. Some platforms offer free services to researchers and/or collaborative projects at a reduced or pro bono rate. Still need to consider the costs to participants in terms of devices and/or mobile data charges.	Potentially very high. Cost of app will be determined by the features and capabilities that researchers opt to include. Additional costs such as creating apps for both IOS and Android platforms, cost to launch apps on platforms, and maintenance costs. Need to consider whether the cost of developing an app is warranted for your sample size and length of study. Some developers may offer a discounted or pro bono rate to develop (and maintain) the app. Still need to consider the costs to participants in terms of devices and/or mobile data charges. Important to note that developing apps is a significant time investment and may delay projects.

Benefits/ Challenges	Adapt/Adopt an Existing App	Tailor an App (FFR Apps)	Develop an App (Bespoke App)
Customizability	Low. Depends on the app selected, but most common messenger apps (e.g., WhatsApp) enable multimodal data collection (text, photos, videos, audio).	Dependent on the platform and what they offer. Increased functionality will incur additional costs.	Dependent on the design of the app and capabilities of the developers. Increased functionality will incur additional costs.
Familiarity	App-dependent. Existing social media/messenger apps typically have high familiarity with participants as they are already in use. Training likely to focus on content of the diary (e.g., what to report and when) rather than how to use app functions.	Low. But novelty of app can help recruitment of participants and/or organizational collaboration, as well as public interest in your research. Scope to develop/tailor apps so that they reflect more common app interfaces. Likely to require training to ensure participants are comfortable using the app and its functions, in addition to ensuring participants know what and when to report.	
Privacy	Dependent on the app. Some apps offer secure encryption, but important to ensure the app is compliant with institutional research ethics. Use of social media/messenger apps may encroach on participants' personal spheres. Smartphone devices offer password protection, which can protect participants' data.	Dependent on the app and the specifics of the platform/developers (e.g., what servers or data management protocols they have in place). Important to consider how platform/developers use the data derived through your research project and if this is compliant with institutional research ethics. Use of "separate" app on participants' device may overcome tensions with encroaching on participants' private spheres. In addition to devices offering password protection, potential to password protect apps.	

APP DIARY CHECKLIST

In addition to considering the factors in Table 5.3, please ensure that you also consult each of the checklists in Chapters 3 and 4 that are relevant to the type of data your app will be collecting.

APP DIARY CHECKLIST

Diary Study Design Question	Y/N
Have I consulted the **required legal and ethical guidance and advice** pertaining to app usage and digital data storage and storage (e.g., is my intended app GDPR compliant)?	
Have I designed a clear and detailed **diary information sheet** and an informative **diary briefing session** (which may involve a presentation), incorporating guidance regarding what (not) to record as well as details about using required technology and how to obtain support should technical challenges arise?	
Have I considered participant **privacy and anonymity** (and the privacy of others), as well as **potential "participant as researcher" burden**, and been transparent about this in participant-facing information, including consent forms, and providing participants the opportunity to ask questions and express comfort levels?	
Have I developed a clear **data storage and transfer plan for large data** that is in line with local ethical protocols? And have I planned to discuss this with my participants?	
Have I considered the costs to my participants (e.g., data, devices)? And have I secured a separate smartphone for research use only?	
Have I developed and agreed on a clear communication protocol with participants? And have I established a clear schedule of communication and how this communication will take place with participants through the app?	

APPLICATION ACTIVITY
USING APP-BASED DIARIES

Reflecting on QDM design considerations discussed throughout this chapter, use this worksheet to consider the design choices you will need to make in your own QDM project. These questions are intended to help you to effectively prepare your QDM study but also to help you structure and think about your rationale and justifications for your design choices when submitting to ethical review boards, discussing your project with supervisors/coauthors, and also writing up your QDM methodology. In completing this worksheet, we encourage you think about the potential limitations of each design choice but importantly how these align with your research question(s) and how your personal philosophical choices inform these decisions.

Worksheet 2

1. **Should I use an app-based diary?**
   - Briefly justify why an app-based diary is appropriate and desirable for your research project (e.g., why do you want to use an app-based diary?).
     1A. Sample
     - Is an app-based diary appropriate for my target sample? (e.g., Are there any potential issues with access, cost, usability?)
     - Do my participants want to use an app-based diary? (e.g., Is there the potential that participants may feel like it is intrusive?)

     1B. Features
     - What kind of functions will your app include? How do these link to your research questions?
     - Does your research project require multimodal diary data? (e.g., Is there the risk of data for data's sake; how will different modes of data be combined; how do the different modes data enable you to address your research question(s)?)

     1C. Time and cost
     - Does your project have the budget to develop an app and cover ongoing costs? Does your sample size and research design (e.g., length of diary keeping period) warrant developing or tailoring an app?

2. **Is there (already) an app for that?**
   - Why is an app-based diary appropriate?
   - Is there an existing subscription (paid or free) platform app service that would be appropriate and feasible for my study (e.g., associated costs; degree to which you need the app to be tailored/changeable; ease of access for participants)?
   - Is there an existing app that would be appropriate and feasible for my study? (e.g., Are there any limitations to existing apps; does the app have the functionality I need for my project?)

FURTHER READING

García, B., Welford, J., & Smith, B. (2016). Using a smartphone app in qualitative research: The good, the bad and the ugly. *Qualitative Research, 16*(5), 508–525.

Hadfield-Hill, S., & Zara, C. (2018). Being participatory through the use of app-based research tools. In B. Carter & I. Coyne (Eds)., *Being participatory: Researching with children and young people: Co-constructing knowledge using creative techniques* (pp. 147–169). Springer International.

Seide, K., Casanova, F. O., Ramirez, E., McKenna, M., Cepeda, A., & Nowotny, K. M. (2023). Piloting a flexible solicited diary study with marginalized Latina women during the COVID-19 pandemic. *International Journal of Qualitative Methods, 22*, 16094069231183119.

ENDNOTES

1 https://42matters.com/ios-apple-app-store-statistics-and-trends

2 Data privacy and protection laws vary between countries and institutions and are subject to changes. For specific guidance, please consult your institution for guidance and advice.

3 https://gdpr.eu/what-is-data-processing-agreement/

4 Also, it is important to ensure that how participants register and consent to using the app (e.g., is this done within the app) is compliant with your institution's ethical review board.

5 https://five.epicollect.net/

6 ANALYZING DATA FROM QDMs
Thematic Analysis and Beyond

Having progressed through the key design considerations and different types of qualitative diaries, our attention now shifts to the analysis of qualitative diary data. In this chapter, we will consider the core elements of analyzing these data, from data management and preparation, the types of analytical approaches available and how to select the "right" analytical approach depending on a study's particular philosophical underpinnings, and, importantly, the research questions, initial aims of the research, and the reason for employing QDMs in the first place. The chapter will review the challenges and limitations of employing traditional analytical methods for QDM analysis alone, setting the scene for Chapter 7, which will introduce QDM-specific analytical approaches. Finally, given that QDMs are often used in tandem with other qualitative methods (e.g., the diary-interview method; Zimmerman & Wieder, 1977), the chapter will also provide guidance on analytical integration with other types of qualitative data. By the end of this chapter, readers will have a good understanding of how to prepare QDM data for analysis and of the strengths, challenges, and limitations of employing different traditional analytical methods to QDM data.

ANALYZING QDMs: AN INTRODUCTION

As should be evident from the preceding chapters, QDMs represent a diverse data collection method that offers researchers both creative and unique means to collect their data. As a result of the diversity in potential QDM designs, be it *how* the data are collected (e.g., what medium of diary is used) or *when* the data are collected (e.g., length of study, reporting/recording schedules), QDM data are often complex, potentially multimodal, and typically temporal. As a result of this complexity, a key challenge faced by many QDM researchers is how best to analyze their study data. This challenge is arguably amplified by the scarcity of "QDM-specific" analysis methods (cf. Radcliffe, 2013;

Spencer et al., 2021), but equally, it has been previously acknowledged that in the QDM methodological literature, while QDM design practices are relatively well explained (see Chapters 2–5), far less has been written about analytical procedures, which are key in improving rigor in qualitative diary research (Filep et al., 2018).

While the subsequent chapter outlines two QDM-specific analysis methods, developed through our own use of QDMs (e.g., Radcliffe, 2013; Spencer et al., 2021), we would like to encourage flexibility and creativity in the use of QDMs and, in particular, the potential development of new analytical approaches to address the aforementioned paucity of QDM-specific analysis methods. As such, in this chapter, we illustrate and discuss how traditional qualitative analysis methods may be, and indeed have been, drawn upon in extant QDM studies. Before doing so, however, it is necessary to discuss the pragmatics of managing and preparing your QDM data for analysis.

DATA MANAGEMENT AND PREPARATION

Fundamental to any qualitative research project is an effective, coherent, and rigorous approach to managing your data. This is particularly pertinent in the context of QDM studies, given the complexity and voluminous nature of the data. For example, depending on the design of your QDM study, you may have several months of diary entries, these data may be multimodal, and you may have participants completing diaries at different times or phases in your research. These design complexities can quickly become a challenge and potentially unmanageable if you do not have a clear and consistent protocol for managing your research process and resultant study data. As Guest et al. (2013) provide valuable and comprehensive guidance on data management processes for qualitative research projects more broadly, here we offer QDM project-specific guidance for managing your data during the phases of your project.

Pre- and Ongoing Data Collection

Before commencing your data collection, we strongly recommend developing a *dynamic participant tracking table* that you regularly and systematically update throughout your diary data collection. Doing so will enable you to manage your QDM project effectively, but it is equally a key means through which you develop an effective audit trail of your research process, which in turn supports ensuring the rigor, transparency, and trustworthiness of your study (Bowen, 2009; Tuval-Mashiach, 2017). More pragmatically, a rigorous participant tracking system will enable you to monitor your project's progress but also coordinate, share, and communicate said progress with collaborators and/or project supervisors in an efficient way.

Participant tracking tables serve as a structured and organized means to store, manage, and track participant-related information and typically consist of rows and columns, where each row represents an individual participant, and each column represents a specific attribute or characteristic associated with the participants. The columns may include details such as participant ID, name, contact information and preferences, demographics, interview date(s), diary-keeping status, and any other relevant information. Accordingly, your participant tracking table should align with the key aspects of your QDM study design (see Chapter 2) and be structured in a way that enables you to track each participant's participation journey.

To illustrate, Figure 6.1 is a segment of a participant tracking table from a project following an interview-diary-interview protocol (cf. Zimmerman & Wieder, 1977). Within this protocol, diaries were collected daily over a period of 3 weeks (21 days) and therefore reflective of a "shortidunal" interval-contingent design. Participants were provided an electronic diary (e.g., text-based design) via email, yet in line with guidance that participants be offered the choice of audio recording their entries (see Chapter 2). To reduce the risk of data loss, participants were instructed to return their diaries *during* the diary completion period (e.g., every 5–7 days) and were reminded to do so at each weekly check-in with the researcher. Figure 6.1 illustrates how the design features of your study may be reflected in your participant tracking table.

In addition to maintaining a rigorous participant tracking table, it is equally important that you maintain good data storage practices to avoid potential data loss and reduce any delays due to inefficient data organization. Guest et al. (2013) once again provide comprehensive and detailed guidance for qualitative data management,[1] so our focus here remains on diary-specific considerations.

First, it is important to remember that diary data are typically voluminous (e.g., a 2-week daily diary study with a relatively small sample of 10 participants would still result in ±140 unique diary entries). It is therefore important that you have a coherent and consistent data storage approach and, ideally, enact this storage management from the start of your data collection and on an ongoing basis. In our own research projects, we have found it useful to create folders for each participant (folder name should reflect anonymized identifiers)

158 Qualitative Diary Methods

FIGURE 6.1 ■ Participant Tracking Table

Annotations:
- Anonymized participant identifiers – e.g., participant 1; male, participant 2; female
- Each data collection method in the study along with their scheduled dates
- Project progress indicators
- Researcher keeping track of participant engagement and participant-specific tasks

ID	Partici-pant status	Consent form retrieved and stored?	Pre-diary interview	Diary start & medium	Agreed contact arrange-ments	Diaries returned?	Diary data analyzed?	Post-diary interview	Data transcribed?	Any issues/notes?	To do?
P01_M	Complete	Y	Y; 11/07/22	12/08/22 Electronic; text	Weekly email	Y; 21/21 entries	Y	Y; 11/08/22	Y; all	n/a	None
P02_F	Ongoing	Y	Y; 14/08/22	20/02/22 Electronic; audio & text	Weekly phone call, after 4pm, email to schedule	Ongoing; 11/21 returned	Ongoing; awaiting final entries		Ongoing; interview 1 dome, diaries ongoing	n/a	- Week 2 check-in - ongoing analysis of returned diaries
P03_F	Ongoing	Y	Y; 14/08/22	16/08/22 Electronic; Audio	Weekly email	N	N	N	N	Not replying to emails, Suspected drop out	Try contacting again
P04_M	Recruited	N	TBC	TBC	TBC	TBC	TBC	TBC	TBC	TBC	Schedule interview 1

wherein all their data, including different types of data (e.g., photos, text), are stored. It is useful to label each file according to its temporal unit and data type (e.g., diary day 1_text, diary day 2_text, diary day 2_photo). Alternatively, given the potential for diaries to be multimodal, you may also find it useful to create a folder for each participant, wherein you can store all the data types in subfolders that reflect the temporal unit (e.g., "diary day 1" would contain all relevant data for the first diary entry for the given participant). For diaries that are not temporally bound (e.g., signal-contingent designs), we encourage you to impose some kind of logical sequencing in lieu of an explicit temporal unit (e.g., diary 1, 2, 3 or diary A, B, C, etc., potentially also adding the date and time of the entry where this might be useful) for each participant to maintain a coherent data storage system. Regardless of your labeling conventions, it is imperative that your approach is consistent across all study participants and that data are stored as soon as you retrieve/receive them from participants to avoid data loss.

We also recommend transcribing relevant diary data as soon as possible following receipt of diary entries (e.g., transcribing audio diary entries as they are collected). The transcribed files can then be stored alongside or in place of audio diary data (depending on research ethics expectations/commitments). Where audio files are to be deleted upon transcription of entries, remember to also make any pertinent auditory notes (e.g., regarding emotions or other noises in the room) where relevant. If diary entries have been handwritten via a pen-and-paper–based approach, these entries will usually also require electronic transcription as soon as possible, subsequently ensuring original paper copies are safely destroyed. Where relevant, we recommend anonymizing data during this transcription process, for instance, by deciding upon and consistently employing pseudonyms or other identifiers for participants and other people or organizations mentioned within their accounts. Ensuring data are transcribed, anonymized, organized, and stored in a logical and consistent manner throughout the course of the QDM study will make subsequent data analysis much easier. Preliminary stages of analysis, such as data immersion, can also commence during this time, which is particularly useful where post-diary interviews are to be used and/or where diary questions posed shift over the course of the study in response to prior entries (e.g., see Zundel et al., 2018). Here, a thorough reading of the data and note taking can be particularly useful during ongoing data organization and transcription, which will not only aid any further stages of data collection but also effectively prepare you for subsequent, in-depth analysis post-data collection.

Post-data Collection

Once your data collection is complete, it is advisable to conduct a thorough audit of all your study participants and their associated data (inclusive of different types of data) to ensure that there are no missing data and that each participant's data repository is complete and accurate. It is here where the importance of maintaining the participant tracking table comes to the fore, as this table will be fundamental to being able to audit your data repository by cross-referencing "expected" data files (e.g., as indicated by the participant tracking table) with "actual" data files (e.g., how many files you have for each participant). But equally, it is important to store study data as you go along rather than wait until you have completed your data collection to organize your data management system and store your data files. Where you identify missing data (e.g., unable to locate one or more participants' entries), we recommend, where possible, re-engaging with the given participant(s) to try and retrieve the entries. Where this is not possible/feasible, you should ensure that any missing data are recorded. This is equally the case for participants whose entries are incomplete due to withdrawal and/or attrition (see Chapter 2).

Once you have self-audited your data and ensured that your records are complete and accurate, you can start to organize your data for analysis. While your specific data organization approach may be dependent on your analytical method (e.g., see Chapter 7) and medium (e.g., use of qualitative data analysis software (QDAS) vs. manual analysis; for extensive guidance on using QDAS, see Jackson, 2019), when conducting QDM research, it is advisable that all analyses are preceded by the development of descriptive participant summaries and thereby detailed and rich description of each participant's experiences, perspectives, and behaviors (Patton, 2014). Doing so not only aids data immersion and familiarization, as is typical with qualitative analysis more broadly (Miles & Huberman, 1994; Patton, 2014), but is particularly useful in the specific context of QDM as a means to summarize complex and voluminous data.

In preparing these summaries, in addition to providing a brief biographical sketch of participants, you should aim to provide a descriptive account of participants' diaries, in line with your research question(s). For example, if the aim of your diary study was to understand the daily experience of mistreatment at work (e.g., Spencer, 2019; Spencer et al., 2021), then your participant summaries would focus on providing a summarized account of what the diaries captured in relation to this overarching research question. Alternatively, you may wish to take a more structured approach and segment participant summaries according to the questions your diary posed. How you structure participant summaries is determined by researcher preference, but it is important that your approach is consistent and, ideally, that these summaries remain "descriptive" in orientation, wherein the aim is to provide a description of participants' diaries that aids immersion and provides context for subsequent interpretative analysis. As Patton (2014, p. 534) notes, it can be tempting to rush into the creative work of interpretation, but *description* comes first. In the context of QDMs, these summaries can also be a useful place to make note of participants' attrition (e.g., if they withdrew from the study mid-diary keeping, as this may provide important interpretive context for subsequent analysis). For example, within the aforementioned project (i.e., Spencer, 2019), it became evident when developing participant summaries that attrition was often preceded by a worsening of the interactions reported, which, in turn, was an important finding in the context of this study.

CHOOSING AN ANALYTICAL APPROACH: KEY CONSIDERATIONS

In QDM research, it is advisable that you consider your analytical approach at the design stage of your diaries. As with any qualitative or, indeed, quantitative project, it is of fundamental importance that your research questions and methods (collection and analysis) are commensurate with your specific philosophical and theoretical commitments (Patton, 2014; Willig, 2013). While an in-depth discussion of research paradigms is beyond the scope of this book, and readers should consult the wealth of available literature (e.g., Crotty, 1998; Denzin & Lincoln, 2011; Patton, 2014), here we discuss three QDM-specific considerations that are bound to issues of commensurability:

What Are Your Ontological and Epistemological Positions?

The first point of consideration in how you will analyze your QDM data, particularly textual data, is whether the desired analytical approach is tied to particular paradigmatic commitments. Indeed, while many qualitative analysis methods are positioned as paradigmatically neutral and espouse flexibility in their application across a range of ontological and epistemological positions[2] (e.g., thematic analysis, Braun & Clarke, 2006; template analysis, King, 2004), there are analytical approaches that have strong paradigmatic commitments. Here it is important to remember the difference between "method" and "methodologies" and be cognizant that some analytical *methods* constitute, or are part of, specific method*ologies* that specify package of theory, analytic method, and (elements of) research design (Braun & Clarke, 2021), so-called "off-the-shelf" methodologies (see Chamberlain, 2012). For example, grounded theory, discourse analysis, and interpretive phenomenological analysis are typically considered "methodologies" rather than methods and thereby "theoretically informed and delimited frameworks for research" (Braun & Clarke, 2021, p. 38).

As such, it is imperative that researchers seeking to use QDMs in their research do so in a manner that is devoid of "methodological muddling" (see Goulding, 2002). This, however, can be avoided by having a rigorous research design wherein there is a coherent thread from research question(s), data collection methods, and analysis methods, and as such, it is strongly advised that you explore potential analytical methods *prior* to collecting any data, ideally in the very early stages of your research.[3]

Research Question-Analysis Alignment: Why Did You Use QDMs in the First Place?

The second point of consideration in selecting your analytical approach is to reflect on your diary usage in relation to your research question(s) (i.e., why you used diaries in the first place). In doing so, we encourage you to think about your initial motivations and justifications for their inclusion/use, particularly how they align with your research aims and question(s). As we discussed in Chapter 1, we conceptualize QDMs as an approach that enables researchers to collect rich qualitative data that enable us to capture both the "down" (i.e., in-depth reflections in the moment) and "across" (i.e., change over time) of participants' experiences. Thus, in thinking about how you may analyze your diary data and to aid this reflection, we suggest researchers consider the following prompts:

A. *Did you aim to capture details of events/experiences/thoughts/emotions in the moment (i.e., a "down" focus)?*

B. *Did you aim to capture changes in events/experiences/thoughts/emotions over time (i.e., an "across" focus)?*

C. *A combination of both (i.e., both a "down" and "across" focus)?*

If your research aims and questions align most strongly with Prompt A, wherein diaries were used primarily as a means to reduce retrospection (Bolger et al., 2003) and to capitalize on the "down" affordances of QDMs in proving rich contextual and relational details, and/or your diaries were signal/

event contingent (see Chapter 1), your analytical approach is most likely to be primarily content driven. Due to this focus on content (e.g., "what" events/experiences/thoughts/emotions are your participants reporting in a given moment), many traditional qualitative analysis methods may be appropriate. In contrast, if your project aligns more strongly with Prompt B or perhaps Prompt C, wherein there is an emphasis on change, an "across" focus on "how" events/experiences/thoughts/emotions change over a given period, your analytical approach will need to account for these temporalities in your data. Capitalizing on the affordances of QDMs, particularly temporal elements of the data, however, can be challenging when relying on traditional qualitative analysis methods relative to diary-specific approaches, which are outlined in Chapter 7.

Are You Integrating Diary and Other Types of Qualitative Data?

As noted in Chapter 2, it is common for QDMs to be employed in tandem with other qualitative methods, typically interviews (e.g., Gibson et al., 2013; Guo & Sun, 2023; Radcliffe & Cassell, 2014, 2015; Radcliffe et al., 2023; Spencer et al., 2022), as part of multimethod qualitative designs. As such, the third potential point of consideration is how you will integrate your diary data with other qualitative data types (e.g., interview data). Given the diversity in diary designs and mediums (see Chapters 2–5), integrating these data requires careful consideration so that your analysis and subsequent findings remain commensurate with your overarching philosophical commitments, but equally, that integration of your data is done in a way that enables you to address your research questions in a rigorous and meaningful way.

As diaries are most frequently used in conjunction with interviews, here we focus on how you may approach integrating interview and diary data. Key to doing so is to reflect on your research questions and rationale for using QDMs in conjunction with interviews. For example, if your research was guided by a singular, overarching, research question, then it is likely that you intended to integrate the two data sources. For example, in Leighann's study exploring the ways in which managers integrate scholarship in their everyday management practice (Spencer et al., 2022), she, alongside her coauthors, combined interviews with text-based diaries, justifying their use of diaries as a means to elaborate/enrich the thematic findings from the interview data. Accordingly, diary data were analyzed in line with the thematic template derived from the interview data. In contrast, multimethod studies may progress with multiple research questions that are distinctly focused on each data collection method; thereby, diaries are used to address a specific research question (or aim), and interviews focus on another (see, e.g., Litovuo et al., 2019; MacDonald et al., 2018). In addition, if your study is collecting different types of data (e.g., textual data through interviews and photos through visual diaries; e.g., Ashman et al., 2022; Cassell et al., 2020; Gibson et al., 2013; Latham, 2003), it is likely that you will need different analysis approaches for these different data modalities (see, e.g., Pinilla et al., 2023; Shortt & Warren, 2019). It is therefore important that you consider how you envision integrating your different sources of data or not by reflecting on the alignment between the methods and your research questions, but equally, how different types of data will need to be analyzed.

To contextualize the importance of these three considerations, we now discuss how existing QDM studies have approached their analysis. We first explore QDM studies that have drawn on traditional qualitative analysis approaches. In doing so, we illustrate the diversity of approaches adopted in QDM research by splitting our discussion to include both "generic" and "methodologically wed" analytical approaches. We then progress to the overarching strengths and limitations of these approaches before discussing visual-specific analysis methods.

USING TRADITIONAL QUALITATIVE ANALYSIS APPROACHES

Generic Thematic Analysis Approaches for QDM Analysis

As is the case for qualitative research more broadly, most existing QDM studies have tended to rely on theme-based analytical approaches, predicated on the idea of identifying patterns in the data that are common, recurrent, or in some way significant and/or meaningful. As such, a wealth of QDM research has drawn on established, yet paradigmatically neutral, theme-based analysis approaches, such as template analysis (King, 2004; King & Brooks, 2016) and thematic analysis (Braun & Clarke, 2006).

In our own QDM research projects, we have tended toward template analysis (TA; King, 2004). TA is predicated on a hierarchical approach to data coding, which does not impose specific levels of coding or differentiate themes as descriptive or interpretative (King, 2004). Rather, it focuses on grouping codes together to form broader, higher-order themes, allowing for overarching themes to be refined by more specific aspects within them (King, 2004). Put simply, in this type of analysis, a primary, "first-level" theme represents a significant element of the data, further detailed by several sub-themes (i.e., second-, third-order themes, etc.), which clarify aspects of the main theme. Therefore, the goal of this analysis is to create a "thematic template" for the study that captures the main areas of interest (first-level themes) and their associated detailed themes (second-level, third-level themes).

In our own research, we have found template analysis particularly useful in studies combining interview and diary data but equally as a result of its paradigmatic flexibility. For example, Laura and colleagues have illustrated the efficacy of template analysis in a series of studies exploring work–family experiences when adopting an inductive stance (e.g., Radcliffe & Cassell, 2014, 2015) but equally when approaching the data in a more abductive manner (e.g., Radcliffe et al., 2021; Radcliffe et al., 2023). In the latter, as prompted by the review process, Radcliffe et al. (2023) provide a detailed account of their analysis, illustrating the movement between existing theory and the data through the combination of a priori (theory-driven) and emergent (data-driven) codes as they developed and refined their study thematic template following a three-stage process. Similarly, Spencer et al. (2022) detail their abductive analysis using template analysis over four stages. However, where the studies differ is the stage at which the interview and diary data were integrated, with Radcliffe et al. (2023) integrating the data at the outset, whereas Spencer et al. (2022) followed a sequential integration approach wherein they developed the study template on the basis of the interview data (Stages 1 and 2) and then integrated the diary data in Stage 3. As such, these studies illustrate the flexibility of template analysis in integrating different sources of data, but equally, the corpus of Laura and colleagues' QDM research further illustrates how template analysis is an efficacious method when dealing with relatively large QDM sample sizes and the resultant voluminous data (e.g., $N = 60$; Radcliffe et al., 2023).

Given the proliferation of Braun and Clarke's (2006) six-step thematic analysis, numerous examples of QDM studies from a range of disciplines have also drawn upon the approach. For example, sociologists Neves, Colón Cabrera, et al. (2023) drew on thematic analysis in their study exploring the lived experience of loneliness among 32 older adults during the initial phases of the COVID-19 pandemic. In their study, diaries were semi-structured, handwritten, or digital depending on participant preference (see p. 122), kept for a period of 7 days with participants instructed to complete the diary twice daily (morning and evening), guided by a series of prompts provided to participants. In a similar vein to Radcliffe et al. (2023) and Spencer et al. (2022), Neves, Colón Cabrera, et al. (2023) provide a detailed and thorough account of their analysis, which they typify as "mixed coding" inclusive of both inductive and deductive codes (p. 124) and as such indicate to the reader which themes were inductive and/or deductive but equally how they adopted the six-step approach outlined by Braun and Clarke (2006).

In the context of health research, Dennett et al. (2020) used thematic analysis in their study exploring the experiences of people with progressive multiple sclerosis (MS) during their participation in a 36-week trial of a home-based standing frame (see p. 3 for trial details). Corresponding to the needs and capabilities of their participants, audio diaries were collected wherein participants were instructed to record their experiences of how it felt to stand and use the frame over the course of the 36-week trial. While it is not specified how many diaries were collected from each respective participant,[4] the authors do note that in line with their interest in collecting contemporaneous data, participants were asked to record standing experiences during each stand or as near to the completed standing period as possible. However, they equally note that participants were free to record "as many times as they wanted and when they wanted" (Dennett, 2020, p. 3), resulting in 155 total diaries for analysis. Similar to Neves, Colón Cabrera, et al. (2023), the authors outline their use of Braun and Clarke's (2006) six-step approach, albeit in slightly less detail. From their analysis, the authors demonstrate the impact of the standing frame on the participants with MS, such as how standing engendered a sense of freedom and normality. Interestingly, while the analysis is largely thematic, the authors note that they considered the "narrative trajectories" in participants' diaries by viewing entries as "a whole series rather than solely as fragmented entries." To this end, within the findings, the authors occasionally draw attention to changes in participants' experiences and reflections over time within the findings. However, there is limited detail as to how or whether the authors explored these narrative trajectories by drawing on a particular approach.

In contrast, once more in the context of health research and audio diaries, MacDonald et al. (2018), in their study exploring family food practices, provide a more detailed account of their combination of thematic analysis (Braun & Clarke, 2006) and discourse analysis (Alvesson & Kärreman, 2000). Through this combination, the authors note how the different analysis approaches allowed them to explore different dimensions of the data, noting how "[the] thematic analysis highlighted the complexity of family food practices . . . discourse analysis drew out more about how control was embedded within practices, revealing different dynamics of parent and child control within food negotiations" (MacDonald et al., 2018, p. 784). In doing so, the study illustrates how generic theme–based approaches, owing to their flexibility and paradigmatic neutrality, may be combined with "methodologically wed" approaches such as discourse analysis when analyzing diary data. However, as noted earlier in the chapter, it is imperative that such combinations are well justified and do not broach issues of incommensurability.

In summary, generic thematic approaches, such as those discussed here (e.g., Braun & Clarke, 2006; King, 2004), offer researchers valuable analytical approaches for QDM data that are suited to a range of reasoning strategies (e.g., inductive, deductive, abductive), sample sizes, use with other data sources, and in combination with analytical approaches (see also Cassell & Bishop, 2019). In addition, as both approaches, thematic and template analysis, are stage-based approaches, with both King (2004) and Braun and Clarke (2006) offering clear analytical guidance (or steps), they may be particularly suited to more novice researchers and/or those who may be new to QDMs more broadly. However, while both approaches offer analytical steps, both King (2004, 2012) and Braun and Clarke (2006) note that these steps are not prescriptive, and researchers should adapt their process to suit their specific research and data. In our view and as illustrated in the next chapter, these "generic" analytical approaches, owing to their flexibility, offer QDM researchers significant opportunities to be creative and potentially develop new QDM analysis approaches (see, e.g., Spencer et al., 2021).

"Methodologically Wed" Analytical Approaches and QDM Analysis

In addition to the paradigmatically neutral approaches discussed above, analytical approaches that are more appropriately considered constituents of particular *methodologies* are equally popular in QDM studies. Here we will focus on three dominant approaches: grounded theory, phenomenological analysis, and narrative analysis.

Grounded Theory

Studies employing grounded theory (GT) are typically interested in phenomena that are not well understood and are (complex) social processes and/or wherein the researcher intends to develop a grounded theory from the data and analysis (Glaser & Strauss, 1967; see also Braun & Clarke, 2021; Suddaby, 2006). These commitments are reflected in Flanders et al. (2016), who employed daily qualitative diaries to explore bisexual people's negative experiences related to their sexual identity. To do so, online diaries were administered every 24 hours to a sample of 91 participants for a period of 28 days. Participants were provided with two questions: "In the past 24 hours, I had an experience that affirmed my bisexual identity in a negative way," and "In the past 24 hours, I had an experience that threatened my bisexual identity in a negative way" (p. 156); participants were asked to report whether these experiences had occurred (yes/no) and to write a brief narrative describing the negative or threatening experience.[5] In addition to adhering to the tenets of grounded theory in the analysis, an interesting aspect of the authors' constructivist analysis and subsequent findings was that the authors organized their findings according to the social-ecological model of Brofenbrenner (1979, p. 157). Doing so enabled a nuanced analysis of participants' negative experiences at intrapersonal-, interpersonal-, and social-structure levels and, in turn, a more fine-grained understanding of the experiences of participants.

However, where this study arguably diverges from many studies employing GT approaches is that it does not inductively generate a particular "theory." In contrast, Rauch and Ansari (2022b) conducted an inductive multimethod study of military personnel operating drones in the U.S. Air Force, comprising interviews, unsolicited diaries, documents, and observations. In analyzing their data, the authors followed a "theoretically sensitive inductive approach" and the analytical processes of GT to develop a model of "technology-induced emotional ambivalence and coping at work" that explains how an emerging technology changed the meaning and morality of work and how these workers respond to such disruption to their work, which they identify with strongly. Overall, in addition to providing a clear explication of a theoretical model derived from GT analysis, the authors provide a highly detailed and transparent account of their analysis and, therefore, provide those interested in adopting GT to analyze diary data as a valuable reference point. GT is therefore a particularly valuable approach for QDM researchers seeking in-depth exploration of social processes, but equally, it may be of particular use when there is limited existing theory that explains a given phenomenon.

Phenomenological Approaches

Whereas GT can be particularly suited to studies exploring social processes, studies adopting phenomenological approaches are typically concerned with understanding individuals' lived, subjective experiences (see Gill, 2014) or, more simply, concerned with the phenomenological question, "What it is like to experience *something*?" (Larsen & Adu, 2021). As such, QDMs employing a phenomenological perspective or approach typically employ diaries as a means to explore complex, often sensitive experiences. For example, Cudjoe (2022)[6] used diaries to explore "what it is like" for children whose parents have mental illnesses, drawing on interpretive phenomenological analysis (IPA). Perhaps due to the parallels between the affordances of QDMs and IPA (see Cudjoe, 2022), IPA is a relatively popular *form* of phenomenology (see Gill, 2014, for discussion) in extant QDM studies. For instance, Hannekom and Shymko (2020) explore coping strategies of individuals during COVID-19 confinement, Dunham et al. (2017) examine the experience of pain in elderly patients with cancer, and Hodgkins (2022) investigates perceptions of empathy among early childhood practitioners. In the latter, the authors illustrate a clear alignment to the tenets of IPA, for example, including participants' own subjective definitions of "empathy," which provides the reader with a foundation with which to interpret subsequent sections of the findings. In addition, Hodgkins (2022) provides a detailed account of their analysis process and adoption of the six steps put forward by Smith et al. (2009) to conduct IPA, which researchers seeking to adopt a phenomenological approach in their own diary research may find particularly useful, given it is a relatively structured and proceduralized approach. In addition, given the challenges in relation to sample recruitment and retention within QDM (see Chapter 2), IPA may be particularly propitious wherein there is a relatively small sample size given the idiographic emphasis in IPA (see Gill, 2014; Smith, 2011).

Narrative Approaches

Hitherto, the analysis approaches discussed have all largely focused on the generation, development, or perhaps "emergence" of "themes" (e.g., GT) from diary data and therefore arguably involve the "fragmentation" of participants' accounts into units of meaning (i.e., themes). In contrast to this, researchers drawing on narrative analysis approaches are often interested in the contingency of the data (i.e., *A* happened because of *B*, thereby the temporal and sequential linking of events, actions, and actors) and, therefore, consider the data as "whole" (for a detailed discussion, see McAllum et al., 2019). In line with this, Egerod and Christensen (2009) drew on narrative analysis in their study of patient diaries in Danish intensive care units. An interesting methodological feature of this kind of study is that in contrast to most solicited diary research, which relies on first-person accounts, "patient diaries" are written vicariously by nurses, hospital staff, family, or friends. In Egerod and Christensen's (2009) study, diaries were written by nurses on the ward, with the purpose of helping patients fill in the gaps when their memory fails. In this way, the diaries uniquely offer the double perspective of the patient and narrator (nurse) but equally include perspectives of the patients. Owing to this, within their findings, the authors include "parallel plots": the nurse's, patient's, and family's storylines across three stages of the narrative. For example, in the first "crisis" stage of the narrative, the analysis illustrates how nurses' plots would focus on tasks (e.g., setting up tubes, machines), patients' plots would be passive often due to them being unconscious, and families' plots were positioned as concerned/worried spectators, as the following excerpt illustrates:

> Finally we have put a catheter in your bladder, so urine can accumulate in a bag. You were unstable and doing poorly during this procedure. This meant that we had to set up a lot of medicine for you. You get pain medication and sleeping medication and then you get a lot of medication to keep up your blood pressure. But it took a long while before the medicine began to work as we hoped, we were very worried for you. But you made it through the first most critical phase. Yesterday your condition was again extremely critical and your wife, who had gone home to sleep, was called back after just a few hours. Again you made it through, and today has been less critical. . . . Sincerely, Cathy Miller" (#20, entry 1). (Egerod & Christensen, 2009, p. 273)

The multilayered narratives, derived through their use of narrative analysis, enabled the researchers to delve into the structure of patient diaries but equally highlighted how the patient diary also became the nurses' stories. In a similar yet more recent study, Maagaard and Laerkner (2022) drew on patient diaries and interviews to understand the narrative choices nurses make when tasked with patient diary keeping. By analyzing the diary data through a structural narrative approach (e.g., Riessman, 2008), the authors focused on content, organization, and language and what these indicated about the nurses' narrative processes. Their findings focus on three prominent strategies that characterize nurses' narrative choices: (1) making the situation of intensive care more manageable, (2) showing acts of perceiving the patient, and (3) constituting relations through actions and interactions (Maagaard & Laerkner, 2022, p. 7). In this way, the authors illustrate how, on one hand, these strategies engage the patient and depict nurses' care, empathy, and support yet, on the other, reveal the nurses' power to interpret, passivize, and downplay the patient's experiences.

While these studies are somewhat unique in their use of patient diaries rather than first-person solicited diaries, both studies illustrate how narrative analysis may be used to delve deeper into the stories present in diaries. For example, the parallel plot and storyline approach of Egerod and Christensen (2009) illustrates the rich potential of diaries to gain an understanding of the different actors and their experiences that may be present for a given event/experience and how these change over time from the perspective of the diarist. In contrast, the structural approach adopted by Maagaard and Laerkner (2022) enables researchers to focus on the linguistic devices drawn upon by diarists, for example, revealing power dynamics through pronoun usage. In this way, narrative approaches may be of particular benefit to studies seeking to understand the multifaceted nature of participants' experiences through the content they provide (see also Hagan et al., 2020; Nielsen et al., 2019) but equally delve into the nuances of how the stories themselves are constructed linguistically.

Using Traditional Qualitative Analysis Approaches: Strengths and Limitations

Overall, these traditional, established, qualitative analysis approaches offer QDM researchers a rich toolkit to draw on when it comes to designing diary studies and the subsequent analysis of these data. As noted earlier, when selecting your analytical approach, we advise consideration of the three prompt questions: What are your ontological and epistemological positions, why are you using QDMs in the first place (e.g., for in the moment [down focus] vs. over time [across focus]), and are you integrating your diary data with other sources of data? Working through these considerations will provide you with useful criteria to narrow down your decision-making. However, having reviewed the dominant traditional qualitative analysis approaches, it should now be evident how your paradigmatic underpinnings should be the primary influence in these decisions. As noted, some of these approaches, particularly grounded theory and phenomenologically informed analysis approaches, should not be adopted without commensurate and coherent research designs and therefore devoid of "methodological muddling" (Goulding, 2002).

Traditional qualitative analysis approaches offer QDM researchers a range of strengths, including being able to identify recurrent patterns across and within their data (e.g., generic thematic approaches, such as TA; King, 2004), explore idiographic lived experiences (e.g., IPA; Smith et al., 2009), or perhaps develop "grounded" theories in the face of new/unexplained phenomena (GT; Glaser & Strauss, 1967). However, the overarching strength of these traditional, established approaches is arguably their *familiarity*. For example, many of these traditional approaches are considered "methodological templates" for analysis, given their propensity to be adopted as standardized protocols and/or overly proceduralized (Kohler et al., 2022). Now while there is significant debate among qualitative researchers regarding the dis/advantages of methodological templates (see, e.g., Kohler et al., 2022) and the use of "templates" has in itself become somewhat pejorative, there is the argument that the use of an established analysis process may be beneficial in the context of QDM research, specifically because they offer proceduralized approaches. For example, developing qualitative expertise can be both challenging and time-consuming (see, e.g., Cassell, 2018), and as such, these "methodological templates" can be beneficial for more novice researchers (e.g., doctoral students) or those who may not have conducted *qualitative* research before. Therefore, drawing on templates may be attractive due to them providing accessible and structured guidance, often in the forms of "analytical steps" that can be advantageous when facing complex and voluminous diary data, and given the proliferation of these approaches, there is a wealth of resources to help researchers hone their practice. In addition, given the relative novelty of QDMs as a data collection tool, it might be the case that while your reviewers (or examiners) have expertise in qualitative research, they may be unfamiliar with QDMs. As such, using a more familiar, traditional analysis approach may help to convey the legitimacy of your research. Indeed, in our own experiences of publishing QDM research, being able to signpost template analysis as an established method has been beneficial in convincing reviewers of the legitimacy and rigor of our research, typically through providing detailed "steps" of our analysis that elaborate how we adopted TA (see, e.g., Radcliffe et al., 2023; Spencer et al., 2022).

In terms of the limitations of traditional approaches, regardless of their paradigmatic underpinning (i.e., whether they are generic or "methodologically wed" analysis approaches), there are two key limitations. First, while traditional qualitative analysis methods are adept in enabling exploitation of the "down" benefits of QDMs (see Chapter 1), a potential limitation of these traditional approaches is that it can be challenging to explore and/or account for the relationship/links between particular themes at within- and between-person levels. For example, if diaries are event-focused and thereby interested in how individuals experience and respond to a given type of "event," it is likely that researchers would have an interest in understanding the relationship between, for instance, events, actions, experiences, outcomes, and emotions and potential interdependencies between these "in the moment."

Second, with the arguable exception of *some* narrative approaches (see, e.g., Vidaillet, 2007), traditional approaches are perhaps limited in terms of their ability to account for the temporal elements of diary data. As such, those adopting QDMs for their benefits in providing longitudinal/shortitudinal data may need to combine analytical approaches to account for the temporal elements. For example, in our review of diary studies in organizational research (Spencer et al., 2021), we identified that a frequent analytical combination was that of GT (i.e., Glaser & Strauss, 1967; Strauss & Corbin, 1998) or contemporary derivatives (i.e., "Gioia method"; Gioia et al., 2013) with the analytical tools associated with "process research" (see Langley, 1999). For example, Balogun and Johnson (2004) and Fisher et al. (2018) draw on Langley's "temporal bracketing," "visual mapping," and/or "narrative" strategies, which enables the data to be organized as occurring over time or phases. While these combinations may result in rich temporally sensitive findings, our review identified that these may not always be suitable or feasible in micro-level studies, particularly where you have an interest in within-person changes. More simply, if you have an interest in how an *individual's* experiences and/or perceptions change over time, adapting existing approaches may be tricky, particularly if we consider the space limitations of journals and the inherent complexity of diary data. Indeed, it was these challenges that led us to develop thematic trajectory analysis (TTA) as a direct response to our own struggles adapting traditional approaches, which we discuss in detail in the next chapter.

The third overarching limitation of traditional analytical approaches is their potential shortcomings in analyzing nontextual data, particularly visual data. As discussed in Chapter 4, owing to the proliferation and everydayness of photographic devices (e.g., smartphones) and proverbial "visual" turn(s) in the social sciences (e.g., Bell et al., 2014; Jewitt, 2008), multimodal diaries that collect photo and/or photo data are increasingly common. However, while there is a multitude of benefits of these data (see Chapter 4), the inclusion of visual data adds further complexity to the analysis and dissemination of findings. This, in turn, often means that researchers give primacy to text-based data that have been collected in tandem with the visual data (e.g., discussions of/prompted by photographs) or restrict their analysis to textual data that are derived from the visual diary (e.g., transcripts of video diaries; Cooley et al., 2014; Rodd et al., 2014). In this way, many analysis sections of photo/video diary studies often provide limited insight into how one may analyze the *visual*. For this reason, in the section that follows, we focus specifically on studies that have explicitly included the visual in their analysis.

ANALYZING MULTIMODAL/VISUAL DIARY DATA

As noted, while diverse traditional analytical approaches are often drawn on to analyze multimodal diary data, there are arguable constraints in doing so, as these methods are primarily textual in orientation. As a result, it is often the case that the text is given primacy in these studies. For example, in their study exploring how mental health recovery in homeless clients is shaped by shelter type (temporary or emergency accommodation), Karadzhov (2023) drew on IPA to analyze interview and multimodal diary data. Drawing on the guidance of Rose (2016), the researcher assigned one or more codes to each image while remaining attentive to the function the images had in each participant's interview accounts. In this way, Karadzhov did not treat the images as independent artifacts, but instead, interpretations remained grounded in participants' accounts of their meaning and significance. Analyzing the visual data in this way enabled Karadzhov (2023) to integrate the visual and textual data in their findings but equally foreground the importance of grounding the meaning of images in participants' accounts. This is illustrated within the findings wherein an image of a plastic bag hanging from a door captured in response to the prompt "What is something that best captures your life now?" could arguably be perceived as quite somber, instead reflecting a positive experience and representation of the theme "restoration of homelikeness," as the participant recounts, "Because once upon a time, I didn't have no door to hang no bag on you see what I'm saying? I didn't have no door to close. I'm saying it's the little things you gotta be grateful for" (Karadzhov, 2023, p. 182).

Similarly, King and Dickinson (2023), in their study of how the COVID-19 pandemic restrictions reconfigured leisure practices, note the importance of grounding visual data in the meanings and accounts of participants. Here, drawing on the guidance of Pink (2007), the authors note that "visual content alone is not enough without locating the social, cultural and personal contexts which give it meaning, and the subjective agendas through which they are produced" (p. 12). Accordingly, visual data were coded alongside the written entries "to add an additional layer of meaning." However, in coding the visual data, the authors do highlight their use of "visual coding questions" proposed by Banks and Zeitlyn (2015), which include descriptive coding prompts (e.g., what is the image content?) and more interpretive prompts (e.g., when, how, and why is it made and for whom?).

In addition to the adoption, and indeed adaption, of established theme-based analysis methods (for further examples, see Palmer et al., 2022; Pilcher et al., 2016), there are also examples of researchers drawing on visual-specific methodologies and arguably giving the visual parity with the textual. For example, once more in the context of the COVID-19 pandemic, Pinilla et al. (2023) sought to capture the impact of the pandemic on family routines and intimate relationships in Chile by exploring the changes in productive and non-productive activities and pastimes. Drawing on data collected through an app-based diary (see Chapter 5 for further detail), the authors combined visual content analysis to code and subsequently quantify their visual data (e.g., frequency counts of activities photographed) in tandem with socio-semiotic analysis following the guidance of Kress and Van Leeuwen (2020). Doing so enabled Pinilla et al. (2023) to explore the semiotic resources present in the photographs, for example, gender differences in expressions of "forgone activities," wherein male participants would photograph objects with brief captions, whereas female participants would more often refer to other people with whom they share close ties and do so with more detailed emotion-focused captions. The authors contend that their analysis enabled them to gain insight into how participants used a variety of "semiotic resources" and the significance of these semiotic choices.

A further illustration of a study that adopted a semiotically informed approach is the video diary study of Iivari et al. (2014), exploring children's (10–11 years) technology use in their everyday life. In their article, the authors provide a detailed account of their grounding in "nexus analysis" (Scollon & Scollon, 2014), a methodological framework that aims to understand complex social and cultural issues by examining connections (nexuses) between discourse, social action, and the broader social environment. In practice, what this entails according to Iivari et al. (2014) is "viewing social action as a cross-section of three aspects: historical body (Nishida, 1958), interaction order (Goffman, 1971) and discourses in place (Scollon & Scollon, 2003). . . . The crucial aspect is to look at what is being done in the social action in focus and how the dimensions of historical body, interaction order, and discourses in place can be seen to intersect in this action" (p. 511). Owing to the arguable complexity of nexus analysis, the authors present an in-depth account of their analysis, parsed over four phases. In Phase 1, the authors performed a content analysis to examine what the children were reporting before progressing to the nexus analysis framework across Phases 2 to 4. Briefly, what this entailed was reviewing the diaries through a series of lenses: discourse-focused (Phase 2), multimodel aspects of the data by viewing the transcript beside the speech, inclusive of facial expressions, movement, gestures, and so on, and finally the formal nexus analytical lens wherein the authors state they were sensitized by the concepts of historical body, interaction order, and discourses in place and describing aspects of the social action. This led Iivari et al. (2014) to rich findings that were connected with (1) the different subject positions that the children enacted in relation to different kinds of audiences during the production of the video clips and (2) the variety of genres that the children invoked. To contextualize this, the findings illustrate how the children, despite being given the same assignment, invoked a variety of subject positions, such as "a diarist," "a news anchor," and "a stage performer," and a range of popularized genres, such as "an intimate, confessional diary entry," "a news broadcast," and "a homework assignment," but equally how they transitioned between these positions and genres, sometimes changing them several times even during one video clip.

These semiotic-focused approaches (e.g., Iivari et al. 2014; Pinilla et al., 2023) may be particularly useful for researchers seeking to delve into meanings underpinning the *construction* and *performance* of, and within, visual diaries—that is, how participants opt to capture, represent, or stylize an event/experience in a given photo/video, in isolation or as an additional interpretive layer to the "what" (content) of the photo/visual. However, owing to the complexity of these approaches, we strongly advise researchers seeking to employ these approaches to consult the primary methodological texts (e.g., Kress & Van Leeuwen, 2020; Scollon & Scollon, 2014) and importantly ensure that the design of their diaries enables such analysis in the first place (see Chapter 4 for guidance).

Those researchers who, like us, may lean toward the comfort of more proceduralized approaches may find value in grounded visual pattern analysis (GVPA; Shortt & Warren, 2019). As discussed in Chapter 4, GVPA is a *dialogic* and *archaeological* approach to visual analysis and therefore incorporates both discursive and content-focused analysis, thereby equally privileging narratives (that accompany images) and the content of images. In explicating the process of GVPA, Shortt and Warren (2019) provide detailed information and illustrations of how researchers should progress through the five steps of the process, which researchers seeking to draw on GVPA should consult in the first instance. Briefly, the process initially entails a *dialogic stage* (Step 1), which entails interrogating the meaning of the photo(s) rather than what is *in* the image(s) by drawing on the narratives (e.g., derived from interviews or text-based diary data) *about* the photographs. Through this process, researchers identify patterns from the narratives and, in turn, derive "image sets"—collections of photographs that reflect a given theme (e.g., what the photos mean)—rather than being based on the content of the photos themselves (e.g., similar objects or aesthetics). Following this, the analysis process progresses to the "archaeological stage," which encompasses "grouping" (Step 2), "ordering" (Step 3), "structured viewing" (Step 4), and "theorizing" (Step 5):

In Step 2, grouping, researchers should group together all the photographs associated with a particular theme, which offers a chance to *look* at how the dialogical meaning has been visualized (Shortt & Warren, 2019). In Step 3, ordering, researchers decide how the photographs in a given "group," or set, will be laid out (e.g., chronologically, by photographer, randomly). Decisions on how to order the set is at the discretion of the researcher and should be informed by their research questions. For example, if you have an interest in temporality and/or change over time, then it may be logical to order the photos chronologically, or perhaps if you are interested in individual differences, then ordering by the photographer (or diarist) may make the most sense. Following this, in Step 4, "structured viewing," the process progresses to focusing on the content, symbolism, and aesthetics of the photos; Shortt and Warren (2019) advise looking for patterns across the images, commenting on both the content and symbolic nature of the images (what they are of) and the compositional nature of the images. In doing so, they provide a series of prompts to guide this process, including "symbolic viewing" (e.g., *"What is striking or unusual? What has been foregrounded or placed in the background?"*) and "compositional viewing" (*"How has the photographer . . . framed the photo? . . . placed themselves in relation to the scene?"* (see Shortt & Warren, 2019, p. 546, Table 2). Finally, in Step 5, researchers engage in the process of "theorizing" by asking, *"How have the patterns identified in the image-sets above extended the dialogical data?"* (p. 552).

To illustrate the potential of GVPA, we now focus on a recent article that adopted the method to explore the concept of "liquid liminality" to problematize dominant conceptions of "work–life" balance and, in turn, better understand contemporary flexible working life. In their study, Izak et al. (2023) drew on an autoethnographic visual diary exploring one of the authors (Harriet hereinafter) for the first 12 months of full-time work as an academic after 14 months of maternity leave, thereby enabling an exploration of the return to work but also "the lived experience of the everyday tensions and ambiguities felt between work/non-work, professional/mother/wife, public/private, work life/home life and all the complexities in-between these spaces and role" (p. 207). In their findings, the authors interweave the narrative and visual data and focus on two themes derived from their use of GVPA: *ambiguous space* and *transitioning-learning anew who I am at work*. For example, in the ambiguous space theme, we are provided with rich multimodal accounts that illustrate the tensions between and blending of work and life, such as a work handbag that contains baby wipes and an old pacifier juxtaposed with an academic textbook and papers, illustrating how Harriet's handbag itself became a liminal space between "work" and "home" life. As a result of their analysis, the findings lead Izak et al. (2023) to contribute the concept of liquid liminality as a means to problematize previously assumed structural distinctions between "work" and "home" in the context of flexible working. Therefore, Izak et al. (2023) illustrate the utility of GVPA as an analytical approach, both practically and theoretically.

However, it is noteworthy that GVPA is relatively new approach, and as such, limited QDM studies have adopted the approach, yet perhaps with the potential for methodological contributions in this regard. Researchers seeking to adopt the approach may find the studies of Cotton et al. (2023) and Shortt and Warren (2019) valuable resources.

In summary, and as illustrated across the discussion of analysis approaches adopted, there are varied visual-analysis options available, and thus selecting your approach will once again depend on the specifics of your study, but in particular how you envision the role of the visual in your research. For example, if you are drawing on the visual as elicitation devices and, therefore, giving the textual data primacy, then using traditional qualitative approaches such as those discussed may be appropriate—for example, in isolation, as illustrated by Karadzhov (2023), or perhaps in combination with visual analysis techniques, such as the approach used by King and Dickinson (2023). In contrast, if you seek to privilege the "visual," for example, how participants draw on "semiotic resources" and/or the meaning structures of and within visual media, then semiotic approaches (e.g., Iivari et al. 2014; Pinilla et al., 2023) may be most suitable. Finally, it may be the case that you are equally interested in both the visual and textual, in which case GVPA (Shortt & Warren, 2019) is a highly recommended approach.

INTEGRATING DIARY AND OTHER FORMS OF DATA

As discussed extensively in Chapter 2, diaries are very frequently used with other sources of data, most notably interviews. As such, earlier in this chapter, we noted that how you intend or envision integrating these forms of data is the third key consideration when selecting your analysis approach. As discussed, consideration needs to be given as to what purpose you envisioned the diary data to serve in your study in relation to your research questions. But equally, as illustrated in the discussion of visual analysis, if you are drawing on visual data, it is likely that you will need to consider how your analysis will account for different modalities of data. To help you in this process, Table 6.1 outlines existing studies that have drawn on different sources and forms of data in their studies across a continuum of analytical integration.

TABLE 6.1 ■ Examples of Different Data Integration Strategies

Integration Orientation	Fully Integrated	Partly Integrated	Non-integrated
Definition	Studies that have subsumed diary and other sources of data into a singular data set for analysis	Studies that have adopted separate analysis methods to analyze data sources but use the combined findings to address the research question(s)	Studies that have analyzed diary and other sources of data separately and to address distinct research questions
Potential logic/rationale	• Diaries and other sources of data are the same type of data (e.g., all textual data) • Diaries and other sources of data are analyzed together • Diaries and other sources are used to address a singular research question • Diaries and other sources of data are combined to build an overarching understanding of a given phenomenon (e.g., building a picture of X) • **Analyzed together**	• Diaries and other sources of data are different types of data (e.g., textual and visual data) • Diaries and other sources of data are *analyzed separately* but drawn on to address the same research questions and/or combined in the interpretation of the findings • **Analyzed separately but findings combined**	• Diaries and other sources of data are different types of data (e.g., textual and visual data) • Diaries and other sources are analyzed separately • Diaries and other sources of data are used to address distinct research questions • **Analyzed separately *and* findings kept distinct**
Example studies	Rauch and Ansari (2022); Radcliffe and Cassell (2015)	Iivari et al. (2014); King and Dickinson (2022)	MacDonald et al. (2018); Litovuo et al. (2019)

In summary, in this chapter, we have provided insight into how you might go about analyzing your QDM data, from data management and preparing for analysis, to the key considerations you should take into account when selecting your analysis method and the diverse analytical methods available to analyze your diary data. In doing so, we have considered both textual and visual data but equally different types of textual and visual analysis approaches, including the strengths and limitations of these approaches. We have also considered how you might go about integrating diary data with other forms of data, particularly interview data. Below you will find a checklist and decision-making prompt table based on this discussion to help you think about your data management and preparation, as well as guide you in selecting your analysis approach. We hope that this chapter has provided you with both practical guidance on how to approach your analysis while also highlighting the analytical opportunities and possibilities providing inspiration for your own QDM research. In the next chapter, we discuss two QDM-specific analysis approaches, which address some of the limitations of traditional analysis approaches when applied to QDM research as discussed in this chapter.

APPLICATION ACTIVITY
HOW WILL I MANAGE MY DIARY DATA ANALYSIS?

As might be evident from this chapter, going about analyzing your diary data can be quite complex and involves numerous decisions and points of consideration. While these decisions can seem quite obvious, such as keeping track of your data collection to folder naming conventions, oftentimes these are the things that researchers learn to do over time rather than feature in methodological texts or classes. So, to help you in this process, we have provided a checklist and decision prompt table to help you think about how you will manage your diary data and how you will go about analyzing your data. As with other checklists in this book, we have designed this to help you with your decision-making in designing your diary study but also to help you reflect on your methodological decisions when developing and writing up the justifications in your methodological choices within ethics applications, funding bids, and within the Methodology section of your final project write-up.

MANAGING YOUR DIARY DATA FOR ANALYSIS: A STEP-BY-STEP CHECKLIST WITH DECISION-MAKING PROMPTS

Project Phase	Step #	Task	Steps and Decision Prompts
Before and during your data collection	Step 1	Keeping track of data collection	• Have you created a dynamic and systematized participant tracking table that you keep updated regularly? (e.g., see Figure 6.1)
	Step 2	Collating, transcribing, and storing your data	• Is your data storage plan compliant with your ethical approval? • Have you got a logical and consistent organization scheme for your data? • For example, have you created a folder for each participant? Are all data files, for said participants, clearly named and organized according to temporal unit (e.g., diary day 1, week 1, etc.)? • Have you converted all written and/or digital diaries into a Word file or similar? • Have you transcribed any and all audio data into a Word file or similar? • Have you stored all nontextual data? • Have you thoroughly anonymized all your data? • Is your approach consistent across all participants (e.g., same file formats)?
After data collection	Step 3	Organizing your data for analysis	• Have you self-audited your data repository and accounted for any missing data? • Have you created participant summaries? • Have you got a data organization system in place? • Have you organized your data in a meaningful way (as determined by your RQs and LOA)? For example, have you created a data display matrix (see Chapter 7) and an organized system in the analysis software (e.g., Nvivo cases, if relevant)? • Have you combined all the different types and sources of data in a coherent and logical way?

(Continued)

(Continued)

Project Phase	Step #	Task	Steps and Decision Prompts
	Step 4	Choosing your analysis approach	• What are your ontological and epistemological positions? 　○ Is your research design reflective of a particular "methodology" (i.e., grounded theory, phenomenology)? 　○ Can you use a generic analysis method (i.e., thematic analysis, template analysis)? • Why did you use QDMs in the first place (research question-analysis alignment)? 　○ Did you aim to capture details of events/experiences/thoughts/emotions in the moment? 　○ Did you aim to capture changes in events/experiences/thoughts/emotions over time? 　○ A combination of both? • Are you integrating diary and other types of data? 　○ Are you looking to follow a fully integrated, partly integrated, or non-integrated strategy? • Are you collecting visual data and want to analyze the "visual" itself or combine visual and textual analyses? • Have you, your supervisors, or your collaborators got expertise in a particular method? Is this method suitable for your diary study? • Are you new to qualitative research? Will a more structured approach be helpful? • Is your analysis method feasible in the time frame you have available? • Can you justify and defend your analysis method?

Project Phase	Step #	Task	Steps and Decision Prompts

	Step 5	Analyzing your data	• Have you consulted the methodological literature for your given approach?
			• Have you read other diary studies that have used the approach?
			• Are you keeping an audit trail of your analysis and your analytical decisions? (important for writing up your method and findings section and to demonstrate the rigor of your analysis)
			  ○ Have you followed your chosen analysis methods steps appropriately and rigorously?
			  ○ Have you kept record of any adaptions you made to your chosen method procedures?

FURTHER READING

Bowen, G. A. (2009). Supporting a grounded theory with an audit trail: An illustration. *International Journal of Social Research Methodology*, *12*(4), 305–316.

Braun, V., & Clarke, V. (2006). Using thematic analysis in psychology. *Qualitative Research in Psychology*, *3*(2), 77–101.

Braun, V., & Clarke, V. (2021). Can I use TA? Should I use TA? Should I not use TA? Comparing reflexive thematic analysis and other pattern-based qualitative analytic approaches. *Counselling and Psychotherapy Research*, *21*(1), 37–47.

Guest, G., Namey, E. E., & Mitchell, M. L. (2013). *Collecting qualitative data: A field manual for applied research*. Sage.

Patton, M. Q. (2015). *Qualitative research & evaluation methods: Integrating theory and practice*. Sage.

Shortt, H. L., & Warren, S. K. (2019). Grounded visual pattern analysis: Photographs in organizational field studies. *Organizational Research Methods*, *22*(2), 539–563.

ENDNOTES

1 Please ensure that your data management and storage protocol adhere to your institutional and/or ethical review board requirements and regulations.
2 Note that there is still the need for ontological and epistemological positions themselves to be commensurate.
3 For a helpful comparative discussion of when and why you may use TA, DA, GA, or IPA, please see Braun and Clarke (2006).
4 Includes both MS patients (n = 12) and their standing assistants (n = 8); total sample N = 20.
5 Participants were also asked to report positive experiences from the past 24 hours, findings of which can be found in Flanders et al. (2016).
6 This article provides an extensive discussion of the methodological and theoretical justifications for using QDMs within IPA, but note that the discussion of analysis procedures is very limited. Substantive findings can be found in Cudjoe et al. (2022).

7 QDM-FOCUSED ANALYSIS APPROACHES

Having reviewed the use of traditional qualitative analytical methods and their application to QDMs in the previous chapter, in this chapter, we focus on two QDM-focused analytical approaches that were developed specifically to address some of the limitations of adopting traditional qualitative analysis methods to analyze diary data. Specifically, in this chapter, we delve into Radcliffe's (2013) "event diagrams" approach and Spencer et al.'s (2021) "thematic trajectory analysis" approach, which we developed as a response to the challenges we faced in analyzing our diary data. This chapter will, therefore, provide readers with an enhanced understanding of when and why the use of either approach might be appropriate and the strengths and limitations of each of these approaches. We also provide clear and detailed step-by-step guidance for employing each approach, as well as providing clear guidance on how to report the analytical output when using each of these analytical methods in the write-up of your research findings. By the end of this chapter, you will, therefore, be able to select the most appropriate analytical approach for your QDM study and be able to carry out QDM-focused analysis to fully capitalize on the benefits of your QDM data for your specific research project.

INTRODUCING QDM-FOCUSED ANALYTICAL APPROACHES: CAPTURING THE "DOWN" AND "ACROSS" BENEFITS OF QDMs

As noted throughout this book, in our view, QDMs are a particularly valuable method within the qualitative toolkit as they offer an approach that, depending on the specific research focus and design, enables contextually rich data to be collected in the moment but equally with the opportunity to collect temporally sensitive, longitudinal/shortitudinal data (i.e., the "down" and "across" benefits of QDMs, respectively) (see Chapter 1 for further discussion). As we have noted in the previous chapter and elsewhere (e.g., Spencer et al., 2021), while the use of traditional/established analysis methods offers researchers a wealth of benefits and strengths, our review of these approaches highlighted their limitations with respect to fully capitalizing on the "down" and "across" benefits of QDMs. Notably, how they often render QDM data atemporal is a significant oversight given diaries are an inherently temporal method, thereby negating the "across" benefit of QDMs. However, while traditional/established qualitative methods are arguably more adept in enabling exploitation of the "down" benefits of QDMs, an additional, perhaps more nuanced, limitation of existing approaches is that it can be challenging to explore and/or account for the relationship/links between particular themes at within- and between-person levels. For example, if diaries are event-focused, thereby how individuals experience and respond to a given type of "event," it is likely that researchers would have an interest in understanding the relationship between different momentary occurrences, experiences, or event components and the potential interdependencies between these.

To this end, in this chapter, we focus on the two approaches that we developed through our own efforts and struggles during our respective doctoral research projects. We first focus on Laura's event diagrams approach (EDA; Radcliffe, 2013), which enables a fine-grained analysis of the *"down"* aspects of diary data, before discussing our more recent analysis method, thematic trajectory analysis (TTA; Spencer et al., 2021) that we collaboratively developed during Leighann's doctoral research, which focuses on capitalizing on the *"across"* aspects of diary data. While we acknowledge our inevitable bias here, in our view, the strengths of both these approaches lie in the fact that they were developed specifically for analyzing qualitative diary data. They, therefore, inherently overcome some of the issues of retrofitting, or adapting, traditional approaches to the complexities of diary data. However, as both build on template analysis (King, 2004), an established analysis method, they retain the rigor and recognizability of an already established and popular approach. As such, any researchers seeking to draw on EDA or TTA should in the first instance consult the primary methodological texts; for detailed explanations of how to conduct template analysis, see King (2004) and King and Brooks (2017) (see also Chapter 6 for studies that have used TA). In addition, both approaches incorporate steps that enable the visualization of qualitative data and therefore harness the power of visualized data to provide engaging and succinct means to communicate findings in the write-up of your projects (see Langley & Ravasi, 2019). To explicate these benefits in more specific detail, we now discuss both approaches, beginning first with EDA.

Embracing the "Down": Analyzing QDMs Using Event Diagrams Analysis

Laura developed her EDA (Radcliffe, 2013) during her doctoral research, which was focused on gaining an in-depth insight into the decision-making processes that dual-earner couples engage in when faced with daily work–family conflicts. To gain these insights, as discussed in detail in Chapter 3, Laura drew on event-contingent QDMs, completed over a period of 28 consecutive days by both members of heterosexual couples. In analyzing these data, Laura initially relied on TA (King, 2004) because of its utility in studies examining different perspectives, thereby enabling Laura to explore the perspectives of individual couple members, as well as perspectives across couples and across time (Radcliffe, 2013). As such, Laura initially analyzed all her data (diaries and interviews) into a single thematic template according to the procedures of TA.

However, owing to her focus on the *decision-making processes*, Laura realized that she needed an additional means to organize her data to (1) enable comparisons between individuals and couples and (2) explore the links between different stages in the decision-making process. In other words, while the study template derived from TA enabled holistic understanding of the kinds of conflicts experienced, the types of decisions made, the factors that influenced these decisions (e.g., why), and the outcomes of these decisions across the study sample, it did not enable Laura to explore the relationships, or "event chains," between these themes. For instance, when an individual encounters a particular type of work–family conflict, what decisions do they make and why, and what are the outcomes of these decisions? As such, Laura decided to build on TA by generating flowchart-style diagrammatical representations of each of these event chains captured in daily diaries, leading to the development EDA (Radcliffe, 2013).

EDA is an approach that is focused on the relationships and/or links between *events or activities* and is therefore particularly useful in understanding how events unfold in a particular moment, including what people do and why they do it, as well as the associated momentary outcomes. In addition, as noted, EDA is predicated on the analytical procedures of TA (King, 2004) but adapted to include the visualization of thematic content through the generation of "event" diagrams. The process unfolds over three main steps, which are depicted in Figure 7.1 and detailed below.

Conducting EDA: A Three-Step Process

Step 1: Conduct a Thematic Template Analysis

The first step in EDA is to conduct a thematic template analysis of your diary data (see below for integrating the approach with other diary data) following the procedures of King (2004).[1] In Laura's study, this process involved developing an initial template of four major themes that reflected the four questions asked in the study diaries (see Chapter 3)—"type of conflict," "decision made," "reason for decision," and "outcome of decision"—and then conducting a full thematic template analysis, wherein she iteratively worked through her data to develop and refine the final study template (see Figure 7.1), which served as the basis for interpreting the data. It is important here that this study template contains some kind of explicit logical sequencing system, wherein the major themes (Level 1) and constituent (Level 2, Level 3, etc.) themes are numbered (and/or alphanumerical), as indicated in Figure 7.1.

Step 2: Create Event (or Activity) Diagrams

The second step of the analysis is to create the event diagrams by "zooming in" to the level of the events or activities at the focus of your research. For example, in Laura's study, the "event" or "activity" she was interested in was decision-making in the context of work–family conflicts. Thus, in Step 2 of EDA, Laura went back to her diary data and focused on each of the 224 decisions reported in participant diary entries to create flowchart-style diagrams of each. Each diagram included the type of conflict, the decision that was made, the reasons expressed for making this decision, and the subsequent outcomes (Radcliffe, 2013). Importantly, within each of the diagrams, the codes from the final template (derived in Step 1) relating to the specific decision, decision-making factor, or outcome represented in that diagram were reported, therefore making links between the two easily apparent (see Figure 7.1). In this way, these diagrams show the relationship between the themes (derived from the thematic template) and maintain the detail of each incident. This, in turn, enabled Laura to explore what led to what and why (i.e., event chains), thereby being able to "see" the factors that tend to lead to particular decisions in particular circumstances or the kinds of decisions that lead to particular outcomes.

Step 3: Comparative Analysis Within and Between Participants

The final step of EDA is to conduct within- and between-person level analysis by drawing on the event diagrams developed in Step 2. Here, you can engage in different kinds of comparative analysis depending on your RQs and/or what seems most interesting in your data, for example:

Within-person comparisons: How does the same individual experience different activities and/or events at different times, when is this similar or different, and why?

Between-person comparisons: How have different individuals responded to the same event? Is this similar or different, and why?

In Laura's study, the diagrammatical representations enabled the comparison of decision-making within and between individuals and couples, as well as the exploration of links between different stages in the decision-making process. For instance, as demonstrated in Figure 7.1, at the between-person level, the decision-making process reported by both partners regarding the same decision could easily be compared side by side, or those outcomes most commonly associated with particular types of decisions or decision-making factors could be more easily explored. At the within-person level, the diagrams enable comparison of how the same conflict led to different decisions and outcomes on different days. In this way, the event diagrams aided an effective and detailed analysis of the data regarding how couples made decisions in incidents of work–family conflict.

Integrating Event Diagrams With Other Qualitative Data

In Laura's original research in which she first developed EDA, and in much of her subsequent QDM research, she has drawn upon Zimmerman and Wieder's (1977) diary-interview method and thereby combined qualitative diary data with qualitative interview data. Within initial interviews, to help prepare participants for subsequent diary completion (see Chapter 2), she also often draws upon the critical incident technique (CIT; Chell, 1998; Flannagan, 1954). As a result, Laura has also used EDA to analyze qualitative interview data derived from employing the CIT, alongside any other instances during the interviews in which participants had provided detailed depictions of particular work–family conflict incidents and subsequent decision-making processes. To do so, she highlighted all such incidents discussed within the interview data and performed EDA in the same way as she did for those focused upon within the diary data. While importantly acknowledging that the critical incident technique is retrospective, thereby potentially influencing the type of events likely to be recalled as well as the way in which the associated details are recalled (Schwarz, 1999; see also Chapter 1 for a discussion of the complex implications of retrospective

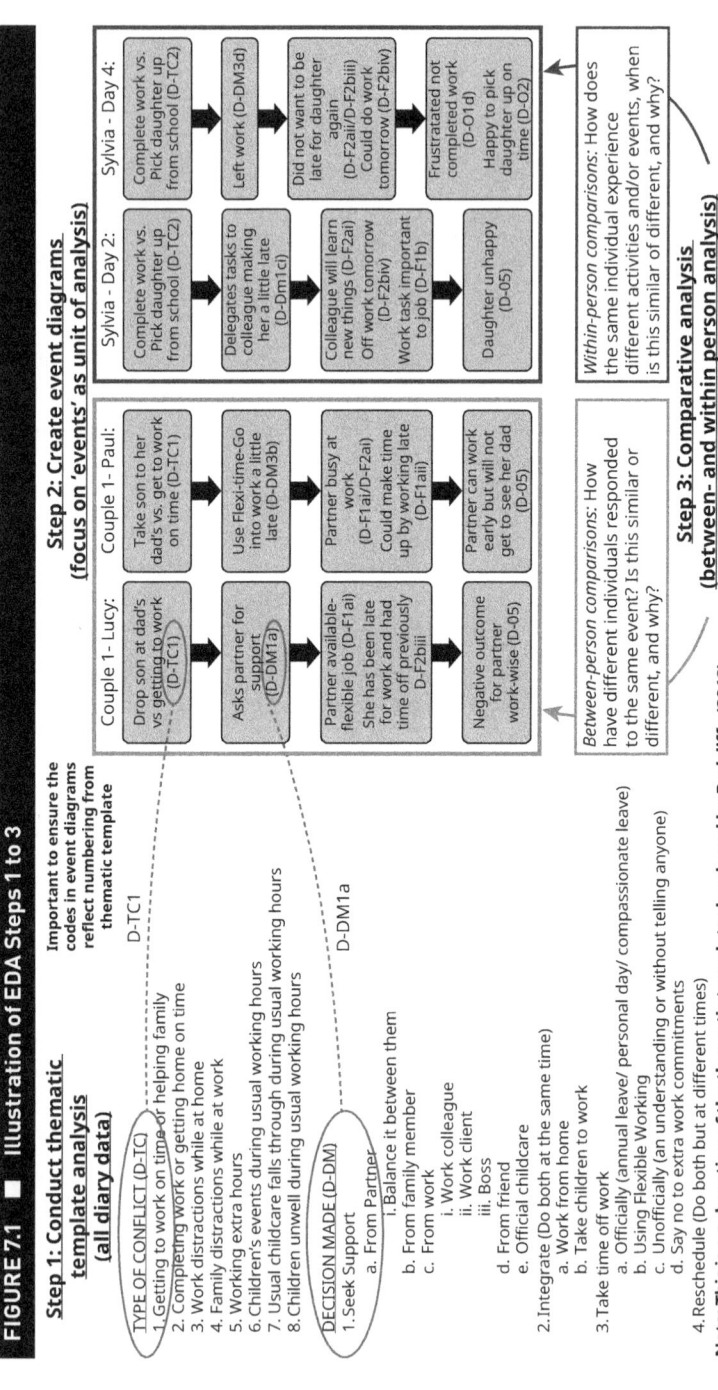

190 Qualitative Diary Methods

FIGURE 7.1 ■ Illustration of EDA Steps 1 to 3

Step 1: Conduct thematic template analysis (all diary data)

Important to ensure the codes in event diagrams reflect numbering from thematic template

TYPE OF CONFLICT (D-TC)
1. Getting to work on time or helping family — D-TC1
2. Completing work or getting home on time
3. Work distractions while at home
4. Family distractions while at work
5. Working extra hours
6. Children's events during usual working hours
7. Usual childcare falls through during usual working hours
8. Children unwell during usual working hours

DECISION MADE (D-DM)
1. Seek Support — D-DM1a
   a. From Partner
      I. Balance it between them
   b. From family member
   c. From work
      i. Work colleague
      ii. Work client
      iii. Boss
   d. From friend
   e. Official childcare
2. Integrate (Do both at the same time)
   a. Work from home
   b. Take children to work
3. Take time off work
   a. Officially (annual leave/ personal day/ compassionate leave)
   b. Using Flexible Working
   c. Unofficially (an understanding or without telling anyone)
   d. Say no to extra work commitments
4. Reschedule (Do both but at different times)

Note: This is a subsection of the thematic template developed by Radcliffe (2012)

Step 2: Create event diagrams (focus on 'events' as unit of analysis)

Couple 1 - Lucy:
- Drop son at dad's vs getting to work (D-TC1)
- Asks partner for support (D-DM1a)
- Partner available-flexible job (D-F1ai). She has been late for work and had time off previously D-F2bii
- Negative outcome for partner work-wise (D-O5)

Couple 1 - Paul:
- Take son to her dad's vs. get to work on time (D-TC1)
- Use Flexi-time-Go into work a little late (D-DM3b)
- Partner busy at work (D-F1ai/D-F2ai). Could make time up by working late (D-F1aii)
- Partner can work early but will not get to see her dad (D-O5)

Sylvia - Day 2:
- Complete work vs. Pick daughter up from school (D-TC2)
- Delegates tasks to colleague making her a little late (D-DM1c)
- Colleague will learn new things (D-F2ai) Off work tomorrow (D-F2biv) Work task important to job (D-F1b)
- Daughter unhappy (D-O5)

Sylvia - Day 4:
- Complete work vs. Pick daughter up from school (D-TC2)
- Left work (D-DM3d)
- Did not want to be late for daughter again (D-F2ai/D-F2biii) Could do work tomorrow (D-F2biv)
- Frustrated not completed work (D-O1d) Happy to pick daughter up on time (D-O2)

Step 3: Comparative analysis (between- and within person analysis)

Between-person comparisons: How have different individuals responded to the same event? Is this similar or different, and why?

Within-person comparisons: How does the same individual experience different activities and/or events, when is this similar of different, and why?

accounts), EDA also proved effective in terms of enabling a more detailed analysis of specific events discussed in interview data. In this way, while designed for and, therefore, being particularly well aligned with the analysis of QDM data, EDA can be used to analyze qualitative data more broadly, where (at least some of) these data are focused upon attaining an in-depth understanding of a particular event and how it unfolded in the moment. In other words, EDA adds an additional interpretive layer to the traditional output of most thematic analysis approaches (such as TA), enabling researchers to analytically "zoom in" on particular events highlighted in the data. A pertinent point to note here is that particular interview techniques at the point of data collection would usually be required to make later EDA analysis feasible in which there is a line of questioning focused upon drawing out, in quite some detail, the particularities of specific events or experiences and how they evolved in that moment.

More broadly, EDA-derived analytical output or insights can be helpfully contextualized by broader interview data or indeed by data collected by other means, enabling a more contextualized understanding of the particular events or experiences focused upon via EDA. Here, the combination of data derived from different methods, alongside the combination of analytical strategies, lends itself to producing a fine-grained understanding of specific events without losing contextual insight.

Limitations

As with all methods of analysis, there are inevitable challenges and limitations of using EDA. First, given that this is a method building upon existing thematic analysis approaches, it is inevitably more time-consuming than using such traditional thematic analysis alone as it involves additional steps beyond the initial creation of an overarching thematic structure representative of your entire participant sample. EDA involves subsequent detailed steps that involve creating organized thematic structures (or event diagrams) for each event recorded within each participant diary. While this is particularly useful in enabling researchers to fully realize the "down" benefits of QDMs, as discussed above, it is important to build in additional time for analysis when developing your project plan or timetable.

Another important limitation of EDA is that it does not readily enable full realization of the "across" benefits of QDMs. This approach may go some way to enabling pattern spotting in terms of how themes may be changing over time by enabling you to line up all the event diagrams for one particular participant in a temporally relevant order. However, further steps are ideally required if your main reason for employing QDMs is to capture and understand change over time, as was the case in Leighann's research investigating experiences of mistreatment. As a result, we created TTA, which we will outline below, specifically for projects in which temporality is central to answering the research question posed.

EMBRACING THE "ACROSS": ANALYZING QDMs USING THEMATIC TRAJECTORY ANALYSIS

As discussed in the introduction of this chapter, both EDA and TTA were developed as responses to the challenges we faced during our respective doctoral projects when it came to analyzing our data. For Laura, it was the challenge of being able to account for links between momentary thematic content, as well as understand and compare decision-making processes and how and why individuals made the decisions they did in the context of work–family conflicts. For Leighann, it was her struggles trying to analyze her diary data in a way that sufficiently enabled her to account for the daily *dynamics* of mistreatment at work (for further details, see Chapters 3 and 5). Here, the main challenge was that despite diaries being the most appropriate method to capture these daily dynamics (e.g., an apt means to collect contemporaneous and longitudinal data to understand what it is like going to work every day when you are being mistreated), when it came to analyzing the data, Leighann struggled with traditional qualitative approaches, essentially rendering her diary data atemporal and undermining the rationale for using them in the first place. As such, with Laura's existing experience using QDMs (at the time Leighann's PhD supervisor) and Leighann's interest in narrative analysis, particularly visual plotlines (see Spencer, 2020), we collaboratively developed TTA as a diary-specific and temporally sensitive analysis method.

To illustrate TTA, we first discuss the philosophical positioning of the approach and then a detailed account of the four-step process. As in the above discussion of EDA, we have provided a visual representation of the process to aid comprehension. However, as in the case with EDA, TTA (Spencer et al., 2021) builds on King's (2004) thematic template analysis, and as such, it is imperative that researchers seeking to adopt TTA, and indeed EDA, consult the primary methodological texts (e.g., for detailed explanations of how to conduct template analysis before attempting TTA, see King, 2004; King & Brooks, 2017) but ideally as an interpretive companion to the sections that follow.

Philosophical Positioning of TTA

Owing to the methodological heritage of TA (King & Brooks, 2017), TTA (and, indeed, EDA) should be understood as a *generic* form of analysis (see Chapter 6), not exclusively wedded to any one philosophical position. Instead, as with any generic form of analysis, the "philosophical freedom" of TTA means that you must ensure that the analysis and subsequent interpretation of the data using TTA are done in a philosophically commensurate manner, particularly in terms of how trajectories are interpreted and how meaning is theorized (Braun & Clarke, 2006). However, to aid you in understanding how your philosophical commitments might influence how you conduct TTA and interpret TTA outputs, Table 7.1 illustrates the potential implications for using TTA under different philosophical positions, namely, *neo-positivism, limited realism, contextualism,* and *radical constructionism* (King & Brooks, 2017).

TABLE 7.1 ■ Philosophical Considerations and Implications When Using TTA

Philosophical Position	Ontology	Epistemology	Guiding Principles	Implications for Use of TTA
Neo-positivism	Realist	Realist	• Seeks to build or test theory, minimizing impact of researcher subjectivity	• Use of independent coders to generate thematic templates and map trajectories • Trajectory mapping likely to involve standardized procedure and structure across themes • Use of strong theory linked a priori themes • May use findings of TTA to generate testable hypotheses or combine with quantitative methods

(Continued)

TABLE 7.1 ■ Philosophical Considerations and Implications When Using TTA *(Continued)*			
Philosophical Position	Ontology	Epistemology	Guiding Principles	Implications for Use of TTA
Limited realism	Realist	Constructivist/ relativist	• Seeks to develop an account that is credible and potentially transferrable while recognizing conclusions are tentative	• Use of a priori themes common, likely combined with emergent themes • May use trajectories to triangulate with other forms of data • May use trajectories to develop propositions and/or hypotheses in sequential mixed methods • Methodological reflexivity encouraged
Contextualism	Relativist	Constructivist/ relativist	• Seeks to understand participants' meaning-making within the specific research context	• Strong preference for inductive coding and emergent themes • Interpretations strongly grounded in textual data, rather than trajectories in isolation • Discussion of thematic trajectories will include consideration of social

Philosophical Position	Ontology	Epistemology	Guiding Principles	Implications for Use of TTA
				context and acknowledge the potential of multiple interpretations • Personal and methodological reflexivity encouraged
Radical constructionism	Relativist	Strongly relativist	• Seeks to examine how phenomena are constructed (e.g., language creates reality) and how research itself constructs knowledge	• Limited to studies focusing on patterns, or aspects, of discourse rather than how discourse is constructed in interactions (cf. discourse analysis) • Use of TTA must be strongly justified (e.g., emphasize themes defined in terms of aspects of discourse rather than personal experience)

Source. Reproduced from Table 3 from "Thematic Trajectory Analysis: A Temporal Method for Analysing Dynamic Qualitative Data" by L. Spencer, L. Radcliffe, R. Spence, & N. King, 2021, *Journal of Occupational and Organizational Psychology, 94*(3), 531–567 (https://doi.org/10.1111/joop.12359). Licensed under CC BY-SA 4.0 (https://creativecommons.org/licenses/by/4.0/). Original content adapted from *Template analysis for business and management students* (p. 17), by N. King & J. Brooks, 2017, SAGE Publications Ltd. Copyright 2017 by Nigel King and Johanna Brooks.

Conducting TTA: A Four-Step Process

To demonstrate how to conduct TTA, we turn to a discussion of the four steps, each of which draws on illustrative examples from Leighann's doctoral research project (see Chapters 3 and 5). For clarity, the process is depicted as linear, but as with most qualitative analysis approaches, in reality, it is a highly iterative process that involves frequently moving back and forth between steps. As such, we highlight potential moments of iteration throughout.

Step 1: Create Data Display Matrices

The first step of TTA is to prepare the diary data for analysis by organizing them in a way that is expedient to examining changes over time (see Chapter 6). To do so, we suggest the creation of a data display matrix (Miles & Huberman, 1994) for each participant. Here specifically, time-ordered display matrices help preserve "chronological flow" and permit understanding of what led to what (Miles & Huberman, 1994). The primary purpose of this step is to arrange the data in a way that enables an accessible means to thematically code data in Step 2. Thus, columns denote the temporal unit (e.g., day/week/month of entry), rows represent the questions or topic areas posed in the diary nested for each participant, and, at this stage, the raw data from participants' diaries can simply be transposed[2] into the relevant boxes in preparation for Step 2, as illustrated in Figure 7.2.

It is important to note that if your diaries follow an unstructured rather than semi-structured design (see Chapter 2), that is, an open journal-style diary (e.g., Wechtler, 2018), different options could be used to denote the rows. For example, theory-driven concepts could be employed in studies with an established theoretical lens. Alternatively, for studies that are more inductive in nature, tentative areas of interest may be identified based on initial familiarization with the data and modified as further analysis is undertaken. It is important to highlight the iterative nature of the four steps that constitute TTA, wherein you may return to this initial step to amend the labels denoting different rows used to organize your data. In practice, it is likely that a combination of the above might be appropriate for many studies, depending on philosophical positioning (see Table 7.1). We once more encourage that this approach is used flexibly and importantly in a way that is commensurate with your project's specific philosophical perspective, research approach, and design (see Chapter 6).

Step 2: Thematic Template Analysis at Micro-, Meso-, and Macro-Levels

While Step 1 enables the ordering of diary data in a temporal manner, this is not sufficient to enable fine-grained analysis at the individual level in a way that permits insights into how important themes change over time or how they relate to one another. Thus, within Step 2, the process turns to thematically coding

FIGURE 7.2 ■ Diary Data Display Matrix

Temporal unit ──── Diary questions

Day of entry	1	2	3		7	8	
1. Emotion evaluation	5	4	5		5	5	
2. How was work today? Did you have a positive or not so positive day and why?	Not so positive. Helping boss master student	Neutral day. I did not enjoy the day but there were no major problems	Neutral		Not so positive. Had a conversation with my second line manager.	Stress.	
3. Did you experience any negative interactions or mistreatment today at work? If so, tell me about it, please try and be as detailed as possible about the event(s):	Follow up meeting of a project I was following from start. My boss met the collaborators without telling me anything in her office. No response for me. I will have again to chase for information. If there will not be any follow with my boss about what happened today	Only thing, I asked one of the staff about details of a procedure that in the workflow I am supposed to manage and the staff said he did not have time. So I will have to chase it.	Usual issues. Waiting for 4 days to meet one of my bosses regarding one project with a company	<<< Collapsed days 4–6 >>>	The conversation with the second line manager, although not negative as I was not bullied, was disappointing, as my worries were answered with very empathic face expression, the reassurance that action will be taken, and then he disappeared and I will not be able to see him despite reminders for days	I was notified only yesterday night of an important skype meeting with a multinational company for this morning by one of my line managers. I wanted to prepare properly for this meeting that could mean more external funding for the facility. The other line manager, despite me saying I was really busy, requested my presence in a morning meeting that I normally can skip as not very relevant with my work/ Afternoon quieter	<<< Collapsed days 9–16 >>>
4. In what ways did this impact you? i.e. how did you feel directly after? Did it have any effect on your work and/or your mood for the rest of the day?	Feel lagging behind respect to the work	Mood unaffected for the rest of the day, but I see workload increasing because of a lot of new things to chase	Keep chasing with mails and visiting offices, to do list getting bigger because of lack of communication		Problems still lingering and not tackled	To do list ever increasing and impossibility to plan, just firefighting	
5. How do you feel about going to work tomorrow?	Not so positive	Not so positive	Bad		Bad, no changes in positive on the landscape	Tired.	

Participant data

Note. Reproduced from Figure 1 from "Thematic Trajectory Analysis: A Temporal Method for Analysing Dynamic Qualitative Data" by L. Spencer, L. Radcliffe, R. Spence, & N. King, 2021, *Journal of Occupational and Organizational Psychology, 94*(3), 531–567 (https://doi.org/10.1111/joop.12359). Licensed under CC BY-SA 4.0 (https://creativecommons.org/licenses/by/4.0/).

the content of the participant diary entries that draws on, yet extends, the procedures of TA (King, 2004). In line with the procedures of TA, researchers may begin with initial a priori codes or take a more inductive approach to derive data-driven themes of interest depending on epistemological positioning and study aims (see King & Brooks, 2017). Importantly, where TTA diverges from TA is that rather than only creating one template representing all study data, TTA involves the creation of three levels of templates:

Level 1: Micro-templates (template for each diary entry)
First, the creation of a series of *"micro-templates"* for each individual diary entry, allows researchers to understand key themes reported at each specific temporal unit or within each diary entry (e.g., day, week, etc.). In this way, the creation of micro-templates during TTA shares similarities with EDA, and indeed, the output of EDA (i.e., event diagrams) could be used here within studies in which both the "down" and "across" benefits of QDMs are pertinent to answering research questions posed. We have found it useful for micro-templates to be contained within the matrix created at Step 1, so that micro-templates are positioned side by side and thematic comparisons across temporal units can begin to highlight thematic variation over time (see Figure 7.3). Again, at this stage, you may draw similarities to EDA as described above, enabling both approaches to be used together where necessary or useful for a particular study.

Level 2: Meso-templates (template for each participant)
The next step within TTA is the creation of a *"meso-template,"* a composite template of the full set of diary entries for each participant by combining all micro-templates from a given participant. It is important that researchers include the day/week (i.e., relevant temporal unit) during which particular themes were experienced in order to retain temporal grounding of the themes, an example of which can be seen in the meso-template in Figure 7.3. For example, if the temporal unit of interest is the day of entry (i.e., daily interval design; Iida et al. 2012), researchers should include the day's number next to the relevant themes to represent the particular time points at which that (sub)theme was discussed (i.e., theme X—1,3,7, where 1, 3, and 7 represent the days that this (sub)theme was present). We recommend developing the meso-template at the same time as you work through each micro-template. These meso-templates provide an interpretive template for each complete diary, giving an overview of the data for each participant in a thematically meaningful structure.

Chapter 7 • QDM-Focused Analysis Approaches   199

FIGURE 7.3 ■ Translation Across the Three Levels of Thematic Templates

Micro-template (template/diary entry)

	Day 1 – micro-template	Day 2 – micro-template	Day 3 – micro-template	Day 4 – micro-template
A. Evaluation of day	• 5 – somewhat negative	• 4 – neutral	• 5 – somewhat negative	• 7 – very negative
B. Interaction/events	• IWN – left out of meeting	• IWN – Request for help denied	• IWN – meeting delays; lack of communication	• IWN – last minute change; left out of meeting
C. Impact of interaction	• IWPN – lagging behind	• IWPN – feel like have to chase things	• IWPN – work progress hindered	• IPSP – demotivated
D. Anticipation (eval)	• ANU – neutral	• ANU – neutral	• AN – negative	• AN – negative
E. Locus of anticipation	• LAN – evaluative only	• LAN – evaluative only	• LAN – evaluative only	• LAN – evaluative only

Numbers denote days theme was present; derived from micro-templates

Meso-template (template/participant)

A. **Evaluation of day (uses 7pt Likert scale - reversed)**
   i. Very negative (4, 10, 15)
   ii. Somewhat negative (1, 3, 7, 8, 14)
   iii. Neutral (2, 5, 6, 9, 12, 13)
   iv. Positive (11, 16)

B. **Interactions/events (Informed by Bartlett & Bartlett (2011) typology**
   i. Person-related
      a. Positive interaction/event (IPP)
      b. Negative interaction/event (IPN) (5, 7, 10, 15, 15)
   ii. Work-related
      a. Positive interaction/event (IWP) (11, 13)
      b. Negative interaction/event (IWN) (1, 2, 3, 4, 5, 6, 8, 8, 12)
   iii. None reported (IO) (9, 14, 16)

C. **Impact of interactions/event**
   i. Impact on self
      a. Positive impact IPSP (5, 11, 13, 16)
      b. Negative impact IPSN (4, 5, 7, 10, 15)
   ii. Impact on work
      a. Positive impact IPWP
      b. Negative impact IPWN (1, 2, 3, 6, 8, 12)
   iii. None reported IPO (M9) (M16)

D. **Anticipation of next day**
   i. Positive AP (5, 11, 13)
   ii. Neutral ANU (1, 2, 6, 9, 12, 14, 16)
   iii. Negative AN (3, 4, 7, 10, 15)

E. **Locus of anticipation**
   i. Retrospective (LAR) (13, 15)
   ii. Prospective (LAP) (7, 14)
   iii. 'Friday' effect (TGIF) (5)
   iv. None/evaluative only (LAN) (1, 2, 3, 4, 6, 8, 9, 10, 11, 12, 16)

Combine all participant micro-templates to create meso-template

Combine all participants meso-templates to create macro-template

Macro-template (template/sample)

A. **Evaluation of day (uses 7pt Likert scale - reversed)**
   i. Very negative
   ii. Negative
   iii. Somewhat negative
   iv. Neutral
   v. Positive
   vi. Somewhat positive
   vii. Positive
   viii. Very positive

B. **Interactions/events (Informed by Bartlett & Bartlett (2011) typology**
   i. Person-related
      a. Positive interaction/event (IPP)
      b. Negative interaction/event (IPN)
   ii. Work-related
      a. Positive interaction/event (IWP)
      b. Negative interaction/event (IWN)
   iii. None reported (IO)

C. **Impact of interactions/event**
   i. Impact on self (IPS)
      a. Positive impact (IPSP)
      b. Negative impact (IPSN)
   ii. Impact on work (IPW)
      a. Positive impact (IPWP)
      b. Negative impact (IPWN)
   iii. None reported IPO

D. **Anticipation of next day**
   i. Positive (AP)
   ii. Neutral (ANU)
   iii. Negative (AN)

E. **Locus of anticipation**
   i. Retrospective (LAR)
   ii. Prospective (LAP)
   iii. Friday effect (TGIF)
   iv. None/evaluative only (LAN)

Iterative movement back and forth between templates to refine coding and themes (see King & Brookes, 2016)

Note. Reproduced from Figure 2 from "Thematic Trajectory Analysis: A Temporal Method for Analysing Dynamic Qualitative Data" by L. Spencer, L. Radcliffe, R. Spence, & N. King, 2021, *Journal of Occupational and Organizational Psychology*, 94(3), 531–567 (https://doi.org/10.1111/joop.12359). Licensed under CC BY-SA 4.0 (https://creativecommons.org/licenses/by/4.0/).

Level 3: Macro-templates (template for all diary data)
Following creation of the micro- and meso-templates, you can next consolidate all the meso-templates to create a final *"macro-template"* of the entire study's diary data (i.e., all participants), which reflects the usual output of TA (King & Brooks, 2017). Here, there is the option to generate more than one macro-template where research questions aim to explore how experiences and changes over time may vary among subgroups of the study sample. For instance, separate macro-templates may be created for "men" and "women," where the research seeks to examine gender differences. In practice, the three levels of templates are best created concurrently, enabling you to "zoom in" to the day-to-day accounts (micro-templates) and "zoom out" to participant (meso-templates) and study-level data (macro-templates). Insights into the data that occur during the later stages may necessitate changes in the earlier analysis. In this way, moving back and forth between the different template levels is a key part of the TTA process. Figure 7.3 illustrates the three levels of templates and how participants' data translate across the templates.

Step 3: Visualization of Thematic Trajectories

The outputs of Steps 1 and 2 provide highly detailed representations of thematic data by retaining the complexity and temporal grounding of the data, and at this point, some temporal patterns may already begin to emerge. However, given the volume of data produced in many QDM studies, it is likely that patterns of change over time within specific themes will remain difficult to visualize and even more difficult to compare across participants (or groups of participants). TTA therefore offers a final important step: the creation of trajectory diagrams for individual themes (and their subthemes) that enable researchers to easily and quickly visualize how participants' conceptualization/experience of a particular major theme changes over time, as well as to compare such temporal patterns across participants.

Visualization in TTA is distinct from comparable approaches that rely on the frequency of themes (e.g., Cain et al., 2018), in that rather than focusing on the number of times a theme is mentioned, TTA instead maps how individuals' different experiences or understandings of a particular major theme shift over time by mapping its subthemes, thereby highlighting how this theme was framed by participants on different days. These subthemes therefore become "plot points" on the trajectory diagram representing a particular major theme from your template.

To map these trajectories, first select the major theme(s) from your macro-template (see Step 2) that are particularly relevant to understanding change over time within your study (i.e., for which major themes is it important for you to understand how they change over time?). The key themes of focus for exploring variation over time might be defined by research questions or emerge as an interesting aspect of the data through the analysis process.

Once you have decided on the theme(s) of focus, a Cartesian-style diagram is next created for each participant, where this diagram represents one particular major theme, with the x-axis denoting the movement over time (e.g., temporal unit; day of entry) and the y-axis reflects the subthemes of the selected major theme for temporal visualization. Here, you can use the data contained in participants' meso-templates (i.e., the day or week of (non)occurrence of each of the subthemes) to enable you to plot each of the subthemes related to the selected major theme along the y-axis. See, for example, Figure 7.4, in which the major theme, *"locus of anticipation,"* has been visually represented for a participant over the course of their diary. Here we can see that the subthemes associated with this major theme, *"retrospective," "prospective," "Friday effect,"* and *"none reported,"* have been plotted along the y-axis so that we can see "at a glance" the different ways in which this participant framed their anticipation and how this changed over time. This means that you will end up with as many trajectory analysis diagrams as you have participants in your study, plotting a diagram for each participant to enable subsequent comparison.

Visualization of thematic trajectories may also be carried out with as many themes as you deem relevant to answering your study research question(s). We suggest that you first map trajectories by hand for speed and to determine the layout of themes before moving to digitalization of these trajectories where required (e.g., selected trajectory diagrams that will be included within the write-up of your study), using your preferred software.[3]

The key value in visualizing thematic trajectories is in enabling the identification of patterns of thematic content over time, which will usually be lost when analytical processes remain focused on static themes. While data reduction is necessary to afford this additional layer of insight, data complexity is maintained within the three levels of templates and by returning to the original data source to help explain and add rich contextual details to observed patterns, as discussed in Step 4. When creating these trajectory diagrams, how themes are coded is an important consideration:

Evaluative or Categorical Themes
Themes may be evaluative, wherein the thematic content reflects an evaluative dimension (e.g., increasing/decreasing; positive/negative), or categorical, meaning they reflect no progressive or evaluative element. To illustrate, in Leighann's

mistreatment project, the final question of the diary assessed the anticipatory effects of experiences on a given day in impacting the next day, asking participants, "How do you feel about going to work tomorrow?" Given the framing of this question, participants often responded with explicit evaluative statements, "I feel good," "Dreading it, because of the issues mentioned above," as well as concise entries: "bad," "fine," and so on. Accordingly, in developing the initial coding template, the a priori theme "anticipation of the next day" was succeeded by three second-level subthemes—"positive evaluation," "neutral evaluation," and "negative evaluation," respectively. Therefore, in mapping the thematic trajectories for "anticipation of the next day," the process involved annotating the three evaluative themes along the x-axis following the logical progression of negative–neutral–positive (see Figure 7.4).

Importantly, however, often themes will reflect no progressive or evaluative element and instead reflect distinct categories, thereby having no preestablished or possible logical hierarchical order. In this way, peaks and troughs within trajectory diagrams are not reflective of an increase/decrease in severity or intensity, but rather the focus here is on being able to visualize a thematic pattern over time (see Söderström, 2020). Drawing once more on participant entries for the question "anticipation of next day," participants would at times rationalize their anticipations, which enabled us to develop the major theme "locus of anticipation." For example, participants would frame these entries either retrospectively (e.g., their discussions focus on the events of the current day) or prospectively (e.g., their discussions focus on events that were due to take place the next day). To illustrate, a retrospective framing would entail the participant coupling their anticipation to events of the given day that had already occurred (e.g., "Not good at all, I am just thinking about what happened today"). In contrast, in prospective framings, participants would shift their attention away from the events of the given day and instead focus on an imagined version of the next day at work (e.g., "I think that I will probably be not as positive tomorrow, as I am in the office all day and it will be a stark comparison to today"). A further dimension of participants' anticipations was the anchoring effect of predictive absences from work, such as the weekend or planned days off. On these days, participants would couch their anticipations in the absence from the workplace, rather than an experienced (retrospective) or imagined (prospective) event (e.g., "Happy that tomorrow is Friday"; "Three days off. I feel good!"). Accordingly, data here were coded to reflect four categorical subthemes— "retrospective," "prospective," "Friday effect," and a "none reported" theme— to ensure continuity in the trajectory diagram when participants may not have

Chapter 7 • QDM-Focused Analysis Approaches 203

FIGURE 7.4 ■ Translation of Thematic Data to Thematic Trajectory: Examples of Evaluative and Categorical Themes

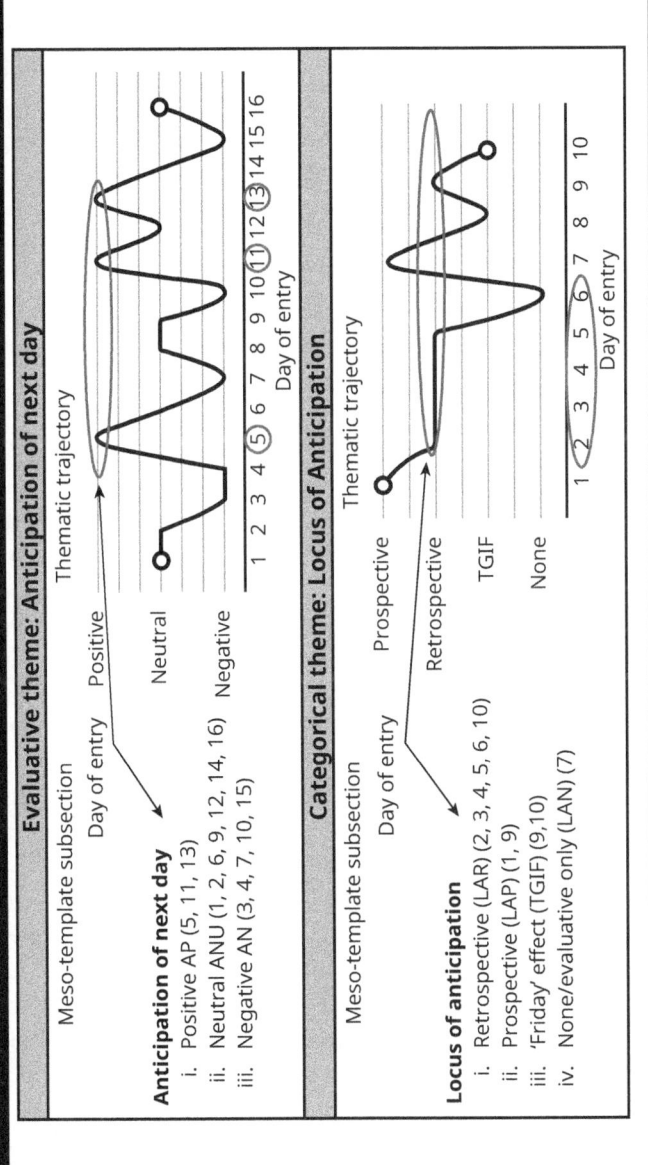

Evaluative theme: Anticipation of next day

Meso-template subsection

Day of entry → Positive / Neutral / Negative — Thematic trajectory

Anticipation of next day
  i. Positive AP (5, 11, 13)
  ii. Neutral ANU (1, 2, 6, 9, 12, 14, 16)
  iii. Negative AN (3, 4, 7, 10, 15)

Day of entry: 1 2 3 4 ⑤ 6 7 8 9 10 ⑪ 12 ⑬ 14 15 16

Categorical theme: Locus of Anticipation

Meso-template subsection

Day of entry → Prospective / Retrospective / TGIF / None — Thematic trajectory

Locus of anticipation
  i. Retrospective (LAR) (2, 3, 4, 5, 6, 10)
  ii. Prospective (LAP) (1, 9)
  iii. 'Friday' effect (TGIF) (9,10)
  iv. None/evaluative only (LAN) (7)

Day of entry: 1 ② ③ 4 5 ⑥ ⑦ 8 9 10

Note. Reproduced from Figure 3 from "Thematic Trajectory Analysis: A Temporal Method for Analysing Dynamic Qualitative Data" by L. Spencer, L. Radcliffe, R. Spence, & N. King, 2021. *Journal of Occupational and Organizational Psychology*, 94(3), 531–567 (https://doi.org/10.1111/joop.12359). Licensed under CC BY-SA 4.0 (https://creativecommons.org/licenses/by/4.0/).

provided thematic content for this theme (e.g., providing evaluative statements only). Thus, in mapping the trajectories of these four subthemes, the process follows the plotting of the relevant subtheme on each day/week, and where no data are available for that theme, this is plotted as "none reported." Figure 7.4 illustrates examples of the trajectories of evaluative and categorical themes from Leighann's mistreatment project.

The same data may, therefore, be coded in both ways, and thus the decision to code data in an evaluative and/or categorical manner is also often at the discretion of the researcher.

Step 4: Intra- and Inter-theme Trajectory Analysis

Having visualized your thematic trajectories, you are now able to use these to conduct in-depth, temporally sensitive analysis both at within- and between-person levels. Similar to Söderström (2019), who considered the "overall shape" of life diagrams drawn during life history interviews and made comparisons across participants, the impetus here is to *examine the shape of trajectories over time*. For example, you might ask whether particular patterns appear temporally significant—are there periods of stability and/or flux? Are there clear patterns where, for example, a particular subtheme tends to precede another subtheme, therefore suggesting potential connections between these themes? Or, how does the participant's trajectory change over time (within-person), and how does this pattern compare to the patterns of others (between-person)? In all cases, you will be asking, "What is meaningful about this pattern?" and move back and forth between identified patterns and the qualitative data in order to answer this question and research questions.

Where you have visualized more than one major theme in this way, you may also wish to compare these different thematic trajectories to further aid the interpretation of your data. For example, researchers might explore if one subtheme being present tends to align with another subtheme also being present. Alternatively, if a particular categorical theme is reported, is there an increase/decrease in an evaluative theme? Once more, it is imperative to move back and forth between such patterns and the relevant rich textual data to enable explanation and understanding. Rather than trajectory diagrams being relied upon alone to draw any kind of conclusions, these are instead devices to enable the identification and communication of interesting temporal patterns that could otherwise have been missed but *should be interpreted only by returning to the rich qualitative data*. Thematic trajectories should therefore be presented alongside textual quotes in the write-up of findings.

Integrating TTA Output With Other Qualitative Data

While our discussion of TTA reflects TTA's use as an analytical approach after data collection, the thematic trajectories derived through the process would arguably serve as rich elicitation devices within qualitative interviews. Indeed, Laura has previously recommended that diaries be used in conjunction with interviews and, in particular, the importance of post-diary interviews (Radcliffe, 2013, 2018). Here we propose that researchers could use the trajectory diagrams to further stimulate participants' reflections on their diary content. For example, researchers could, where appropriate, focus follow-up questions for participants on the overall patterning (e.g., peaks and troughs) of evaluative themes but equally the recurrence or rarity of particular subthemes in categorical trajectories. This would provide undoubtedly rich context and depth while offering a visual means to aid participants' reflections in post-diary interviews.

Additionally, while TTA has so far been developed specifically for data collected using QDMs, the applicability of the approach to different forms of longitudinal qualitative data could be considered in future research. For example, we envisage how this might be applied to longitudinal qualitative data collected using multiple interviews over time or researchers' notes collected as part of longitudinal participant observations. We suggest that exploring the applicability of this analytical approach across diverse longitudinal data sets has the potential to yield exciting new theoretical and methodological insights.

Limitations

As discussed above when considering the limitations of EDA, where analytical methods involve the extension of existing approaches, this inevitably involves additional time requirements. This is particularly the case when employing TTA, which extends TA and even EDA, taking these approaches a step further to enable a temporally focused analysis that enables QDM researchers to really capitalize on the "across" benefits of QDMs. It is, therefore, important for us to acknowledge here the additional time required when embarking on TTA. We argue that the valuable, novel insights that can be attained by adopting TTA make the additional time investment worthwhile, but we urge anyone considering this approach to ensure that adequate time (and/or resources) is built into project planning to support feasibility. Other elements to consider here, as discussed in previous chapters, are the number of participants you require to keep diaries in the first place, particularly if your study requires a temporal understanding of your data. TTA will inevitably involve a much lengthier process where diary participant numbers become quite large, which should again form a key part of feasibility considerations.

Another challenge when using TTA revolves around the diary design employed to collect your QDM data, specifically whether you have used an interval- or event-contingent design (see Chapter 2). TTA naturally lends itself well to interval-contingent designs in which a predictable number of diary entries will be recorded over particular intervals of time (e.g., one diary entry recorded each day over a 2-week period). Such interval-contingent designs make the plotting of thematic trajectories more straightforward as the x-axis can readily denote predictable temporal units (e.g., days or weeks). However, this becomes more challenging where event-contingent diaries have been used. For example, an important part of the process of developing TTA was employing or "testing" this approach across different diary projects. During this phase, we used TTA to reanalyze some of Laura's existing work–family conflict diary data, collected using an event-contingent design (i.e., participants were asked to record an entry every time they experienced a conflict between work and family). This meant that there were numerous instances when participants had reported more than one event a day (e.g., more than one entry per temporal unit), which made Step 3 of TTA more challenging in terms of how to plot temporal units along the x-axis. To resolve this, while developing the method, for Laura's data, we opted to plot multiple temporal units along the x-axis to reflect that for some participants, they experienced multiple conflicts, as illustrated in Figure 7.5, which contains both members of the couple.

As illustrated in Figure 7.5, we plotted multiple entries for days 3 and 5, as there were multiple events reported on these days. While this worked well in that we were able to explore participants' experiences visually and was particularly useful at the within-couple level—as illustrated in Figure 7.5, we were able to visually compare the conflicts experienced within the couple—it does add a significant degree of complexity to the analysis, which might make comparative analysis challenging but equally be confusing for your reader. An alternative strategy when using TTA for event-contingent designs is to draw on the method primarily for within-person analysis, thereby using the trajectory diagrams to understand and illustrate a given participant's experiences over time, rather than comparing between participants. It is therefore important to acknowledge that when diaries have followed an event-contingent design, TTA is more challenging to employ in such cases. This is something to keep in mind when designing your diary study, particularly when you are using QDMs with the "across" benefits in mind and are, therefore, likely to want to use TTA when analyzing your data.

Chapter 7 • QDM-Focused Analysis Approaches 207

FIGURE 7.5 ■ Thematic Trajectory Diagram Based on Event-Contingent Diary Data

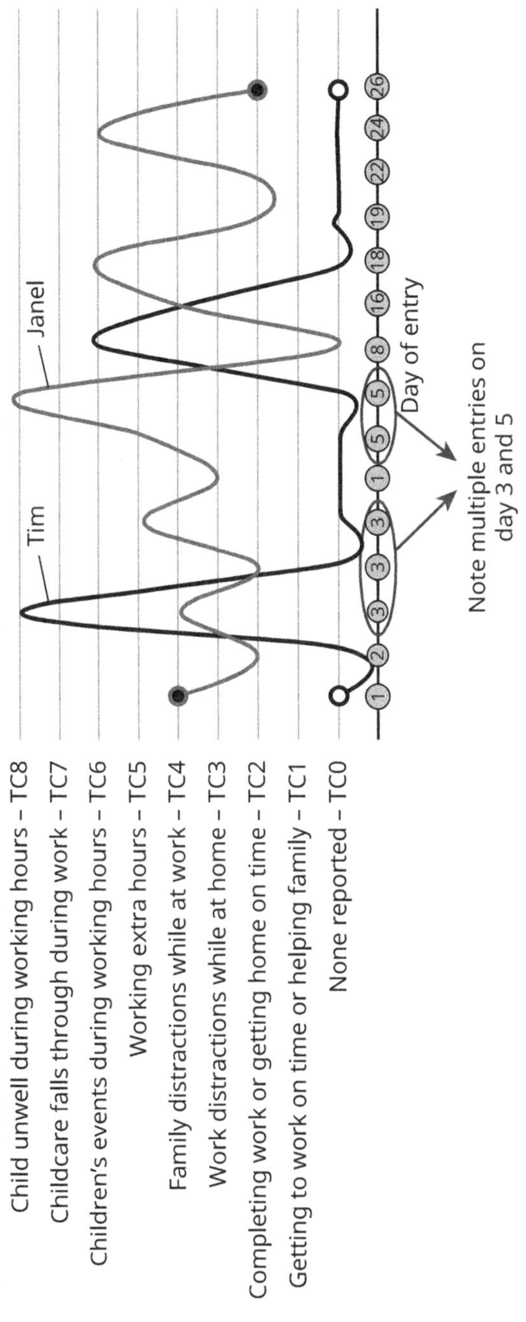

Child unwell during working hours – TC8
Childcare falls through during work – TC7
Children's events during working hours – TC6
Working extra hours – TC5
Family distractions while at work – TC4
Work distractions while at home – TC3
Completing work or getting home on time – TC2
Getting to work on time or helping family – TC1
None reported – TC0

Tim
Janel

Day of entry
Note multiple entries on day 3 and 5

REPORTING AND INTERPRETING TTA AND EDA: REDUCTION VERSUS REDUCTIVE

A valid question, and at times criticism, we often received when we were developing TTA and during subsequent presentations/workshops is whether TTA is overly "reductive" and, thereby, whether it is appropriate to reduce and represent participants' experiences as visualized thematic trajectories. Our answer to this has always been, and always will be, a resounding no because we agree that participants' experiences should not be reduced solely to the trajectories, and this does not align with the steps outlined in TTA. But equally, the same holds for event diagrams derived through EDA.

Indeed, for TTA, we strongly discourage interpretation of the trajectory diagrams in isolation and instead encourage that they be used as an important tool only in spotting patterns of change over time before returning to the rich textual data to enable understanding of the context of, and reasons for, these patterns, thereby ensuring interpretations are grounded in the qualitative content of the diaries. In the same way, in EDA, the combination of analytic strategies allows for the examination of the data without losing sight of the big picture, as well as allowing the examination of the big picture without losing sight of each individual voice. It is important to move between the event diagrams and the rich qualitative data related to the event.

Consequently, we suggest that both trajectory diagrams and event diagrams are *always* presented alongside rich thematic content rather than as a sole analytical output. Visualizations derived from both TTA and EDA should therefore be viewed as a process of data *reduction*, providing an extra and, we would argue, valuable layer of interpretive power that is key to enabling temporally or event-sensitive focused findings and theorization, respectively. But these visualizations are not and should not be considered sufficient alone without concurrent contextualization within the rich qualitative diary data.

To conclude, EDA and TTA are diary-specific analysis processes and have therefore been designed, developed, and refined to enable researchers to analyze their diary data in way that capitalizes on the key benefits of diary data—that is, in-depth exploration of the *"down"* (i.e., in-depth reflections in the moment) and *"across"* (i.e., change over time) of participants' experiences. As we have discussed in this chapter, while both EDA and TTA enable *some* exploration of both the "down" and "across" (e.g., in EDA, you could compare participants' event diagrams over time), the approaches are more naturally allied to a "down" or "across" focus, respectively. In this way, if your project is focused on capturing experiences in the moment (i.e., the "down" of QDMs), which are essential to be able to provide in-depth answers to your research questions, then EDA is likely the most appropriate approach. Conversely, if your project (and thereby research questions) is more focused on changes over time (i.e., the "across" of QDMs), then TTA is more appropriate. However, as we noted early in this chapter, we urge both flexibility and creativity in using these approaches and therefore encourage methodological development and innovation but to do so in a way that remains sensitive to the importance of contextualizing diagrams within the rich qualitative diary data.

APPLICATION ACTIVITY
USING TTA OR EDA

In the exercise that follows, we ask you to consider two different research studies, each with a distinct research question, and, drawing on insights attained in this book so far, consider the potential challenges and benefits of analyzing the data with both TTA and EDA, as well as which would be most suitable. (Note: You can find an outline for suggested answers in the Appendix.)

Exercise: Identify Challenges and Benefits of TTA or EDA

Project Brief	Analytical Considerations
RQ: How do employees with long-term health conditions decide to work while unwell? • How do these decisions impact their daily well-being? • How do these decisions impact their daily experience of work? Sample: Forty individuals with a range of long-term health conditions (e.g., Crohn's disease, fibromyalgia, endometriosis, etc.) Study design: Diary-interview method, combined interval- and event-contingent diaries (participants to record once a day at a time that is convenient for a 1-month period, alongside event-contingent, requiring them to record a diary entry when they feel they have had to make a work-based decision, e.g., to work or to take time off) Adapted from Hannah Musiyarira's PhD project	The researcher has decided to analyze their data using EDA because of the analytical focus on decision-making, here when and why individuals with long-term health conditions decide to work/not work while they are unwell. What are the benefits of using EDA to analyze these data? What are the potential challenges in using EDA to analyze these data? How can the researcher integrate the diary and interview data? Could the researcher use TTA? What are the potential limitations of using TTA for these data?

(Continued)

(Continued)

Project Brief	Analytical Considerations
RQ: How do first-time parents experience the first month of parenthood?	Which analysis method (e.g., EDA or TTA) is most appropriate and why?
• What emotions do they experience and why?	What are the benefits of analyzing the data using this method?
• What challenges do they report?	What are the potential challenges of analyzing the data using this method? How can the researcher overcome these challenges?
• What benefits/positive experiences do they report?	
Sample: Thirty first-time parents	
Study design: Interval-contingent diary; participants asked to reflect on their experiences each day for a 1-month period	

FURTHER READING

King, N., & Brooks, J. M. (2017). *Template analysis for business and management students*. Sage. https://doi.org/10.4135/9781473983304

Radcliffe, L. S. (2013). Qualitative diaries: Uncovering the complexities of work-life decision-making. *Qualitative Research in Organizations and Management: An International Journal*, 8(2), 163–180.

Spencer, L., Radcliffe, L., Spence, R., & King, N. (2021). Thematic trajectory analysis: A temporal method for analysing dynamic qualitative data. *Journal of Occupational and Organizational Psychology*, 94(3), 531–567.

ENDNOTES

1 For detailed explanations of how to conduct template analysis, please consult the primary methodological texts (e.g., King, 2004; King & Brooks, 2017).

2 Or transcribed if an audio/handwritten diary.

3 For example, PowerPoint, Lucidchart, and Vectr enable efficient digitization of trajectory diagrams.

8 CONCLUDING CHAPTER AND THE FUTURE OF QDMs

In this chapter, we bring the book to a conclusion by providing a summary overview of learning about QDMs, particularly focusing on recapping the important considerations to pay attention to when developing QDM projects, including the importance of research question-method fit. We also include a summary of the progression of QDMs over the past few decades and a consideration of the future of the method. The chapter concludes with a reflection task to encourage readers to reflect on, and consolidate, their learning and think about the possibilities for their own QDM research projects. By the end of this chapter (and book), you should have a strong understanding of when and why to use QDMs, the wide range of methods encompassed within QDM research, and the benefits, challenges, and important practical considerations associated with each, including the importance of employing commensurate analytical approaches. Therefore, you should be able to plan and successfully conduct your own innovative QDM research project.

RECAPITULATION: KEY POINTS FROM PREVIOUS CHAPTERS

As introduced in Chapter 1, QDMs are a broad range of multimodal methods that allow researchers to capture events, experiences, and emotions in the moment and over a particular time period. As we have discussed, and indeed demonstrated, throughout this book, QDMs have numerous significant benefits for social science researchers. In our view, the overarching benefit of QDMs is that they are a method that harnesses both the "depth" and richness of qualitative data captured in the moment, alongside the "breadth" afforded by adopting a longitudinal approach, which allows a detailed exploration of how (and why) things change over time. Throughout this book, we referred to this as the capacity of QDMs to collect rich qualitative data that enable us to capture both the "down" (i.e., in-depth reflections in the moment) and "across" (i.e., change over time) of participants' experiences.

In this way, QDMs arguably offer researchers a unique means to overcome some of the limitations of other, more traditional, qualitative methods. For example, relative to interviews and focus groups, which capture participants' reflections at specific points in time, QDMs provide continuous, real-time insights into participants' daily lives and experiences. They therefore offer a temporal dimension that is valuable for understanding processes and changes over time, often offering a richer, more nuanced picture of the phenomena under study. In addition, diaries have been suggested to be less intrusive than traditional ethnographic observation (Zimmerman & Wieder, 1977), permitting participants themselves to document their own experiences, within their own time and space, potentially leading to more authentic data (Bolger et al., 2003). QDMs are therefore an excellent method for capturing real-time, temporally sensitive, in-depth data that enable understanding and comparison of participants' experiences in a way that is contextually sensitive.

In addition to these "data-focused" benefits, as discussed at length in Chapter 1, QDMs are beneficial to both researchers and the researched alike. Indeed, they are a participant-led approach (e.g., Hacker, 2013; O'Reilly et al., 2022) that encourages participants' reflexivity and is particularly suited to sensitive research. As we have argued throughout, a core strength of QDMs is that they are good at overcoming, at least to some extent, researcher/researched power relations. As QDMs enable participants to record their experiences without the presence of the researcher, they empower the participant to record whatever they choose and do so without the pressure that might arise from the physical presence of the researcher and the related demands of maintaining a particular flow of conversation (Monrouxe, 2009). As such, they are also typified as a more inclusive research method, enabling, for example, the research process to be conceptualized in a way that enables participants to be "researchers" in their own contexts, and thereby agentic producers of knowledge, rather than researchers producing knowledge about them (Budworth, 2023; Hayes et al., 2024; Islam, 2015). As is hopefully evident from our discussions throughout this book, a further fundamental way in which QDM studies can be participant-led is through their flexible potential and capacity to enable participants to complete their entries in a way that suits their needs generally but also their specific needs in a given moment.

However, as with all research methods, there are challenges in employing QDMs, and indeed different types of QDMs, that require careful consideration.

In relation to QDMs more broadly, owing to the enhanced commitment of QDMs required by participants (Bolger et al., 2003), participant recruitment, retention, and engagement are core challenges. Here, as discussed in Chapter 2, it is therefore important that your sample is considered carefully in terms of the additional burden your study and specific diary design may be placing on them. It is important to keep this in mind in terms of retention rates and appropriate supports that can be put in place to make the experience of engaging in your QDM project as easy, flexible, and enjoyable as possible. As such, in Chapter 2, we discussed the key considerations allied to retaining participants—notably, the importance of designing the diary with your participants in mind, prioritizing their needs above your own desires for data (e.g., Gatrell, 2009). But equally, the importance of maintaining contact with participants through an agreed communication strategy (i.e., when, how, and why you will contact participants and when, how, and why they should contact you). Doing so should go some way to enhancing and maintaining participants' engagement in your QDM study.

Owing to the enhanced commitment involved in QDMs, and indeed the different types of data that can be collected with QDMs discussed in Chapters 3 through 5, there are important ethical considerations that are specific to QDMs. For example, as QDMs are a method that encourages and instigates participants' reflexivity (Cassell et al., 2020; Radcliffe, 2018), while a benefit of their use, it is also important that researchers are aware of the potential unintended impact this may have on participants (i.e., potential for emotional discomfort). As discussed in Chapter 2, it is therefore important that researchers within QDM studies provide the opportunity for participants to explore and develop their reflexivity and emotions in a safe space (Cassell et al., 2020; Hibbert & Cunliffe, 2015), in so doing, enabling the learning process that accompanies reflexivity to move beyond the level of disturbance and doubt to create new forms of understanding (Hibbert & Cunliffe, 2015). It is, therefore, paramount that when agreeing to take part in a diary study, participants feel safe and that care is taken to support privacy and confidentiality (Plowman, 2010). Further important ethical considerations are tied to the specific type of QDM and the resultant data (e.g., photos, video), as discussed in Chapters 3 through 5, which researchers should consult when designing their study.

Regardless of the type of QDM and resultant data, it should now be evident to readers that the data derived through QDM studies are voluminous and complex, which can be a significant challenge in employing QDMs. Therefore, as advised in Chapter 6, it is important that researchers have a clear data management process from the very start of data collection and that this is rigorously maintained throughout. Indeed, researchers need to consider how they will retrieve participant data (in a way that is appropriate for and agreed by participants) or, in instances where data are immediately available to researchers (e.g., through the use of app diaries), how this will be managed, so as to avoid potential data loss. As noted, depending on the particulars of your study, notably sample size, length of diary-keeping period, and diary design (i.e., signal/interval/event/mixed contingent design; Bolger et al., 2003), data in QDM studies are voluminous and can quickly become challenging for the researcher to keep track of and manage if a clear data management process is not in place from the beginning.

Throughout preceding chapters, we have provided contingencies for these main challenges but have also discussed a wealth of potential challenges that may emerge from across the varied types of diaries across Chapters 3 to 5. However, a key means through which to prevent the emergence of problems is to ensure your QDM study is well designed.

KEY CONSIDERATIONS IN DEVELOPING QDM RESEARCH PROJECTS

When it comes to designing your QDM study, as we discussed in Chapter 2, fundamental considerations cut across all different modalities that are pertinent to ensuring a robust and effective diary design but, equally, one that is participant-led.

Research Question and Method Fit

As with all research projects, ensuring coherence between the research aims and questions is fundamentally important. In the context of QDM research, to determine whether QDMs are appropriate, in Chapter 1, we provide two guiding reflective questions to aid this process:

1. To answer my research questions, is it important that I capture details of events/experiences/thoughts/emotions *"in the moment"*?
2. To answer my research questions, is it important that I capture how experiences/thoughts/emotions/interpretations change (or sometimes remain stable) *"over time"*?

Readers should by now recognize that these two questions are tied to the overarching benefits of QDMs, in that they offer an approach that has the capacity to collect rich qualitative data that enable us to capture both the *"down"* (i.e., in-depth reflections in the moment; Question 1) and *"across"* (i.e., change over time; Question 2) of participants' experiences but equally that researchers may answer "yes" to both of these questions and therefore have an interest in both the "down" and "across" (see, for example, Hannah's project in Chapter 2).

In addition to aiding the initial decision of whether to employ QDMs or not, these questions are also heavily influential in terms of the specific design of your QDMs—in particular, whether they are signal-, interval-, event-, or mixed-contingent design (Bolger et al., 2003). Indeed, as discussed in Chapter 2, event-contingent designs are likely to align with studies employing diaries because of an interest in capturing rich, momentary details of specific events (i.e., Question 1), whereas interval-interval contingent designs are often more aligned with studies using diaries because they are interested in examining change over time (i.e., Question 2). In contrast, signal- and mixed-contingent designs are arguably amenable to both. You could, for example, draw on a signal-contingent design to explore "in-the-moment" reflections wherein the "moment" of interest is signal dependent (i.e., what participants are doing/feeling when triggered to report; see, e.g., Consolvo et al., 2017) but equally compare these "moments" over time. In this way, while there is some alignment between your overarching rationale for using QDMs (e.g., Question 1 and/or 2) and the overarching designs (signal, interval, event, or mixed contingent), these are not fixed relationships, and as discussed in Chapter 2, mixed designs are certainly possible. What is, however, important is that your selection or, indeed, combination of designs is commensurate and coherent with your research questions.

Further points of consideration to ensure that your use of QDMs is aligned with your research questions are how the diaries will be structured (e.g., structure, semi-structured), whether you will use QDMs in combination with other methods, how long participants will be required to complete their diaries, and indeed the mode of diary. The worksheet provided in Chapter 2 is a useful means through which to start thinking through these design decisions and importantly how they fit with your research aims and questions.

However, while it is important that there is clear alignment between your design decisions and your research aims and questions, it is equally important that you as researchers approach your QDM study with flexibility and creativity. As with all (qualitative) research, it is likely that your research, or elements thereof, will not go exactly to plan. Accordingly, enabling a degree of adaptability in your design is important. Most notably, your research design, particularly your mode of diary and thereby how participants are to complete their diaries, must also consider your participants and what works best for them as a cohort and individually. Doing so should enable your research project to be participant-led, but equally, your use of diaries should fit with the abilities and needs of your participants. It is therefore our advice to offer participants choice in how they complete their entries where it is feasible to do so and where doing so will not be incommensurate with your research questions. However, keep in mind that there is little point in collecting data for data's sake. For example, unless the visual is pertinent to your research aims (e.g., as indicated in your research question(s)), be it as "data" themselves or as a solicitation device in follow-up interviews, then requesting participants to take photos is likely unnecessary and may lead to additional ethical challenges. You may, however, find through piloting or ongoing contact with participants during formal data collection that they may want to include a mode you had not initially anticipated. It is therefore important you remain open and flexible to amendments in your research design.

A further factor in determining the design of your QDM study and in particular the mode of diary and the type(s) of data you will collect is considering how you will analyze your data. As discussed in this book, a wealth of "traditional" analysis approaches (see Chapter 6) has been effectively drawn upon in different ways to analyze different types of diary data. Thus, the focus of Chapter 6 was to explicate how "traditional" qualitative analysis methods that are typically used for more common types of qualitative data (e.g., interview data) have been applied and arguably adapted to the unique data derived from QDM studies. While the studies reviewed in Chapter 6 illustrated the wealth of insights that can be derived from using these traditional analysis methods, as we discuss in Chapter 7, our own experiences of attempting to apply these traditional analytical approaches in our research were challenging as we found them limited in their ability to enable us to capitalize on the "down" and "across" capacities of QDMs. This, in turn, led to the development of EDA (Radcliffe, 2013) and TTA (Spencer et al., 2021), which enable researchers to fully capitalize on the "down" and "across," respectively. Indeed, in our view, the strengths of both these approaches lie in the fact that they were both specifically developed for analyzing QDM data.

While the choice of analytical method is of course at the discretion of researchers, including their research questions, design, and analytical expertise, in the context of QDMs, it is important that your analysis approach, and thereby how you will analyze your diary data, is something you give consideration in the initial design stages of your study. Doing so will ensure that your design is coherent with your intended analysis method but equally that there is alignment between your method and research questions.

While our discussion here has focused on recapping the core benefits, challenges, and main design considerations in QDM studies, as should be clear from having read the preceding seven chapters, QDMs represent a significant, multifaceted, and at times complex method. Researchers should therefore ensure that each chapter and particularly those that are highly relevant to your own study are read carefully. Our attention now turns to reflecting on the trajectory of QDMs and how we envision the potential future of QDM research.

DEVELOPMENTS IN QDM RESEARCH: LOOKING BACK AND TO THE FUTURE

As discussed in Chapter 1, diaries have a rich history in the social sciences with their (known) use for research purposes evident in Frédéric Le Play's use of diaries for family budget research in the 1800s, with greater expansion of QDM research initially in health care since the 1930s/1940s and a particular proliferation of diary methods more broadly from the 1970s onward. Within the social sciences, interest in and the use of QDMs initially often stemmed from ethnographic approaches, wherein diaries were recognized as an apt observational method where direct observations (typical of ethnographic approaches) were not possible (Zimmerman & Wieder, 1977), for example, within the family home or more "hidden" experiences such as workplace mistreatment (e.g., Spencer, 2019) or "ambient" sexual harassment on college campuses (e.g., Albert et al., 2023).

In more contemporary social science research, QDMs have seen a dramatic increase in the popularity, and their use is on an upward trajectory. This is likely due to the increased demands and needs for more complex research designs (e.g., increased innovation in methods, temporally sensitive designs) to understand more complex phenomena. It is also evident that the marked increased use of QDMs in the past few years is in part explained by the COVID-19 pandemic and the resultant need for researchers to adopt remote research methods. It is arguable that the COVID-19 pandemic catalyzing the increase in QDM studies has equally demonstrated the utility of the approach as a useful remote research method, with the ability to explore complex, emergent experiences and also how they are, and will continue to be, beneficial in permitting exploration of complex, grand societal challenges and real-time monitoring of social trends and changes (e.g., Mueller et al., 2023; Rauch & Ansari, 2022a). Looking forward, we envision that QDMs will continue to include more diverse, cross-cultural studies as they have once again been demonstrated to have value here (e.g., Hayes et al., 2024; Mueller et al., 2023; Rabinovich, 2023; Wechtler, 2018). However, given that much of the extant QDM research has hitherto been largely with and/or on Western samples/contexts, there is scope for further diversification to fully draw on their potential to provide richer insights into global and multicultural perspectives, especially in an increasingly interconnected world.

Such interconnectivity is clearly allied to the rapid increase in technological advancements, which have catalyzed greater use of QDMs in the social sciences. Such advances in technology have enabled QDMs as a "pandemic-friendly" approach, and they are more generally to be employed with greater ease, enabling multimodal options to be used more readily. Of course, people generally being more used to, and therefore comfortable with, recording and capturing their daily lives (e.g., as a result of social media proliferation) also appears to play a role. Technological developments have also expanded the scope and methods of QDMs, most notably the app-based diary studies as discussed in Chapter 5, and we believe that such advancements will likely continue to shape QDM research.

As technological advancements have already had a significant influence on how QDMs can be, and are currently, used to collect data, particularly the different types of data that researchers are now able to collect with ease, we expect that technologically enabled and mediated QDM data collection will continue on an upward trajectory. Indeed, if we reflect on our own experiences of using apps in our QDM studies in the mid-2010s, there were very few studies we could draw on for guidance (i.e., Do & Yagamata-Lynch, 2017; Garcia et al., 2016), but as demonstrated in Chapter 5, there are now a multitude of studies employing apps to conduct innovative and creative QDM studies. It is therefore likely that the use of apps in QDM research will continue to grow, enabling a significant expansion into multimodal data collection and potentially new types of data and new ways of combining data. For example, the advent of both augmented (e.g., Google glass, Apple Vision Pro) and virtual realities (e.g., Second Life, VR headsets) could offer researchers new ways to conduct visual QDM studies. It therefore seems likely that we will see new forms of diaries and diary data emerge as a result. But equally, these new technologies will impact participants' experience of the research process. For example, in Chapter 5, we discussed how incorporating gamification or analytical elements within apps for data collection may enhance participant engagement and retention. Technological advances could therefore make these functionalities easier to incorporate but equally lead to new ways in which participation can be enhanced and therefore lead to better retention rates and, in turn, data quality.

It is equally plausible that the advent of generative artificial intelligence (GAI) (e.g., ChatGPT, Gemini) capable of producing code at the "drop of a prompt" may enable further developments in app usage. For example, if researchers learn *what* to do with the code generated by these models, they could reasonably develop their own apps to collect data. In this way, technological advances such as the rapid proliferation of large language models (LLMs) may level the playing field in terms of being able to employ app-based diaries by significantly reducing the cost and expertise needed to develop an app for research purposes.

We equally envision that these GAI models may lead to technologically enhanced data analysis in the context of QDM studies. Indeed, a recent spate of articles have explored the utility and pitfalls of using LLMs and/or GAI to analyze qualitative data more generally (e.g., Chubb, 2023; Hamilton et al., 2023; Morgan, 2023; Parker et al., 2023; Tai et al., 2024; Weller et al., 2023). These studies broadly conclude that GAI/LLMs *can* be useful for qualitative data analysis, as a "research assistant" (Chubb, 2023) to aid deductive coding (Tai et al., 2024) and help to identify oversights, alternative frames, and personal biases (Hamilton et al., 2023), but they are less successful in locating, subtle interpretive themes (Morgan, 2023). In this way, GAI/LLMs look to be useful tools to *aid* the research process (e.g., enhance speed of descriptive coding) and supplement complex human-centered tasks (Hamilton et al., 2023; Weller et al., 2023), but they remain tools that must be applied within a larger analytic process (Morgan, 2023; Weller et al., 2023), led by *human* researchers.

In the context of QDMs, owing to the voluminous and complex nature of these data (see Chapter 6), the use of GAI/LLM models arguably offers researchers significant potential to expedite some of the processes allied to data storage and the more descriptive elements of the analysis process. For example, as noted in Chapter 6, an important starting point for the analysis of QDMs, regardless of the specific analysis method you go on to use, is to develop descriptive participant summaries (Miles & Huberman, 1994; Patton, 2014). To this end, our PhD student Hannah (see Chapter 2) trialed the use of ChatGPT to do so, importantly adding details the model missed and correcting where necessary; see also Chubb (2023) for a detailed explication of using ChatPDF (a type of ChatGPT) to develop vignettes. While the use of GAI/LLMs is at the discretion of researchers and their individual paradigmatic commitments and views of GAI/LLMs more broadly, we do, however, caution that researchers do not fully "outsource" their QDM analysis to these models and ensure that their analysis retains the value, nuanced sensitivity, and expertise of human researchers.

Finally, while we envisage a continued increase in technological and digital innovations and integrations within QDM studies, it is important that researchers proceed with caution, keeping ethical implications in mind. For example, while advances in technology will lead to new ways of collecting diary data and indeed potentially different types of data, and thereby significant research benefits, it is important that increased technological use does not jeopardize participants' rights to privacy and confidentially. This is particularly pertinent in relation to participants' data security and how personal data are used within the research process (see also Chapter 5). These concerns will need to be reflected within institutional ethical review boards, importantly striking the right balance between regulating technologically and/or digitally mediated research but not stifling the important methodological innovations needed in an increasingly complex and digitized world. Our key argument here is, therefore, that while we think technological advancements will be beneficial in QDM research, as we have noted throughout this book, researchers should avoid unnecessarily doing things just because we are now able to do them. Instead, there will be benefits and challenges, and each innovation should be considered carefully from multiple angles and diverse perspectives at every step of the way, as we have endeavored to do in this book.

CONCLUSION

In conclusion, as is hopefully now evident, QDMs are a valuable part of the wider qualitative research methods toolkit and, in our view, enrich qualitative research by providing researchers with the means to generate insights into participants' experiences, perceptions, and behaviors both in the moment and over time. QDMs are an increasingly important tool in an ever-increasing complex world, given their abilities to address complex questions (e.g., Rauch & Ansari, 2022a) but also as a result of their versatility and multimodality in offering new ways of "seeing" and therefore understanding phenomena. They therefore add value to qualitative research but also to social science more broadly. Indeed, as discussed and evidenced throughout this book, the use of QDMs across the diverse "broadchurch" of the social sciences has led to a wealth of insights, arguably inaccessible through more traditional qualitative approaches. QDMs are therefore an important and increasingly popular part of the qualitative toolkit.

QDMs are equally a method that offer researchers the opportunity to be innovative and creative in their research. As evidenced through our discussions of our own research projects, and indeed those of Hannah Musiyarira and Jo Gregory-Chialton, who contributed their ideas to this book, using QDMs in our research led us to develop new ways of doing research and making contributions to our fields. With the advent of new technologies, the potential to innovate and contribute new important insights is, in our view, increasingly possible. We particularly encourage new approaches to multimodal data collection and analysis but equally to further contribute to QDMs as a core participant-led approach. As is hopefully clear from this book, our view of QDM studies is that they should always be conducted with participants, communities, and ethical conduct at the forefront. Indeed, we see great potential for further expansion and the development of many more important societal insights based on momentary, temporally sensitive data that are often multimodal and captured by participants themselves—thereby seen through the eyes of the participant rather than those of the researcher (at least at the stage of data collection).

In conclusion, having traversed the chapters of this book, you are now equipped with an in-depth resource to plan and execute your own QDM study. We hope that this resource provides you with the knowledge to do so with confidence but equally the inspiration to do so creatively and to innovate in your own research! We look forward to seeing many future QDM projects across the social sciences.

FINAL REFLECTION TASK
LOOKING BACK AND LOOKING AHEAD

Review the diary design worksheets and activities completed throughout the course of this book. Reflecting on these, alongside your broader thoughts, ideas, and learning as you have read this book (and perhaps explored some of the further recommended reading), complete the following table to help solidify your learning and consider future applications.

REFLECT ON AND CONSOLIDATE LEARNING ABOUT QDMS		
Reflection Questions/Prompts	Your Reflections	Future Application Ideas *How will you use this learning in future projects?*
Reflect on the key insights from the three diary design worksheets. • What were the most significant learnings for you? • How has your understanding of QDMs evolved since beginning reading this book?		
Imagine a future project using QDMs. • What research question would you explore? • How would you design the study and why?		
Identify new areas or questions you could explore using QDMs. • How might these align with trends or gaps/problems in your field?		
How do you envision the future of QDM research? • What changes or innovations do you anticipate? • How might you draw on innovations in your own research projects?		

FURTHER READING

Chubb, L. A. (2023). Me and the machines: Possibilities and pitfalls of using artificial intelligence for qualitative data analysis. *International Journal of Qualitative Methods, 22*, 16094069231193593. https://doi.org/10.1177/16094069231193593

Rauch, M., & Ansari, S. (2022). Diaries as a methodological innovation for studying grand challenges. In *Organizing for societal grand challenges* (pp. 205–220). Emerald Publishing Limited.

APPENDIX

We have provided answer keys for the Application Activities for Chapters 3, 4, and 7. Answers appear in boldface and italics in the second column of each of the three tables that follow. (Answers may vary, but the text given lists the main points that should be present in consideration of each topic.)

CHAPTER 3

Application Activity: Which Traditional QDM Approach Would You Use?

In the exercise that follows, we ask you to consider three different research studies, each with a distinct research question, and, drawing on insights attained in this book so far, consider which traditional diary approach you would choose if this was your research project. This exercise should help you to consider the practical application of learning about different QDM modes so far and also to think about how you would rationalize different choices in relation to QDM modality choices.

EXERCISE: CHOOSE AN APPROPRIATE QDM APPROACH	
Project Brief	**Approach & Rationale**
RQ: How do parents experience and navigate living with teenagers diagnosed with obsessive-compulsive disorder (OCD)? • How do parents cope with the challenges on a daily basis? • How (if at all) do these coping strategies develop and change over time? Sample: Cohabiting mothers and fathers with one or more child with OCD	What kind of traditional diary is appropriate for this research project, and why? • *Arguments can be made for both approaches, but in this project, written would likely be preferable for confidentiality and privacy reasons (e.g., to avoid exacerbating existing or causing new tensions in the household).*

(Continued)

223

(Continued)

Project Brief	Approach & Rationale
RQ: How do police officers (POs) make sense of negative interactions with the public directly after their occurrence? • How do POs describe and narrate these experiences? • What emotions do these POs experience? • How do these experiences differ across different POs? Sample: Serving POs with public facing roles	What kind of traditional diary is appropriate for this research project, and why? • *Audio diaries would be preferrable given the affordances of quick, in the moment, reporting, and equally, it would be unlikely that POs would be able to carry a pen-and-paper diary with them and therefore potentially leading to a longer time between event and recall. Finally, the audio recording would give insight into the PO's emotions beyond written text (e.g., tone of voice).*
RQ: How do managers experience leading remote and office-based workers? • What daily challenges do they experience in each context? • What communication strategies do they use and why? Sample: Managers in organizations with remote and/or office-based working arrangements	What kind of traditional diary is appropriate for this research project, and why? • *This project would arguably be suited to both pen-and-paper and audio diaries as managers are typically adept at audio recording/voice notes and therefore may find this a familiar and expedient method. However, this may be context dependent, and audio recording may not be suitable/preferrable and therefore may require a written option. Finally, managers often engage in reflexivity practices and may prefer to write their responses as they are used to keeping journals reflecting on their practice(s).*

CHAPTER 4

Application Activity: Which Ethical Issues Would You Consider?

In the exercise that follows, we ask you to consider two different research studies, each with a distinct research question, and, drawing on insights attained in this book so far, consider the potential ethical issues, challenges, and benefits that it would be pertinent to address.

Appendix

EXERCISE: IDENTIFY PERTINENT ETHICAL CONSIDERATIONS

Project Brief	Ethical, Privacy and Other Considerations
RQ: How do people with food allergies experience and navigate eating outside their homes? • What are the daily eating patterns of these individuals? • What do their meals consist of? • How do they make meal choices in the moment? Sample: Individuals with moderate to severe food allergies Diary design: Photo- and text-based diaries; event contingent—participants instructed to take a photo of meals and/or snacks they consume outside of their homes (e.g., in restaurants, at work)	If you were carrying out this project, what ethical, privacy, and other issues would you need to consider? • *Privacy of others (who have not consented to participate in the research), identifying information of organizations* • *Encouraging negative relationship with food/meals* • *How would participants send you the photos (and other data forms), and how would you anonymize the photos?* • *How will you analyze photos and/or combine with other data formats?*
RQ: How do new parents, recently returned from parental leave, experience daily transitions between their work and home roles? • What are the regular transitions between work and home that new parents make? • How are these transitions between work and family roles experienced? • Are there any gender differences in the type of transitions and the experience thereof? Sample: Working parents (mothers and fathers) who have recently returned to work following parental leave Diary design: Video diaries. Participants instructed to record and verbally explain daily transitions between home and work roles (e.g., daily commute between home and place of work)	If you were carrying out this project, what ethical, privacy, and other issues would you need to consider? • *Privacy of others (who have not consented to participate in the research), identifying information of organizations (e.g., computer screens, emails)* • *Willingness to participate and inclusivity of unexpected transitions (e.g., minor/unexpected/spontaneous interruptions) may not be recorded—consider including another reporting method.* • *Including video content in publications (limited to stills from video)?* • *Data storage and volume of data?* • *How will video diary be sent?*

CHAPTER 7

Application Activity: Using TTA or EDA

In the exercise that follows, we ask you to consider two different research studies, each with a distinct research question, and, drawing on insights attained in this book so far, consider the potential challenges and benefits of analyzing the data with both TTA and EDA, as well as which would be most suitable.

EXERCISE: IDENTIFY CHALLENGES AND BENEFITS OF TTA OR EDA	
Project Brief	**Analytical Considerations**
RQ: How do employees with long-term health conditions make the decision to work while unwell? • How do these decisions impact their daily well-being? • How do these decisions impact their daily experience of work? Sample: Forty individuals with a range of long-term health conditions (e.g., Crohn's disease, fibromyalgia, endometriosis) Study design: Diary-interview method, combined interval- and event-contingent diaries (participants to record once a day at a time that is convenient for a 1-month period, alongside event-contingent, requiring them to record a diary entry when they feel they have had to make a work-based decision, e.g., to work or to take time off) Adapted from Hannah Musiyarira's PhD project	The researcher has decided to analyze their data using EDA because of the analytical focus on decision-making, here when and why individuals with long-term health conditions decide to work/not work while they are unwell. What are the benefits of using EDA to analyze these data? *EDA will enable the researcher to explore the decision-making of participants and the different factors that influence these decisions but equally the outcomes of these decisions in terms of their well-being and work-related outcomes.* What are the potential challenges in using EDA to analyze these data? *The sample is quite large and diaries are kept for a relatively long time. The researcher will have a lot of data to analyze, and this will take a long time. The researcher will therefore need to ensure they have adequate time to analyze the data in this way, or alternatively, the researcher could select a subsample to analyze using EDA to overcome this.* How can the researcher integrate the diary and interview data? *Depending on the design of the interview schedule, the research could integrate the diary and interview data if the interviews relied on the critical incident technique. Alternatively, the researcher can use EDA to supplement the interviews, thereby proving an additional level of interpretive power.*

Project Brief	Analytical Considerations
	Could the researcher use TTA? What are the potential limitations of using TTA for these data?
	The researcher could use TTA, and this would enable interesting within-person insights into how and why decision-making changed over time. This is aided by the research design, including interval- and event-contingent diaries. However, the inclusion of the latter, event-contingent reporting, will add complexity to visualizing the trajectory diagrams. The researcher will need to determine whether it is feasible to include multiple events for a given day in the diagrams and whether this analysis is suitable for between-person comparative analysis.
RQ: How do first-time parents experience the first month of parenthood? • What emotions do they experience and why? • What challenges do they report? • What benefits/positive experiences do they report? Sample: Thirty first-time parents Study design: Interval-contingent diary; participants asked to reflect on their experiences each day for a 1-month period	Which analysis method (e.g., EDA or TTA) is most appropriate and why?
	The research question is specifically focused on garnering temporal insights and so TTA is most suitable.
	What are the benefits of analyzing the data using this method?
	TTA will enable visualizations of thematic content across the first three subquestions (e.g., emotions, challenges, benefits), which will enable both within-person and between-person exploration of the data.
	What are the potential challenges of analyzing the data using this method? How can the researcher overcome these challenges?
	Given the sample size and 1-month time period, the data will be voluminous and require significant time to analyze. The researcher could restrict visualization to one or two themes of interest or a smaller subsample.

GLOSSARY

App diaries: A research method in which participants use a mobile application (or app) as part of a QDM research study. This method is a digital evolution of traditional diary studies, leveraging the convenience and capabilities of mobile devices to collect real-time data.

Apps: Short for "applications," referring to software programs designed to perform specific tasks or functions and typically installed on devices such as smartphones, tablets, computers, or smartwatches. They can serve a wide range of purposes, from productivity to entertainment.

Audio diaries: QDMs wherein participants make audio recordings of their experiences, thoughts, emotions, and reflections over a period of time, as part of a research study.

Autoethnography: A research approach that combines autobiography and ethnography, allowing researchers to explore their own personal experiences in relation to broader sociocultural contexts. In autoethnographic research, the researcher becomes both the subject and the analyst, reflecting on their own life events and experiences to gain insights into cultural phenomena.

Convenience sampling: A sampling technique whereby the researcher uses their own personal networks and contacts to attain participants.

Diary fatigue: A phenomenon where participants taking part in diary studies may become tired or less motivated to maintain their diaries over time, potentially leading to less detailed or less frequent entries or withdrawal from the study altogether.

Epistemology: The branch of philosophy concerned with the theory for knowledge, considering, for instance, what your beliefs are about how knowledge is created, acquired, and validated.

Ethnography: A qualitative research method primarily used in the social sciences that involves the in-depth study of people and cultures involving observation, participation, and researcher immersion within that culture or environment.

Event diagram analysis (EDA): A QDM-specific analysis method, built on TA, that focuses on examining how daily events or experiences unfold by examining how different event elements interact and relate to one another "in the moment" (see Radcliffe, 2013).

Event-contingent diary design: Requires participants to record a diary entry whenever a preestablished event takes place communicated to the participant before data collection.

Fit-for-research (FFR) apps: Platform-based apps that offer free or subscription-based services that enable researchers to tailor an app to their research needs.

Grounded theory: A systematic methodology in qualitative research where the theory is developed inductively from the data.

Grounded visual pattern analysis (GVPA): A qualitative analysis method that involves systematically examining visual materials (such as photographs, videos, or diagrams) in a way that incorporates both discursive and content-focused analysis; thereby an approach that equally privileges narratives (that accompany images) and the content of images themselves.

"In the moment": In the context of QDM studies, this terminology rarely signifies that diaries are recorded literally as events happen but instead generally refers to the capacity of QDMs to capture experiences *much closer to the moment* than would usually be possible with other methods.

Inclusive research: Research that actively seeks to involve and respect the contributions of all relevant stakeholders, particularly those who are often marginalized or excluded from traditional research processes, such as those from underrepresented or marginalized groups.

Interpretative phenomenological analysis (IPA): A qualitative research methodology focused on understanding how individuals make sense of their personal and social experiences. Rooted in phenomenology, it involves an in-depth, highly detailed examination of individual cases.

Interpretivism: A broad research paradigm that argues that (social) reality is socially constructed and, therefore, can only be understood through the subjective interpretation of individuals' experiences and social contexts.

Interval-contingent diary design: Requires participants to record their experiences at regular, predetermined intervals of time communicated to the participant before data collection.

Longitudinal research: A study design that involves repeated observations over an extended period of time, with a focus on capturing change over time.

Multimodal: Methods that involve multiple modes of communication and data, such as text, images, audio, and video.

Narrative inquiry: A research method that focuses on the stories or narratives of participants to understand their experiences and the meanings they ascribe to them.

Nexus analysis: A qualitative research methodology that focuses on understanding the connections (or "nexus") between social actions, discourses, and the broader social practices in which they are embedded. It is a form of discourse analysis that examines how language, actions, and social practices intersect in specific situations to produce meaning and social change.

Ontology: The branch of philosophy that deals with the nature of reality, considering, for instance, what your beliefs are about the nature of (social) reality.

Para-ethnography: An approach in ethnographic research that emphasizes collaboration between researchers and participants in the coproduction of knowledge, involving participants not merely as research subjects but as coresearchers or coanalysts who actively engage in understanding their own realities (see Islam, 2015).

Participant reflexivity: The reflective considerations and critical self-awareness that participants engage in as a result of their involvement in a research study (see Cassell et al., 2020).

Participant-led research: Research that places control over the research process primarily in the hands of participants themselves.

Participatory research: A broad research approach that involves participants in different elements of the research process to varying degrees.

Pen-and-paper diaries: A traditional qualitative research method or QDM wherein participants manually record their thoughts, experiences, behaviors, or activities by writing in a physical notebook or journal.

Photo diaries: QDMs wherein photographs are elicited by participants, across a particular period of time, as part of a research study.

Photo-elicitation: A qualitative research method that involves using photographs or images to evoke, prompt, or guide discussions during interviews.

Purposive sampling: A sampling technique whereby the researcher uses their judgment to deliberately select participants or groups with particular or diverse characteristics to provide as much relevant data as possible to answer their research question(s).

Qualitative diary methods (QDMs): A versatile range of multimodal data collection methods that involve participants themselves recording or capturing events, experiences, emotions, and reflections "in the moment" (or closer to the moment than would otherwise be possible), on multiple occasions, and over a particular time period.

Reflexivity: The process of self-examination and critical reflection on one's own beliefs, actions, and their implications, leading to increasing awareness.

Remote research methods: Methods used to conduct research where the researcher and participants are not required to be in the same physical location.

Researcher diaries/journals or reflective logs: Diaries or journals kept by a researcher when undertaking a research project, focused on the progress of the research and their own personal reflections on this process, including challenges encountered and decisions made.

Semiotic analysis: An analysis method used to interpret and understand the meaning of signs and symbols (which can be anything that conveys meaning, including, for instance, images, gestures, or objects) by deconstructing and examining their elements to uncover deeper meanings, connotations, and cultural significance they carry.

Shortitudinal research: A study design that involves repeated observations over a shorter period of time or, in other words, a short-term longitudinal study. (We would argue that such designs are longitudinal regardless of the time period over which change is captured, but *shortitudinal* is a term that can be used where there is disagreement over the length of time that constitutes longitudinal research.)

Signal-contingent: Requires participants to record a diary entry every time they are alerted to do so by the researcher.

Snowball sampling: A sampling technique based upon participants who have already taken part in the study identifying others in their network who may fit the selection criteria and may be interested in also taking part in the research.

Societal grand challenges: Large-scale, complex, and multifaceted problems that have significant implications for society as a whole and require coordinated, multi-disciplinary, and often global efforts to address.

Socio-semiotic analysis: An analytical approach that examines how social meanings are constructed and communicated through signs and symbols within a particular cultural or social context. It integrates semiotics—the study of signs, symbols, and signification—with social theory to analyze how meaning is produced and interpreted in social interactions, texts, and media.

Solicited diaries: A diary created in response to a specific request from a researcher as part of a research project (cf. unsolicited diaries, diaries people write for personal reasons).

Student diaries/journals or reflective logs: Diaries or journals kept by a student as part of a course syllabus or module assessment, which asks them to reflect on their learning.

Template analysis (TA): A qualitative analysis method used primarily to analyze textual data that involve the creation of a thematic "template"; a hierarchically organized set of codes that represent themes identified in the data (see Kind & Brooks, 2017; King, 2004).

Text-based diaries: QDMs wherein participants record their thoughts, experiences, behaviors, or activities in written form. This might include traditional pen-and-paper diaries but could also include diaries written using digital or electronic means, such as word-processed diaries or email diaries.

The "down" and "across" benefits of QDMs: This terminology depicts key benefits of QDMs as being able to capture the depth and richness of qualitative data captured "in the moment" (the "down"), alongside the "breadth" afforded by adopting a longitudinal approach allowing a detailed exploration of how (and why) things change over time (the "across").

The diary-interview method: A qualitative research method that combines the use of QDMs with follow-up interviews to gather in-depth insights individuals experiences (see Zimmerman & Weider, 1977).

Thematic analysis: A type of qualitative data analysis focused on identifying and interpreting patterns or "themes" within the data.

Thematic trajectory analysis (TTA): A QDM-specific analysis method, built on TA, that focuses on capturing the temporal and dynamic elements of themes identified in QDM data, examining how themes evolve, interact, and change over time (see Spencer et al., 2021).

Video diaries: QDMs wherein videos are taken by participants, who, with various levels of guidance depending on the specific research project, use these cameras to capture their daily lives and experiences from their perspective.

REFERENCES

Alaszewski, A. (2006). Diaries as a source of suffering narratives: A critical commentary. *Health, Risk & Society, 8*(1), 43–58.

Albert, K., Couture-Carron, A., & Schneiderhan, E. (2023). Non-physical and ambient sexual harassment of women undergraduate university students in Canada: A diary study. *Violence Against Women, 30*(9), 2345–2370. https://doi.org/10.1177/10778012231153369

Alford, W. K., Malouff, J. M., & Osland, K. S. (2005). Written emotional expression as a coping method in child protective services officers. *International Journal of Stress Management, 12*(2), 177–187.

Alvesson, M., & Kärreman, D. (2000). Taking the linguistic turn in organizational research: Challenges, responses, consequences. *The Journal of Applied Behavioral Science, 36*(2), 136–158. https://doi.org/10.1177/0021886300362002

Ashman, R., Radcliffe, L., Patterson, A., & Gatrell, C. (2022). Re-ordering motherhood and employment: Mobilizing 'Mums Everywhere' during Covid-19. *British Journal of Management, 33*(3), 1125–1143.

Bai, Q., Dan, Q., Mu, Z., & Yang, M. (2019). A systematic review of emoji: Current research and future perspectives. *Frontiers in Psychology*, 10, Article 476737. https://doi.org/10.3389/fpsyg.2019.02221

Baker, Z. (2021). Reactivity, rationality, emotion and self-protection: Critical reflections on the use and potential of diaries in research on higher education choice and decision-making. In X. Cao & E. F. Henderson (Eds.), *Exploring diary methods in higher education research* (pp. 102–114). Routledge.

Baker, Z. (2023). Young people engaging in event-based diaries: A reflection on the value of diary methods in higher education decision-making research. *Qualitative Research, 23*(3), 686–705.

Baleige, A., Guernut, M., & Moreau, E. (2022). Impact of gender transition on sexuality and diversity of practices: A qualitative analysis of Reddit discussions. *The Journal of Sexual Medicine, 19*(11), S55–S56. https://doi.org/10.1016/j.jsxm.2022.08.050

Balogun, J., Huff, A. S., & Johnson, P. (2003). Three responses to the methodological challenges of studying strategizing. *Journal of Management Studies, 40*(1), 0022-2380.

Balogun, J., & Johnson, G. (2004). Organizational restructuring and middle manager sensemaking. *Academy of Management Journal, 47*(4), 523–549. https://doi.org/10.2307/20159600

Bandini, J. I., Rollison, J., & Etchegaray, J. (2021). Journaling among home care workers during the COVID-19 pandemic: A promising method for qualitative data collection. *Qualitative Social Work, 22*(2), 340–356. 14733250211064812.

Banks, M. H., Beresford, S. A. A., Morrell, D. C., Waller, J. J., & Watkins, C. J. (1975). Factors influencing demand for primary medical care in women aged 20–44 years: A preliminary report. *International Journal of Epidemiology, 4*(3), 189–195.

Banks, M., & Zeitlyn, D. (2015). *Visual methods in social research*. Sage.

Bartlett, R. (2012). Modifying the diary interview method to research the lives of people with dementia. *Qualitative Health Research, 22*(12), 1717–1726.

Bartlett, R., & Milligan, C. (2015). Engaging with diary techniques. In R. Bartlett & C. Milligan (Eds.), *What is diary method* (pp. 13–28). Bloomsbury Academic,

Bates, C. (2013). Video diaries: Audio-visual research methods and the elusive body. *Visual Studies, 28*(1), 29–37.

Bates, C. (2020). Video diaries. In P. Vannini (Ed.), *The Routledge international handbook of ethnographic film and video* (pp. 116–125). Routledge.

Batty, E. (2020). Sorry to say goodbye: The dilemmas of letting go in longitudinal research. *Qualitative Research, 20*(6), 784–799.

Baudrillard, J. (1994). *Simulacra and Simulation*. University of Michigan Press.

Bauman, A., Bittman, M., & Gershuny, J. (2019). A short history of time use research; implications for public health. *BMC Public Health, 19*, 1–7.

Bazerman, C. (2009). *Handbook of research on writing: History, society, school, individual, text*. Routledge.

Beattie, L., & Griffin, B. (2014). Accounting for within-person differences in how people respond to daily incivility at work. *Journal of Occupational and Organizational Psychology, 87*(3), 625–644.

Bell, E., Bryman, A., & Harley, B. (2022). *Business research methods*. Oxford University Press.

Bell, E., & Davison, J. (2013). Visual management studies: Empirical and theoretical approaches. *International Journal of Management Reviews, 15*(2), 167–184.

Bell, E., & King, D. (2010). The elephant in the room: Critical management studies conferences as a site of body pedagogics. *Management Learning, 41*(4), 429–442.

Bell, E., Warren, S., & Schroeder, J. (2014). Introduction: The visual organization. In E. Bell, S. Warren, & J. Schroeder (Eds.), *The Routledge companion to visual organization* (pp. 1–16). Routledge.

Bennett, J. (2014). Researching the intangible: A qualitative phenomenological study of the everyday practices of belonging. *Sociological Research Online, 19*(1), 67–77.

References

Biedermann, N. (2018). The use of Facebook for virtual asynchronous focus groups in qualitative research. *Contemporary Nurse*, *54*(1), 26–34. https://doi.org/10.1080/10376178.2017.1386072

Biernacki, P., & Waldorf, D. (1981). Snowball sampling: Problems and techniques of chain referral sampling. *Sociological Methods & Research*, *10*(2), 141–163.

Bolger, N., Davis, A., & Rafaeli, E. (2003). Diary methods: Capturing life as it is lived. *Annual Review of Psychology*, *54*(1), 579–616.

Bolger, N., DeLongis, A., Kessler, R. C., & Schilling, E. A. (1989). Effects of daily stress on negative mood. *Journal of Personality and Social Psychology*, *57*(5), 808.

Bowen, G. A. (2009). Supporting a grounded theory with an audit trail: An illustration. *International Journal of Social Research Methodology*, *12*(4), 305–316. https://doi.org/10.1080/13645570802156196

Bower, G. H. (1981). Mood and memory. *American Psychologist*, *36*(2), 129.

Boyd, D., Egbu, C. O., Chinyio, E., & Lee, C. C. T. (2004) Audio diary and debriefing for knowledge management in SMEs. *Total Quality Management*, *14*(2), 199–204.

Braun, V., & Clarke, V. (2006). Using thematic analysis in psychology. *Qualitative Research in Psychology*, *3*(2), 77–101. https://doi.org/10.1191/1478088706qp063oa

Braun, V., & Clarke, V. (2021). Can I use TA? Should I use TA? Should I not use TA? Comparing reflexive thematic analysis and other pattern-based qualitative analytic approaches. *Counselling and Psychotherapy Research*, *21*(1), 37–47. https://doi.org/10.1002/capr.12360

Braun, V., & Clarke, V. (2023). Toward good practice in thematic analysis: Avoiding common problems and becoming a knowing researcher. *International Journal of Transgender Health*, *24*(1), 1–6. https://doi.org/10.1080/26895269.2022.2129597

Bronfenbrenner, U. (1979). *The ecology of human development: Experiments by nature and design*. Harvard University Press.

Brown, C., Costley, C., Friend, L., & Varey, R. (2010). Capturing their dream: Video diaries and minority consumers. *Consumption, Markets and Culture*, *13*(4), 419–436.

Brown, K. M., Dilley, R., & Marshall, K. (2008). Using a head-mounted video camera to understand social worlds and experiences. *Sociological Research Online*, *13*(6), 31–40.

Brown, R. C., Fischer, T., & Plener, P. L. (2020). "I just finally wanted to belong somewhere"—Qualitative analysis of experiences with posting pictures of self-injury on Instagram. *Frontiers in Psychiatry*, *11*, Article 510657. https://doi.org/10.3389/fpsyt.2020.00274

Buchanan, D. A. (1991). Vulnerability and agenda: context and process in project management. *British Journal of Management*, *2*(3), 121–132.

Buchwald, D., Schantz-Laursen, B., & Delmar, C. (2009). Video diary data collection in research with children: An alternative method. *International Journal of Qualitative Methods*, *8*(1), 12–20.

Buckingham, D. (2009). Speaking back? In search of the citizen journalist. In D. Buckingham & R. Willett (Eds.), *Video cultures: Media technology and everyday creativity* (pp. 93–114). Palgrave Macmillan UK.

Budworth, P. (2023). Care, comfort, and capacity: The importance of being flexible in research with disabled and chronically ill people. *SSM-Qualitative Research in Health, 4*, 100352.

Burkitt, I. (2012). Emotional reflexivity: Feeling, emotion and imagination in reflexive dialogues. *Sociology, 46*(3), 458–472.

Busby, H. (2000). Writing about health and sickness: An analysis of contemporary autobiographical writing from the British mass-observation archive. *Sociological Research Online, 5*(2), 11–22.

Cain, C. L., Frazer, M., & Kilaberia, T. R. (2018). Identity work within attempts to transform healthcare: Invisible team processes. *Human Relations, 72*, 370–396. https://doi.org/10.1177/0018726718764277

Caliandro, A., Garavaglia, E., Sturiale, V., & Di Leva, A. (2021). Older people and smartphone practices in everyday life: An inquiry on digital sociality of Italian older users. *The Communication Review, 24*(1), 47–78. https://doi.org/10.1080/10714421.2021.1904771

Callon, M. (1986). Some elements of a sociology of translation: Domestication of the scallops and the fishermen of St. Brieuc Bay. In J. Law (Ed.), *Power, action and belief: A new sociology of knowledge* (pp. 196–223). Routledge.

Cao, X., & Henderson, E. F. (2021). The interweaving of diaries and lives: Diary-keeping behaviour in a diary-interview study of international students' employability management. *Qualitative Research, 21*(6), 829–845.

Carlson, E. D., Engebretson, J., & Chamberlain, R. M. (2006). Photovoice as a social process of critical consciousness. *Qualitative Health Research, 16*(6), 836–852.

Cassell, C. (2015). *Conducting research interviews for business and management students*. Sage.

Cassell, C. (2018). "Pushed beyond my comfort zone": MBA student experiences of conducting qualitative research. *Academy of Management Learning & Education, 17*(2), 119–136. https://doi.org/10.5465/amle.2015.0016

Cassell, C., & Bishop, V. (2019). Qualitative data analysis: Exploring themes, metaphors, and stories. *European Management Review, 16*(1), 195–207. https://doi.org/10.1111/emre.12176

Cassell, C., Malik, F., & Radcliffe, L. S. (2016). Using photo-elicitation to understand experiences of work-life balance. In K. Townsend, R. Loudon, & D. Lewin (Eds.), *Handbook of qualitative research methods on human resource management* (pp. 146–162). Edward Elgar.

Cassell, C., Radcliffe, L.S., & Malik, F. (2020). Participant reflexivity in organizational research design. *Organizational Research Methods, 23*(4), 750–773.

Chamakiotis, P., Whiting, R., Symon, G., & Roby, H. (2014). Exploring transitions and work-life balance in the digital era. Research in progress. In *Proceedings of the*

European Conference on Information Systems (ECIS 2014). Open University Research Online. https://oro.open.ac.uk/41333/1/ECIS2014_DBS_paper_final.pdf

Chamberlain, K. (2012). Do you really need a methodology? *QMiP Bulletin, 13*(59), e63. https://doi.org/10.53841/bpsqmip.2012.1.13.59

Chaplin, E. (2004). My visual diary. In C. Knowles & P. Sweetman (Eds.), *Picturing the social landscape: Visual methods and the sociological imagination* (pp. 35–48). Routledge. https://doi.org/10.4324/9780203694527

Chater, N. (1999). The search for simplicity: A fundamental cognitive principle? *The Quarterly Journal of Experimental Psychology: Section A, 52*(2), 273–302.

Chell, E. (1998). Critical incident technique. In G. Symon & C. Cassell (Eds.), *Qualitative methods and analysis in organizational research: A practical guide* (pp. 51–72). Sage.

Chell, E. (2004). Critical incident technique. In C. Cassell & G. Symon (Eds.), *Essential guide to qualitative methods in organisation studies* (pp. 45–60). Sage.

Chen, H., Wang, Y., & Liu, Z. (2022). The experiences of frontline nurses in Wuhan: A qualitative analysis of nurse online diaries during the COVID-19 pandemic. *Journal of Clinical Nursing, 31*(17–18), 2465–2475. https://doi.org/10.1111/jocn.16056

Cherrington, J., & Watson, B. (2010). Shooting a diary, not just a hoop: Using video diaries to explore the embodied everyday contexts of a university basketball team. *Qualitative Research in Sport and Exercise, 2*(2), 267–281.

Christensen, T. C., Wood, J. V., & Barrett, L. F. (2003). Remembering everyday experience through the prism of self-esteem. *Personality and Social Psychology Bulletin, 29*(1), 51–62.

Chubb, L. A. (2023). Me and the machines: Possibilities and pitfalls of using artificial intelligence for qualitative data analysis. *International Journal of Qualitative Methods, 22*, 1–16. https://doi.org/10.1177/16094069231193593

Colom, A. (2022). Using WhatsApp for focus group discussions: Ecological validity, inclusion, and deliberation. *Qualitative Research, 22*(3), 452–467. https://doi.org/10.1177/1468794120986074

Consolvo, S., Bentley, F. R., Hekler, E. B., & Phatak, S. S. (2017). Diary studies and experience sampling. In S. Consolvo, F. R. Bentley, E. B. Hekler, & S. S. Phatak (Eds.), *Mobile user research: A practical guide* (pp. 71–99). Springer International Publishing.

Cooley, S. J., Holland, M. J., Cumming, J., Novakovic, E. G., & Burns, V. E. (2014). Introducing the use of a semi-structured video diary room to investigate students' learning experiences during an outdoor adventure education groupwork skills course. *Higher Education, 67*, 105–121. https://doi.org/10.1007/s10734-013-9645-5

Corti, L. (1993). Using diaries in social research. *Social Research Update*, Issue 2. University of Surrey. https://repository.essex.ac.uk/24606/1/Social%20Research%20Update%202_%20Using%20diaries%20in%20social%20research.pdf

Cottingham, M. D., & Erickson, R. J. (2020). Capturing emotion with audio diaries. *Qualitative Research, 20*(5), 549–564.

Cottingham, M. D., Johnson, A. H., & Erickson, R. J. (2018). "I can never be too comfortable": Race, gender, and emotion at the hospital bedside. *Qualitative Health Research, 28*(1), 145–158.

Cotton, D., Winter, J., Allison, J. A., & Mullee, R. (2023). Visual images of sustainability in higher education: The hidden curriculum of climate change on campus. *International Journal of Sustainability in Higher Education, 24*(7), 1576–1593. https://doi.org/10.1108/IJSHE-09-2022-0315

Crotty, M. J. (1998). *The foundations of social research: Meaning and perspective in the research process.* Sage.

Crozier, S. E., & Cassell, C. M. (2016). Methodological considerations in the use of audio diaries in work psychology: Adding to the qualitative toolkit. *Journal of Occupational and Organizational Psychology, 89*(2), 396–419.

Cudjoe, E. (2022). Using diaries with interpretative phenomenological analysis: Guidelines from a study of children whose parents have mental illness. *International Journal of Qualitative Methods, 21*, 1–9. https://doi.org/10.1177/16094069221084435

Culp-Roche, A., Hampton, D., Hensley, A., Wilson, J., Thaxton-Wiggins, A., Otts, J. A., Fruh, S., & Moser, D. K. (2020). Generational differences in faculty and student comfort with technology use. *SAGE Open Nursing, 6*, 2377960820941394.

Cunliffe, A. L. (2002). Reflexive dialogical practice in management learning. *Management Learning, 33*(1), 35–61.

Danielsson, A. T., & Berge, M. (2020). Using video-diaries in educational research exploring identity: Affordances and constraints. *International Journal of Qualitative Methods, 19*, 1609406920973541.

Dawson, M., McDonnell, L., & Scott, S. (2016). Negotiating the boundaries of intimacy: The personal lives of asexual people. *The Sociological Review, 64*, 349–365. https://doi.org/10.1111/1467-954X.12362

Day, M. C., & Hudson, J. (2012). Reflections on using writing in sport and exercise psychology research and practice. *Qualitative Methods in Psychology Bulletin, 14*, 24–30.

Day, M., & Thatcher, J. (2009). "I'm really embarrassed that you're going to read this...": Reflections on using diaries in qualitative research. *Qualitative Research in Psychology, 6*(4), 249–259.

Dempsey, L., Dowling, M., Larkin, P., & Murphy, K. (2016). Sensitive interviewing in qualitative research. *Research in Nursing & Health, 39*(6), 480–490.

Dennett, R., Hendrie, W., Jarrett, L., Creanor, S., Barton, A., Hawton, A., & Freeman, J. A. (2020). "I'm in a very good frame of mind": A qualitative exploration of the experience of standing frame use in people with progressive multiple sclerosis. *BMJ Open, 10*(10), e037680. https://doi.org/10.1136/bmjopen-2020-037680

Denzin, N. K., & Lincoln, Y. S. (Eds.). (1998). *The landscape of qualitative research: theories and issues.* Sage.

Denzin, N. K., & Lincoln, Y. S. (Eds.). (2011). *The Sage handbook of qualitative research*. Sage.

Do, J., & Yamagata-Lynch, L. C. (2017). Designing and developing cell phone applications for qualitative research. *Qualitative Inquiry*, *23*(10), 757–767. https://doi.org/10.1177/1077800417731085

Dunham, M., Allmark, P., & Collins, K. (2017). Older people's experiences of cancer pain: A qualitative study. *Nursing Older People*, *29*(6), 28–32. https://doi.org/10.7748/nop.2017.e943

Eckenrode, J. (1984). Impact of chronic and acute stressors on daily reports of mood. *Journal of Personality and Social Psychology*, *46*(4), 907.

Eckenrode, J. (1995). *Daily and within-day event measurement*. Oxford University Press.

Egerod, I., & Christensen, D. (2009). Analysis of patient diaries in Danish ICUs: A narrative approach. *Intensive and Critical Care Nursing*, *25*(5), 268–277. https://doi.org/10.1016/j.iccn.2009.06.005

Elliot, H. (1997). The use of diaries in sociological research on health experience. *Sociological Research Online*, *2*(2), U64–U74.

Erickson, F. (2011). Uses of video in social research: a brief history. *International Journal of Social Research Methodology*, *14*(3), 179–189.

Ferguson, E., & Chandler, S. (2005). A stage model of blood donor behaviour: Assessing volunteer behaviour. *Journal of Health Psychology*, *10*(3), 359–372.

Filep, C. V., Thompson-Fawcett, M., Fitzsimons, S., & Turner, S. (2015). Reaching revelatory places: The role of solicited diaries in extending research on emotional geographies into the unfamiliar. *Area*, *47*(4), 459–465.

Filep, C. V., Turner, S., Eidse, N., Thompson-Fawcett, M., & Fitzsimons, S. (2018). Advancing rigour in solicited diary research. *Qualitative Research*, *18*(4), 451–470.

Finkelstein, S. M., Budd, J. R., Warwick, W. J., Kujawa, S. J., Wielinski, C. L., & Ewing, L. B. (1986). Feasibility and compliance studies of a home measurement monitoring program for cystic fibrosis. *Journal of Chronic Diseases*, *39*(3), 195–205.

Fisher, C. M., Pillemer, J., & Amabile, T. M. (2018). Deep help in complex project work: Guiding and path-clearing across difficult terrain. *Academy of Management Journal*, *61*(4), 1524–1553. https://doi.org/10.5465/amj.2016.0207

Fitt, H. (2018). Researching mobile practices: Participant reflection and audio-recording in repeat question diaries. *Qualitative Research*, *18*(6), 654–670.

Flanagan, J. C. (1954). The critical incident technique. *Psychological Bulletin*, *51*(4), 327. https://doi.org/10.1037/h0061470

Flanders, C. E., Robinson, M., Legge, M. M., & Tarasoff, L. A. (2016). Negative identity experiences of bisexual and other non-monosexual people: A qualitative report. *Journal of Gay & Lesbian Mental Health*, *20*(2), 152–172. https://doi.org/10.1080/19359705.2015.1108257

Flick, U. (2022). *The SAGE handbook of qualitative research design*. Sage.

Follick, M. J., Ahern, D. K., & Laser-Wolston, N. (1984). Evaluation of a daily activity diary for chronic pain patients. *Pain, 19*(4), 373–382.

Frąckowiak, M., Rogowski, Ł., & Sommer, V. (2023). Hopes and challenges of creating and using a smartphone application: Working on and working with a digital mobile tool in qualitative sociospatial research. *Qualitative Research, 23*(5), 1378–1397. https://doi.org/10.1177/14687941221098923

Furness, P. J., & Garrud, P. (2010). Adaptation after facial surgery: Using the diary as a research tool. *Qualitative Health Research, 20*(2), 262–272.

Gammack, J. G., & Stephens, R. A. (1994). Repertory grid technique in constructive interaction. In C. M. Cassell & G. Symon (Eds.), *Qualitative methods in organizational research: A practical guide* (pp. 72–90). Sage.

García, B., Welford, J., & Smith, B. (2016). Using a smartphone app in qualitative research: The good, the bad, and the ugly. *Qualitative Research, 16*(5), 508–525. https://doi.org/10.1177/1468794115593335

Gatrell, C. (2009). Safeguarding subjects? A reflexive appraisal of researcher accountability in qualitative interviews. *Qualitative Research in Organizations and Management: An International Journal, 4*(2), 110–122.

Gibson, B. E. (2005). Co-producing video diaries: The presence of the "absent" researcher. *International Journal of Qualitative Methods, 4*(4), 34–43.

Gibson, B. E., Mistry, B., Smith, B., Yoshida, K. K., Abbott, D., Lindsay, S., & Hamdani, Y. (2013). The integrated use of audio diaries, photography, and interviews in research with disabled young men. *International Journal of Qualitative Methods, 12*(1), 382–402. https://doi.org/10.1177/160940691301200118

Gibson, F., Hibbins, S., Grew, T., Morgan, S., Pearce, S., Stark, D., & Fern, L. A. (2016). How young people describe the impact of living with and beyond a cancer diagnosis: Feasibility of using social media as a research method. *Psycho-Oncology, 25*(11), 1317–1323.

Gibson, K. (2022). Bridging the digital divide: Reflections on using WhatsApp instant messenger interviews in youth research. *Qualitative Research in Psychology, 19*(3), 611–631. https://doi.org/10.1080/14780887.2020.1751902

Gill, M. J. (2014). The possibilities of phenomenology for organizational research. *Organizational Research Methods, 17*(2), 118–137. https://doi.org/10.1177/1094428113518348

Gioia, D. A., Corley, K. G., & Hamilton, A. L. (2013). Seeking qualitative rigor in inductive research: Notes on the Gioia methodology. *Organizational Research Methods, 16*(1), 15–31. https://doi.org/10.1177/1094428112452151

Glaser, B. G., & Strauss, A. L. (1967). *The discovery of grounded theory: Strategies for qualitative research*. Aldine de Gruyter.

Gobo, G., & Mauceri, S. (2014). *Constructing survey data: An interactional approach*. Sage.

Goulding, C. (2002). *Grounded theory: A practical guide for management, business and market researchers*. Sage.

Gregorius, S. (2016). Exploring narratives of education: Disabled young people's experiences of educational institutions in Ghana. *Disability & Society, 31*(3), 322–338.

Gubrium, A. C., Hill, A. L., & Flicker, S. (2014). A situated practice of ethics for participatory visual and digital methods in public health research and practice: A focus on digital storytelling. *American Journal of Public Health, 104*(9), 1606–1614.

Guest, G., Namey, E. E., & Mitchell, M. L. (2013). *Collecting qualitative data: A field manual for applied research*. Sage.

Guo, C., Si, L., & Sun, Y. (2023). Research on the process and influencing factors of online diabetes information users' avoidance behavior: A qualitative study. *Behavioural Sciences, 13*, 267. https://doi.org/10.3390/bs13030267

Hacker, K. (2013). *Community-based participatory research*. Sage.

Hadfield-Hill, S., & Zara, C. (2018). Being participatory through the use of app-based research tools. In I. Coyne & B. Carter (Eds.), *Being participatory: Researching with children and young people: Co-constructing knowledge using creative techniques* (pp. 147–169). Springer.

Hagan, R. J., & Manktelow, R. (2021). 'I shall miss the company': Participants' reflections on time-limited day centre programming. *Ageing & Society, 41*(12), 2933–2952.

Hagan, R., Manktelow, R., & Taylor, B. J. (2020). Loneliness, cumulative inequality and social capital in later life: Two stories. *Irish Journal of Sociology, 28*(2), 192–217. https://doi.org/10.1177/0791603520908764

Hamilton, L., Elliott, D., Quick, A., Smith, S., & Choplin, V. (2023). Exploring the use of AI in qualitative analysis: A comparative study of guaranteed income data. *International Journal of Qualitative Methods, 22*, 1–13. https://doi.org/10.1177/16094069231201504

Hammer, L. B., Neal, M. B., Newsom, J. T., Brockwood, K. J., & Colton, C. L. (2005). A longitudinal study of the effects of dual-earner couples' utilization of family-friendly workplace supports on work and family outcomes. *Journal of Applied Psychology, 90*(4), 799.

Hammersley, M., & Atkinson, P. (2019). *Ethnography: Principles in practice*. Routledge.

Hardy, J. (2006). Speaking clearly: A critical review of the self-talk literature. *Psychology of Sport and Exercise, 7*(1), 81–97.

Harper, D. (2002). Talking about pictures: A case for photo elicitation. *Visual Studies, 17*(1), 13–26.

Harvey, L. (2011). Intimate reflections: Private diaries in qualitative research. *Qualitative Research, 11*(6), 664–682.

Hayes, A., Lomer, S., & Taha, S. H. (2024). Epistemological process towards decolonial praxis and epistemic inequality of an international student. *Educational Review, 76*(1), 132–144.

Hayes, J. R., & Flower, L. S. (1986). Writing research and the writer. *American Psychologist*, *41*(10), 1106.

Hayes, J. R., & Flower, L. S. (2016). Identifying the organization of writing processes. In L. W. Gregg & E. R. Steinberg (Eds.), *Cognitive processes in writing* (pp. 3–30). Routledge.

Hays, R., & Daker-White, G. (2015). The care.data consensus? A qualitative analysis of opinions expressed on Twitter. *BMC Public Health*, *15*, Article 1. https://doi.org/10.1186/s12889-015-2180-9

Hayes, A., Lomer, S., & Taha, S. H. (2024). Epistemological process towards decolonial praxis and epistemic inequality of an international student. *Educational Review*, *76*(1), 132–144.

Head, E. (2009). The ethics and implications of paying participants in qualitative research. *International Journal of Social Research Methodology*, *12*(4), 335–344. https://doi.org/10.1080/13645570802246724

Hennekam, S., Ladge, J. J., & Powell, G. N. (2021). Confinement during the COVID-19 pandemic: How multi-domain work-life shock events may result in positive identity change. *Journal of Vocational Behavior*, *130*, 103621.

Hennekam, S., & Shymko, Y. (2020). Coping with the COVID-19 crisis: Force majeure and gender performativity. *Gender, Work, and Organization*, *27*(5), 788–803. https://doi.org/10.1111/gwao.12479

Hershcovis, M. S., & Reich, T. C. (2013). Integrating workplace aggression research: Relational, contextual, and method considerations. *Journal of Organizational Behavior*, *34*(Suppl. 1), S26–S42.

Hibbert, P., Callagher, L., Siedlok, F., Windahl, C., & Kim, H. S. (2019). (Engaging or avoiding) change through reflexive practices. *Journal of Management Inquiry*, *28*(2), 187–203.

Hibbert, P., & Cunliffe, A. (2015). Responsible management: Engaging moral reflexive practice through threshold concepts. *Journal of Business Ethics*, *127*, 177–188.

Hilário, A. P., & Augusto, F. R. (2023). The use of diaries for understanding the experience of health and illness. *Sociology Compass*, *17*(9), e13103.

Hislop, J., Arber, S., Meadows, R., & Venn, S. (2005). Narratives of the night: The use of audio diaries in researching sleep. *Sociological Research Online*, *10*(4), 13–25.

Hodgkins, A. (2022). Exploring early childhood practitioners' perceptions of empathy with children and families: Initial findings. *Educational Review*, *76*(2), 223–241. https://doi.org/10.1080/00131911.2021.2023471

Holliday, R. (2000). We've been framed: Visualising methodology. *The Sociological Review*, *48*(4), 503–521.

Holliday, R. (2004). Filming "The closet": The role of video diaries in researching sexualities. *American Behavioral Scientist*, *47*(12), 1597–1616.

Holliday, R. (2007). Performances, confessions, and identities: Using video diaries to research sexualities. In G. C. Stanczak (Ed.), *Visual research methods: Image, society, and representation* (pp. 255–281). Sage.

Hopkins, N., Ryan, C., Portice, J., Straßburger, V. M., Ahluwalia-McMeddes, A., Dobai, A., & Reicher, S. (2023). Social identity enactment in a pandemic: Scottish Muslims' experiences of restricted access to communal spaces. *British Journal of Social Psychology, 62*(3), 1141–1157. https://doi.org/10.1111/bjso.12625

Hoprekstad, Ø. L., Hetland, J., Bakker, A. B., Olsen, O. K., Espevik, R., Wessel, M., & Einarsen, S. V. (2019). How long does it last? Prior victimization from workplace bullying moderates the relationship between daily exposure to negative acts and subsequent depressed mood. *European Journal of Work and Organizational Psychology, 28*(2), 164–178.

Hunsaker, A., & Hargittai, E. (2018). A review of Internet use among older adults. *New Media & Society, 20*(10), 3937–3954. https://doi.org/10.1177/1461444818787348

Hyers, L. L. (2018). *Diary methods*. Oxford University Press.

Iedema, R., Forsyth, R., Georgiou, A., Braithwaite, J., & Westbrook, J. (2006). Video research in health. *Qualitative Research Journal, 6*(2), 15–30.

Iida, M., Shrout, P., Laurenceau, J. P., & Bolger, N. (2012). Using diary methods in psychological research. In H. Cooper, M. N. Coutanche, L. M. McMullen, A. T. Panter, D. Rindskopf, & K. J. Sher (Eds.), *APA handbook of research methods in psychology: Foundations, planning, measures and psychometrics* (pp. 277–305). American Psychological Association.

Iivari, N., Kinnula, M., Kuure, L., & Molin-Juustila, T. (2014). Video diary as a means for data gathering with children—Encountering identities in the making. *International Journal of Human-Computer Studies, 72*(5), 507–521. https://doi.org/10.1016/j.ijhcs.2014.02.003

Iphofen, R., & Tolich, M. (2018). *The Sage handbook of qualitative research ethics*. Sage.

Islam, G. (2015). Practitioners as theorists: Para-ethnography and the collaborative study of contemporary organizations. *Organizational Research Methods, 18*(2), 231–251.

Izak, M., Shortt, H., & Case, P. (2023). Learning to inhabit the liquid liminal world of work: An auto-ethnographic visual study of work-life boundary transitions. *Management Learning, 54*(2), 198–222. https://doi.org/10.1177/13505076211070359

Jackson, K. (2019). *Qualitative data analysis with NVivo* (3rd ed.). Sage.

Jay, B. (2022). Research with residential childcare practitioners: Early reflections of managing harm in a qualitative diary study. *Scottish Journal of Residential Child Care, 21*(1), 182–194.

Jewitt, C. (2008). *The visual in learning and creativity: A review of the literature*. Arts Council England.

Jewitt, C. (2012). *An introduction to using video for research*. National Centre for Research Methods Working Paper.

Johnson, P., & Duberley, J. (2003). Reflexivity in management research. *Journal of Management Studies, 40*(5), 1279–1303.

Jones, R. L., Fonseca, J., De Martin Silva, L., Davies, G., Morgan, K., & Mesquita, I. (2015). The promise and problems of video diaries: Building on current research. *Qualitative Research in Sport, Exercise and Health*, *7*(3), 395–410.

Karadzhov, D. (2021). Expanding the methodological repertoire of participatory research into homelessness: The utility of the mobile phone diary. *Qualitative Social Work*, *20*(3), 813–831. https://doi.org/10.1177/1473325020913904

Karadzhov, D. (2023). "Recovery is fearful to me . . .": Conceptualizations, concerns and hopes about personal recovery in adults who are chronically homeless. *Social Work in Mental Health*, *21*(3), 285–305.

Karnowski, V. (2013). Befragung in situ: Die Mobile Experience Sampling Method (MESM). In W. Möhring & D. Schlütz (Eds.), *Handbuch standardisierte Erhebungsverfahren in der Kommunikationswissenschaft*. Springer VS. https://doi.org/10.1007/978-3-531-18776-1_13

Kaufmann, K. (2019). Mobile methods: Doing migration research with the help of smartphones. In K. Smets, K. Leurs, M. Georgiou, S. Witteborn, & R. Gajjala (Eds.), *The SAGE handbook of media and migration* (pp. 167–179). Sage.

Kaufmann, K., & Peil, C. (2020). The mobile instant messaging interview (MIMI): Using WhatsApp to enhance self-reporting and explore media usage in situ. *Mobile Media & Communication*, *8*(2), 229–246. https://doi.org/10.1177/2050157919852392

Kaufmann, K., Peil, C., & Bork-Hüffer, T. (2021). Producing in situ data from a distance with mobile instant messaging interviews (MIMIs): Examples from the COVID-19 pandemic. *International Journal of Qualitative Methods*, *20*, 16094069211029697. https://doi.org/10.1177/16094069211029697

Kaur, H., Saukko, P., & Lumsden, K. (2018). Rhythms of moving in and between digital media: A study on video diaries of young people with physical disabilities. *Mobilities*, *13*(3), 397–410.

Keedle, H., Schmied, V., Burns, E., & Dahlen, H. (2018). The design, development, and evaluation of a qualitative data collection application for pregnant women. *Journal of Nursing Scholarship*, *50*(1), 47–55. https://doi.org/10.1111/jnu.12344

Keleher, H. M., & Verrinder, G. K. (2003). Health diaries in a rural Australian study. *Qualitative Health Research*, *13*(3), 435–443.

Kelland, J., Radcliffe, L., Williams, G., & Gregory-Chialton, J. (2025). Synergistic or Siloed? Communicative practices in dual-earner parents' boundary navigation and implications for gendered work-family experiences. *Applied Psychology*, *74*(1), e12586.

King, K., & Dickinson, J. (2023). Nearby nature in lockdown: Practices and affordances for leisure in urban green spaces. *Leisure Studies*, *42*(1), 100–117. https://doi.org/10.1080/02614367.2022.2092646

King, N. (2004). Using templates in the thematic analysis of text. In C. Cassell & G. Symon (Eds.), *Essential guide to qualitative methods in organizational research* (pp. 256–270). Sage.

King, N. (2012). Doing template analysis. In G. Symon & C. Cassell (Eds.), *Qualitative organisational research: Core methods and current challenges* (pp. 426–450). Sage.

King, N., & Brooks, J. M. (2016). *Template analysis for business and management students*. Sage. https://doi.org/10.4135/9781473983304

Knoblauch, H., Schnettler, B., Raab, J., & Soeffner, H. G. (2006). *Video analysis: Methodology and methods*. Peter Lang.

Köhler, T., Smith, A., & Bhakoo, V. (2022). Templates in qualitative research methods: Origins, limitations, and new directions. *Organizational Research Methods, 25*(2), 183–210. https://doi.org/10.1177/10944281211060710

Koopman-Boyden, P., & Richardson, M. (2013). An evaluation of mixed methods (diaries and focus groups) when working with older people. *International Journal of Social Research Methodology, 16*(5), 389–401.

Kress, G., & Van Leeuwen, T. (2020). *Reading images: The grammar of visual design*. Routledge.

Kvale, S., & Brinkmann, S. (2009). *Interviews: Learning the craft of qualitative research interviewing*. Sage.

Langley, A. (1999). Strategies for theorizing from process data. *Academy of Management Review, 24*(4), 691–710. https://doi.org/10.2307/259349

Langley, A., & Ravasi, D. (2019). Visual artifacts as tools for analysis and theorizing. In T. B. Zilber, J. M. Amis, & J. Mair (Eds.), *The production of managerial knowledge and organizational theory: New approaches to writing, producing and consuming theory* (pp. 173–199; Research in the Sociology of Organizations, Vol. 59). Emerald Publishing Limited. https://doi.org/10.1108/S0733-558X20190000059010

Lapierre, L. M., & Allen, T. D. (2006). Work-supportive family, family-supportive supervision, use of organizational benefits, and problem-focused coping: Implications for work-family conflict and employee well-being. *Journal of Occupational Health Psychology, 11*(2), 169.

Larkin, K., & Jorgensen, R. (2016). 'I hate maths: why do we need to do maths?' Using iPad video diaries to investigate attitudes and emotions towards mathematics in year 3 and year 6 students. *International Journal of Science and Mathematics Education, 14*, 925–944.

Larsen, H. G., & Adu, P. (2021). *The theoretical framework in phenomenological research: Development and application*. Routledge.

Latham, A. (2003). Research, performance, and doing human geography: Some reflections on the diary-photograph, diary-interview method. *Environment and Planning A, 35*(11), 1993–2017. https://doi.org/10.1068/a3587

Latham, A. (2004). Researching and writing everyday accounts of the city: An introduction to the diary-photo diary-interview method. In C. Knowles & P. Sweetman (Eds.), *Picturing the social landscape: Visual methods and the sociological imagination* (pp. 117–131). Routledge.

Latour, B. (2005). *Reassembling the social*. Oxford University Press

Law, J. (1994). *Organising modernity*. Blackwell.

Law, J. (2004). *After method: Mess in social science research*. Routledge.

Lawson, A., Robinson, I., & Bakes, C. (1985). Problems in evaluating the consequences of disabling illness: The case of multiple sclerosis. *Psychological Medicine, 15*(3), 555-579.

LeBaron, C. D., & Jones, S. E. (2002). Closing up closings: Showing the relevance of the social and material surround to the completion of interaction. *Journal of Communication, 52*(3), 542-565.

Lev-On, A., & Lowenstein-Barkai, H. (2019). Viewing diaries in an age of new media: An exploratory analysis of mobile phone app diaries versus paper diaries. *Methodological Innovations, 12*(1), Article 2059799119844442. https://doi.org/10.1177/2059799119844442

Linn, S. (2021). Solicited diary methods with urban refugee women: Ethical and practical considerations. *Area, 53*(3), 454-463.

Litovuo, L., Karisalmi, N., Aarikka-Stenroos, L., & Kaipio, J. (2019). Comparing three methods to capture multidimensional service experience in children's health care: Video diaries, narratives, and semi-structured interviews. *International Journal of Qualitative Methods, 18*, 1-13. https://doi.org/10.1177/1609406919835112

Lowson, E., & Arber, S. (2014). Preparing, working, recovering: Gendered experiences of night work among women and their families. *Gender, Work & Organization, 21*(3), 231-243.

Maagaard, C. A., & Laerkner, E. (2022). Writing a diary for "you"—Intensive care nurses' narrative practices in diaries for patients: A qualitative study. *International Journal of Nursing Studies, 136*, 104363. https://doi.org/10.1016/j.ijnurstu.2022.104363

MacDonald, S., Murphy, S., & Elliott, E. (2018). Controlling food, controlling relationships: Exploring the meanings and dynamics of family food practices through the diary-interview approach. *Sociology of Health & Illness, 40*(5), 779-792. https://doi.org/10.1111/1467-9566.12725

Madden, R. (2022). *Being ethnographic: A guide to the theory and practice of ethnography*. Sage.

Manusov, V., & Trees, A. R. (2002). "Are you kidding me?": The role of nonverbal cues in the verbal accounting process. *Journal of Communication, 52*(3), 640-656.

Markham, T., & Couldry, N. (2007). Tracking the reflexivity of the (dis) engaged citizen: Some methodological reflections. *Qualitative Inquiry, 13*(5), 675-695.

Mavhandu-Mudzusi, A. H., Moyo, I., Mthombeni, A., Ndou, A., Mamabolo, L., Ngwenya, T., Marebane, T., &Netshapapame, T. (2022). WhatsApp as a qualitative data collection method in descriptive phenomenological studies. *International Journal of Qualitative Methods, 21*, Article 16094069221111124. https://doi.org/10.1177/16094069221111124

McAllum, K., Fox, S., Simpson, M., & Unson, C. (2019). A comparative tale of two methods: How thematic and narrative analyses author the data story differently. *Communication Research and Practice*, *5*(4), 358–375. https://doi.org/10.1080/22041451.2019.1677068

McClinchy, J., Dickinson, A., & Wills, W. (2023). Developing the diary-interview approach to study the embodied, tacit and mundane nutrition information behaviours of people with type 2 diabetes. *Sociological Research Online*, *28*(2), 482–501.

Mehrotra, A., Pejovic, V., Vermeulen, J., Hendley, R., & Musolesi, M. (2016, May). My phone and me: Understanding people's receptivity to mobile notifications. In *Proceedings of the 2016 CHI Conference on Human Factors in Computing Systems* (pp. 1021–1032). Association for Computing Machinery. https://doi.org/10.1145/2858036.2858566

Mendoza, J., Seguin, M. L., Lasco, G., Palileo-Villanueva, L. M., Amit, A., Renedo, A., McKee, M., Palafox, B., & Balabanova, D. (2021). Strengths and weaknesses of digital diaries as a means to study patient pathways: Experiences with a study of hypertension in the Philippines. *International Journal of Qualitative Methods*, *20*, Article 16094069211002746. https://doi.org/10.1177/16094069211002746

Meth, P. (2003). Entries and omissions: using solicited diaries in geographical research. *Area*, *35*(2), 195–205.

Meyer, R. E., Höllerer, M. A., Jancsary, D., & Van Leeuwen, T. (2013). The visual dimension in organizing, organization, and organization research: Core ideas, current developments, and promising avenues. *Academy of Management Annals*, *7*(1), 489–555.

Miles, M. B., & Huberman, A. M. (1994). *Qualitative data analysis: An expanded sourcebook*. Sage.

Miller, T., Birch, M., Mauthner, M., & Jessop, J. (Eds.). (2012). *Ethics in qualitative research*. Sage.

Miller, T., & Boulton, M. (2007). Changing constructions of informed consent: Qualitative research and complex social worlds. *Social Science & Medicine*, *65*(11), 2199–2211.

Milligan, C., Bingley, A., & Gatrell, A. (2005). Digging deep: Using diary techniques to explore the place of health and well-being amongst older people. *Social Science & Medicine*, *61*(9), 1882–1892.

Moeran, B. (2009). From participant observation to observant participation. *Organizational ethnography: Studying the complexities of everyday life*, 139–155.

Monrouxe, L. V. (2009). Solicited audio diaries in longitudinal narrative research: A view from inside. *Qualitative Research*, *9*(1), 81–103.

Moon, J. A. (2013). *Reflection in learning and professional development: Theory and practice*. Routledge. https://doi.org/10.4324/9780203822296

Mooney, G., McCall, V., & Paton, K. (2015). Exploring the use of large sporting events in the post-crash, post-welfare city: A 'legacy' of increasing insecurity? *Local Economy*, *30*(8), 910–924.

Moran-Ellis, J., & Venn, S. (2007). The sleeping lives of children and teenagers: Night-worlds and arenas of action. *Sociological Research Online*, *12*(5), 133–145.

Morgan, D. L. (1996). *Focus groups as qualitative research* (Vol. 16). Sage.

Morgan, D. L. (2023). Exploring the use of artificial intelligence for qualitative data analysis: The case of ChatGPT. *International Journal of Qualitative Methods*, *22*, 1–10. https://doi.org/10.1177/16094069231211248

Morrison, Z. J., Gregory, D., & Thibodeau, S. (2012). "Thanks for using me": An exploration of exit strategy in qualitative research. *International Journal of Qualitative Methods*, *11*(4), 416–427.

Mueller, G., Barford, A., Osborne, H., Pradhan, K., Proefke, R., Shrestha, S., & Pratiwi, A. M. (2023). Disaster diaries: Qualitative research at a distance. *International Journal of Qualitative Methods*, *22*, 16094069221147163.

Mueller, G., Barford, A., Osborne, H., Pradhan, K., Proefke, R., Shrestha, S., & Pratiwi, A. M. (2023). Disaster diaries: Qualitative research at a distance. *International Journal of Qualitative Methods*, *22*, 1–19. https://doi.org/10.1177/16094069221147163

Muir, S. (2008). *Participant produced video: Giving participants camcorders as a social research methods*. National Centre for Research Methods: Real Life Methods.

Muir, S., & Mason, J. (2012). Capturing Christmas: The sensory potential of data from participant produced video. *Sociological Research Online*, *17*(1), 47–65.

Mupambireyi, Z., & Bernays, S. (2019). Reflections on the use of audio diaries to access young people's lived experiences of HIV in Zimbabwe. *Qualitative Health Research*, *29*(5), 680–692.

Nadin, S., & Cassell, C. (2006). The use of a research diary as a tool for reflexive practice: Some reflections from management research. *Qualitative Research in Accounting & Management*, *3*(3), 208–217.

Nash, M., & Moore, R. (2018). Exploring methodological challenges of using participant-produced digital video diaries in Antarctica. *Sociological Research Online*, *23*(3), 589–605.

Neves, B. B., Colón Cabrera, D., Sanders, A., & Warren, N. (2023). Pandemic diaries: Lived experiences of loneliness, loss, and hope among older adults during COVID-19. *The Gerontologist*, *63*(1), 120–130. https://doi.org/10.1093/geront/gnac104

Neves, B. B., Wilson, J., Sanders, A., Kokanović, R., & Burns, K. (2023). "Live gerontology": Understanding and representing aging, loneliness, and long-term care through science and art. *The Gerontologist*, *63*(10), 1581.

Nielsen, A. H., Angel, S., Hansen, T. B., & Egerod, I. (2019). Structure and content of diaries written by close relatives for intensive care unit patients: A narrative approach (DRIP study). *Journal of Advanced Nursing*, *75*(6), 1296–1305. https://doi.org/10.1111/jan.13956

Nielsen, A. H., Angel, S., Hansen, T. B., & Egerod, I. (2019). Structure and content of diaries written by close relatives for intensive care unit patients: A narrative approach (DRIP study). *Journal of Advanced Nursing*, 75(6), 1296–1305. https://doi.org/10.1111/jan.13956

Nind, M., Boorman, G., & Clarke, G. (2012). Creating spaces to belong: Listening to the voice of girls with behavioural, emotional and social difficulties through digital visual and narrative methods. *International Journal of Inclusive Education*, 16(7), 643–656.

Noyes, A. (2004). Video diary: A method for exploring learning dispositions. *Cambridge Journal of Education*, 34(2), 193–209.

O'Reilly, K., Ramanaik, S., Story, W. T., Gnanaselvam, N. A., Baker, K. K., Cunningham, L. T., Mukherjee, A., & Pujar, A. (2022). Audio diaries: A novel method for water, sanitation, and hygiene-related maternal stress research. *International Journal of Qualitative Methods*, 21, 16094069211073222.

O'Reilly, M., Haffejee, S., Eruyar, S., Sykes, G., & Vostanis, P. (2024). Benefits and challenges of engaging Majority World children in interdisciplinary, multi-qualitative-method, mental health research. *International Journal of Social Research Methodology*, 27(2), 219–233.

O'Dwyer, S., Moyle, W., & Van Wyk, S. (2013). Suicidal ideation and resilience in family carers of people with dementia: A pilot qualitative study. *Aging & Mental Health*, 17(6), 753–760.

Owens, O. L., Beer, J. M., Revels, A., & Levkoff, S. (2019). Feasibility of using a video diary methodology with older African Americans living alone. *Qualitative Social Work*, 18(3), 397–416.

Palmer, T., Waliaula, C., Shannon, G., Salustri, F., Grewal, G., Chelagat, W., Jennings, H. M., & Skordis, J. (2022). Understanding the lived experience of children with type 1 diabetes in Kenya: Daily routines and adaptation over time. *Qualitative Health Research*, 32(1), 145–158. https://doi.org/10.1177/10497323211049775

Papadopoulos, I., & Scanlon, K. (2002). The use of audio diaries in a study with visually impaired people. *Journal of Visual Impairment & Blindness*, 96(6), 456–459.

Parker, R. D., Mancini, K., & Abram, M. D. (2023). Natural language processing enhanced qualitative methods: An opportunity to improve health outcomes. *International Journal of Qualitative Methods*, 22, 1–6. https://doi.org/10.1177/16094069231214144

Patel, V., Nowostawski, M., Thomson, G., Wilson, N., & Medlin, H. (2013). Developing a smartphone 'app' for public health research: The example of measuring observed smoking in vehicles. *Journal of Epidemiology and Community Health*, 67(5), 446–452. https://doi.org/10.1136/jech-2012-201774

Patton, M. Q. (2002). *Qualitative research and evaluation methods* (3rd ed.). Sage.

Patton, M. Q. (2014). *Qualitative research & evaluation methods: Integrating theory and practice*. Sage.

Paulus, T. M., & Lester, J. N. (2021). *Doing qualitative research in a digital world*. Sage.

Piasecki, T. M., Hufford, M. R., Solhan, M., & Trull, T. J. (2007). Assessing clients in their natural environments with electronic diaries: Rationale, benefits, limitations, and barriers. *Psychological Assessment, 19*(1), 25.

Pilcher, K., Martin, W., & Williams, V. (2016). Issues of collaboration, representation, meaning, and emotions: Utilising participant-led visual diaries to capture the everyday lives of people in mid to later life. *International Journal of Social Research Methodology, 19*(6), 677–692. https://doi.org/10.1080/13645579.2015.1086199

Pinilla, J. P., Román Brugnoli, J. A., Leyton Legües, D., & Vergara del Solar, A. (2023). My Home Quarantine on an App: A qualitative visual analysis of changes in family routines during the COVID-19 pandemic in Chile. *Qualitative Sociology, 46*(2), 221–244. https://doi.org/10.1007/s11133-023-09531-z

Pink, S. (2001). More visualising, more methodologies: on video, reflexivity and qualitative research. *The Sociological Review, 49*(4), 586–599.

Pink, S. (2006). *The future of visual anthropology: Engaging the senses*. Routledge.

Pink, S. (2007). Walking with video. *Visual Studies, 22*(3), 240–252.

Pink, S. (2009). *Doing sensory ethnography*. Sage.

Platt, L. (2012). Parks are dangerous and the sidewalk is closer: Children's use of neighborhood space in Milwaukee, Wisconsin. *Children, Youth and Environments, 22*(2), 194–213. https://doi.org/10.7721/chilyoutenvi.22.2.0194

Platt, L., & Rybarczyk, G. (2021). Skateboarder and scooter-rider perceptions of the urban environment: A qualitative analysis of user-generated content. *Urban Geography, 42*(10), 1525–1551.

Plowman, L., & Stevenson, O. (2012). Using mobile phone diaries to explore children's everyday lives. *Childhood, 19*(4), 539–553.

Plowman, P. J. (2010). The diary project: Revealing the gendered organisation. *Qualitative Research in Organizations and Management: An International Journal, 5*(1), 28–46.

Progoff, I. (1992). *At a journal workshop*. Jeremy P. Tarcher, Inc.

Quan-Haase, A., & Sloan, L. (2022). *The SAGE handbook of social media research methods* (2nd ed.). Sage.

Rabinovich, L. (2023). Using solicited audio-recorded diaries to explore the financial lives of low-income women in Kenya during COVID-19: Perspectives, challenges, and lessons. *Oxford Development Studies, 51*(3), 280–290.

Radcliffe, L. (2018). Capturing the complexity of daily workplace experiences using qualitative diaries. In C. A. L. Cunliffe & G. Grandy (Eds.), *The Sage handbook of qualitative business and management research methods* (pp. 188–204). Sage. https://doi.org/10.4135/9781526430236.n12

Radcliffe, L., Cassell, C., & Malik, F. (2022). Providing, performing and protecting: The importance of work identities in negotiating conflicting work–family ideals as a single mother. *British Journal of Management, 33*(2), 890–905.

Radcliffe, L., Cassell, C., & Spencer, L. (2023). Work-family habits? Exploring the persistence of traditional work-family decision making in dual-earner couples. *Journal of Vocational Behavior, 145*, 103914. https://doi.org/10.1016/j.jvb.2023.103914

Radcliffe, L., & Spencer, L. (2018). Diary of an app! Will using mobile devices in qualitative research become the norm? *Impact of Social Sciences Blog*.

Radcliffe, L. S. (2013). Qualitative diaries: Uncovering the complexities of work-life decision-making. *Qualitative Research in Organizations and Management: An International Journal, 8*(2), 163–180. https://doi.org/10.1108/QROM-04-2012-1058

Radcliffe, L. S., & Cassell, C. (2014). Resolving couples' work–family conflicts: The complexity of decision making and the introduction of a new framework. *Human Relations, 67*(7), 793–819.

Radcliffe, L. S., & Cassell, C. (2015). Flexible working, work–family conflict, and maternal gatekeeping: The daily experiences of dual-earner couples. *Journal of Occupational and Organizational Psychology, 88*(4), 835–855.

Rauch, M., & Ansari, S. (2022a). Diaries as a methodological innovation for studying grand challenges. In A. A. Gümüsay, E. Marti, H. Trittin-Ulbrich, & C. Wickert (Eds.), *Organizing for societal grand challenges* (pp. 205–220). Emerald Publishing Limited.

Rauch, M., & Ansari, S. (2022b). Waging war from remote cubicles: How workers cope with technologies that disrupt the meaning and morality of their work. *Organization Science, 33*(1), 83–104. https://doi.org/10.1287/orsc.2021.1555

Ray, J. L., & Smith, A. D. (2012). Using photographs to research organizations: Evidence, considerations, and application in a field study. *Organizational Research Methods, 15*(2), 288–315.

Riessman, C. K. (2008). *Narrative methods for the human sciences*. Sage.

Ritwick, S., & Koljonen, T. (2023, July). *Enter the spiral: The adverse consequences of professional and lay expertise for clients' lived experiences*. Paper presented at the 39th EGOS Colloquium, Cagliari.

Robards, B., & Lincoln, S. (2017). Uncovering longitudinal life narratives: Scrolling back on Facebook. *Qualitative Research, 17*(6), 715–730. https://doi.org/10.1177/1468794117700707

Roberts, J. (2011). Video diaries: A tool to investigate sustainability-related learning in threshold spaces. *Environmental Education Research, 17*(5), 675–688.

Robinson, M. D., & Clore, G. L. (2002). Episodic and semantic knowledge in emotional self-report: Evidence for two judgment processes. *Journal of Personality and Social Psychology, 83*(1), 198.

Robinson, O. C. (2023). Probing in qualitative research interviews: Theory and practice. *Qualitative Research in Psychology, 20*(3), 382–397.

Rodd, H., Hall, M., Deery, C., Gilchrist, F., Gibson, B. J., & Marshman, Z. (2014). 'I felt weird and wobbly.' Child-reported impacts associated with a dental general anaesthetic. *British Dental Journal, 216*(8), E17. https://doi.org/10.1038/sj.bdj.2014.333

Rodgers, H., & Lloyd-Evans, E. C. (2021). Intimate snapshots: TikTok, algorithm, and the recreation of identity. *Anthways*, *1*(1). https://doi.org/10.1177/16094069231221374

Rohn, K. C., Arnold, K. D., & Martini, L. (2022). The 360 diary method: A new approach to student assessment and intervention. *About Campus*, *27*(5), 10–18. https://doi.org/10.1177/10864822221138255

Rosales, A., & Fernández-Ardèvol, M. (2019). Smartphone usage diversity among older people. In S. Sayago (Ed.), *Perspectives on human-computer interaction research with older people* (pp. 51–66). Springer.

Rose, G. (2012). The question of method: Practice, reflexivity and critique in visual culture studies. In I. Heywood & B. Sandywell (Eds.), *The handbook of visual culture* (pp. 542–558). Berg.

Rose, G. (2007). *Visual methodologies* (2nd ed.). Sage.

Rose, G. (2016). *Visual methodologies: An introduction to researching with visual materials*. Sage.

Rose, G. (2023). *Visual methodologies: An introduction to researching with visual materials* (5th ed.). Sage.

Rose, H. (2020). Diaries and journals: Collecting insider perspectives in second language research. In J. McKinley & H. Rose (Eds.), *Routledge handbook of research methods in applied linguistics* (pp. 348–356). Routledge.

Rudrum, S., Casey, R., Frank, L., Brickner, R. K., MacKenzie, S., Carlson, J., & Rondinelli, E. (2022). Qualitative research studies online: Using prompted weekly journal entries during the COVID-19 pandemic. *International Journal of Qualitative Methods*, *21*, 16094069221093138.

Ryan, E. B. (2006). Finding a new voice: Writing through health adversity. *Journal of Language and Social Psychology*, *25*(4), 423–436.

Ryan, E. B., Bannister, K. A., & Anas, A. P. (2009). The dementia narrative: Writing to reclaim social identity. *Journal of Aging Studies*, *23*(3), 145–157.

Sargeant, S., & Gross, H. (2011). Young people learning to live with inflammatory bowel disease: Working with an "unclosed" diary. *Qualitative Health Research*, *21*(10), 1360–1370.

Saunders, M. N. (2012). Choosing research participants. In G. Symon & C. Cassell (Eds.), *Qualitative organizational research: Core methods and current challenges* (pp. 35–52). SAGE Publications, Inc.

Savage, M. (2007). Changing social class identities in post-war Britain: Perspectives from mass-observation. *Sociological Research Online*, *12*(3), 14–26.

Schwarz, N. (1999). Self-reports: How the questions shape the answers. *American Psychologist*, *54*(2), 93. https://doi.org/10.1037/0003-066X.54.2.93

Schwarz, N., & Oyserman, D. (2001). Asking questions about behavior: Cognition, communication, and questionnaire construction. *The American Journal of Evaluation*, *22*(2), 127–160.

Scollon, R., & Scollon, S. W. (2014). *Nexus analysis: Discourse and the emerging internet*. Routledge.

Scott, S., McGowan, V. J., & Visram, S. (2021). 'I'm gonna tell you about how Mrs Rona Has affected me'. Exploring young people's experiences of the COVID-19 pandemic in North East England: A qualitative diary-based study. *International Journal of Environmental Research and Public Health*, *18*(7), 3837.

Seide, K., Casanova, F. O., Ramirez, E., McKenna, M., Cepeda, A., & Nowotny, K. M. (2023). Piloting a flexible solicited diary study with marginalized Latina women during the COVID-19 pandemic. *International Journal of Qualitative Methods*, *22*, 16094069231183119. https://doi.org/10.1177/16094069231183119

Sherliker, L., & Steptoe, A. (2000). Coping with new treatments for cancer: A feasibility study of daily diary measures. *Patient Education and Counselling*, *40*(1), 11–19.

Shortt, H. L., & Warren, S. K. (2019). Grounded visual pattern analysis: Photographs in organizational field studies. *Organizational Research Methods*, *22*(2), 539–563. https://doi.org/10.1177/1094428117742495

Sixsmith, A., Horst, B. R., Simeonov, D., & Mihailidis, A. (2022). Older people's use of digital technology during the COVID-19 pandemic. *Bulletin of Science, Technology & Society*, *42*(1–2), 19–24. https://doi.org/10.1177/02704676221094731

Skolnick, J. H. (1967). *Justice without trial: Law enforcement in dramatic society*. John Wiley.

Slutskaya, N., Simpson, A., & Hughes, J. (2012). Lessons from photo-elicitation: Encouraging working men to speak. *Qualitative Research in Organizations and Management: An International Journal*, *7*(1), 16–33.

Smith, J. (2011). Evaluating the contribution of interpretative phenomenological analysis. *Health Psychology Review*, *5*(1), 9–27. https://doi.org/10.1080/17437199.2010.510659

Smith, J., Flowers, P., & Larkin, M. (2009). *Interpretive phenomenological analysis: theory, method and research*. Sage.

Smith, M. B., Laurie, N., Hopkins, P., & Olson, E. (2013). International volunteering, faith and subjectivity: Negotiating cosmopolitanism, citizenship and development. *Geoforum*, *45*, 126–135.

Smyth, J. M., & Heron, K. E. (2013). Ecological momentary assessment (EMA) in family research. In S. M. McHale, P. Amato, & A. Booth (Eds.), *Emerging methods in family research* (pp. 145–161). Springer International Publishing.

Söderström, J. (2020). Life diagrams: A methodological and analytical tool for accessing life histories. *Qualitative Research*, *20*(1), 3–21.

Sonck, N., & Fernee, H. (2013). *Using smartphones in survey research: A multifunctional tool*. The Netherlands Institute for Social Research.

Soronen, A., & Koivunen, A. (2022). Platformed intimacies: Professional belonging on social media. *European Journal of Cultural Studies*, *25*(5), 1344–1360.

Spencer, L. (2019). *The emergence and evolution of mistreatment in organisations: A sensemaking and gendered perspective* (Doctoral dissertation, University of Liverpool).

Spencer, L., Anderson, L., & Ellwood, P. (2022). Interweaving scholarship and practice: A pathway to scholarly impact. *Academy of Management Learning & Education, 21*(3), 422–448. https://doi.org/10.5465/amle.2021.0266

Spencer, L., Radcliffe, L., Spence, R., & King, N. (2021). Thematic trajectory analysis: A temporal method for analysing dynamic qualitative data. *Journal of Occupational and Organizational Psychology, 94*(3), 531–567. https://doi.org/10.1111/joop.12359

Spencer, S. (2011). *Visual research methods in the social sciences*. Routledge.

Stone, A. A., Shiffman, S., Schwartz, J. E., Broderick, J. E., & Hufford, M. R. (2002). Patient non-compliance with paper diaries. *BMJ, 324*(7347), 1193–1194.

Stowell, A. F., & Warren, S. (2018). The institutionalization of suffering: Embodied inhabitation and the maintenance of health and safety in e-waste recycling. *Organization Studies, 39*(5–6), 785–809.

Strangleman, T. (2004). Ways of (not) seeing work: The visual as a blind spot in WES? *Work, Employment and Society, 18*(1), 179–192.

Strauss, A., & Corbin, J. (1998). *Basics of qualitative research: Techniques and procedures for developing grounded theory*. Sage.

Sudbury-Riley, L. (2014). Unwrapping senior consumers' packaging experiences. *Marketing Intelligence & Planning, 32*(6), 666–686.

Suddaby, R. (2006). From the editors: What grounded theory is not. *Academy of Management Journal, 49*(4), 633–642. https://doi.org/10.5465/amj.2006.22083020

Suedfeld, P., & Pennebaker, J. W. (1997). Health outcomes and cognitive aspects of recalled negative life events. *Psychosomatic Medicine, 59*(2), 172–177.

Symon, G. (2004). Qualitative research diaries. In C. Cassell & G. Symon (Eds.), *Essential guide to qualitative methods in organizational research* (pp. 98–113). Sage. https://doi.org/10.4135/9781446280119

Symon, G., & Whiting, R. (2019). The sociomaterial negotiation of social entrepreneurs' meaningful work. *Journal of Management Studies, 56*(3), 655–684.

Tai, R. H., Bentley, L. R., Xia, X., Sitt, J. M., Fankhauser, S. C., Chicas-Mosier, A. M., & Monteith, B. G. (2024). An examination of the use of large language models to aid analysis of textual data. *International Journal of Qualitative Methods, 23*, 1–14. https://doi.org/10.1177/16094069241231168

Takhar, A., & Chitakunye, P. (2012). Rich descriptions: Evoking informant self-reflexivity in marketing and consumer research. *Journal of Marketing Management, 28*(7–8), 912–935.

Taylor, A. M. (2015). *"It's a relief to talk...": Mothers' experiences of breastfeeding recorded in video diaries* (Doctoral dissertation, Bournemouth University).

Taylor, A. M., van Teijlingen, E., Ryan, K. M., & Alexander, J. (2019). 'Scrutinised, judged and sabotaged': A qualitative video diary study of first-time breastfeeding mothers. *Midwifery, 75*, 16–23.

Thille, P., Chartrand, L., & Brown, C. (2022). Diary-interview studies: Longitudinal, flexible qualitative research design. *Family Practice, 39*(5), 996–999.

Thomas, F. (2006). Stigma, fatigue and social breakdown: exploring the impacts of HIV/AIDS on patient and carer well-being in the Caprivi Region, Namibia. *Social Science & Medicine, 63*(12), 3174–3187.

Thomas, F. (2007). Eliciting emotions in HIV/AIDS research: A diary-based approach. *Area, 39*(1), 74–82.

Thompson, N. (2023). Vygotskian scaffolding techniques as motivational pedagogy for gifted mathematicians in further education: A diary-interview study. *Journal of Further and Higher Education, 47*(4), 492–512.

Toraldo, M. L., Islam, G., & Mangia, G. (2018). Modes of knowing: Video research and the problem of elusive knowledges. *Organizational Research Methods, 21*(2), 438–465.

Travers, C. (2011). Unveiling a reflective diary methodology for exploring the lived experiences of stress and coping. *Journal of Vocational Behavior, 79*(1), 204–216.

Tuval-Mashiach, R. (2017). Raising the curtain: The importance of transparency in qualitative research. *Qualitative Psychology, 4*(2), 126. https://doi.org/10.1037/qup0000062

Tversky, B. (1974). Eye fixations in prediction of recognition and recall. *Memory and Cognition, 2*, 275–278.

Välimäki, T., Vehviläinen-Julkunen, K., & Pietilä, A-M. (2007). Diaries as research data in a study on family caregivers of people with Alzheimer's disease: Methodological issues. *Journal of Advanced Nursing, 59*(1), 68–76.

van Eerde, W., Holman, D., & Totterdell, P. (2005). Special section: Diary studies in work psychology. *Journal of Occupational and Organizational Psychology, 78*(2), 151–154.

Vantilborgh, T., Hofmans, J., & Judge, T. A. (2018). The time has come to study dynamics at work. *Journal of Organizational Behavior, 39*(9), 1045–1049.

Vettini, A., & Bartlett, R. (2022). Using video diaries in social science research: Reflections on past, current, and future ethical trends. In G. Punziano & A. Delli (Eds.), *Handbook of research on advanced research methodologies for a digital society* (pp. 442–460). IGI Global.

Vidaillet, B. (2007). Lacanian theory's contribution to the study of workplace envy. *Human Relations, 60*(11), 1669–1700.

Vince, R., & Warren, S. (2012). Participatory visual methods. In C. Cassell & G. Symon (Eds.), *Qualitative organizational research: Core methods and current challenges* (pp. 275–295). Sage.

Vincett, J. (2018). Researcher self-care in organizational ethnography: Lessons from overcoming compassion fatigue. *Journal of Organizational Ethnography*, 7(1), 44–58.

Vinjamuri, M., Warde, B., & Kolb, P. (2017). The reflective diary: An experiential tool for enhancing social work students' research learning. *Social Work Education*, 36(8), 933–945.

Walker, R., & Weidel, J. (1985). Using photographs in a discipline of words. In R. G. Burgess (Ed.), *Field methods in the study of education* (pp. 191–216). The Falmer Press.

Wallin, P., & Adawi, T. (2018). The reflective diary as a method for the formative assessment of self-regulated learning. *European Journal of Engineering Education*, 43(4), 507–521.

Warren, S. (2002). 'Show me how it feels to work here': Using photography to research organizational aesthetics. *Theory and Politics in Organizations*, 2, 224–245.

Warren, S. (2008). Empirical challenges in organizational aesthetics research: Towards a sensual methodology. *Organization Studies*, 29(4), 559–580.

Warren, S. (2009). Visual methods in organizational research. In D. Buchanan & A. Bryman (Eds.), *The Sage handbook of organizational research methods* (pp. 567–582). Sage.

Wechtler, H. (2018). "Life if elsewhere": A diary study of female self-initiated expatriates' motivations to work abroad. *Career Development International*, 23(3), 291–311. https://doi.org/10.1108/CDI-06-2017-0103

Welford, J., Sandhu, J., Collinson, B., & Blatchford, S. (2022). Collecting qualitative data using a smartphone app: Learning from research involving people with experience of multiple disadvantage. *Methodological Innovations*, 15(3), 193–206. https://doi.org/10.1177/20597991221114570

Weller, S., Davidson, E., Edwards, R., & Jamieson, L. (2023). *Big qual: A guide to breadth-and-depth analysis*. Palgrave Macmillan.

White, M. L. (2012). Turning the camera on yourself: Digital video journals in educational research. In S. Delamont (Ed.), *Handbook of qualitative research in education* (pp. 325–341). Edward Elgar Publishing.

Whiting, R., & Pritchard, K. (2020). *Collecting qualitative data using digital methods*. Sage.

Whiting, R., Symon, G., Roby, H., & Chamakiotis, P. (2018). Who's behind the lens? A reflexive analysis of roles in participatory video research. *Organizational Research Methods*, 21(2), 316–340.

Wiggins, S., Moore-Millar, K., & Thomson, A. (2014). Can you pull it off? Appearance modifying behaviours adopted by wig users with alopecia in social interactions. *Body Image*, 11(2), 156–166.

Wilkinson, C., Carter, B., Bray, L., & Keating, P. (2020). The absent-present researcher: Data analysis of pre-recorded parent-driven campaign videos. *Children's Geographies*, 18(2), 162–175.

Wilkinson, S. (2016). Hold the phone! Culturally credible research 'with' young people. *Children's Geographies*, *14*(2), 232–238. https://doi.org/10.1080/17597269.2015.1134761

Williamson, I., Leeming, D., Lyttle, S., & Johnson, S. (2012). 'It should be the most natural thing in the world': Exploring first-time mothers' breastfeeding difficulties in the UK using audio-diaries and interviews. *Maternal & Child Nutrition*, *8*(4), 434–447.

Williamson, I., Leeming, D., Lyttle, S., & Johnson, S. (2015). Evaluating the audio-diary method in qualitative research. *Qualitative Research Journal*, *15*(1), 20–34.

Willig, C. (2013). *Introducing qualitative research in psychology*. McGraw-Hill Education (UK).

Willig, C., & Rogers, W. S. (Eds.). (2017). *The SAGE handbook of qualitative research in psychology*. Sage.

Wiseman, V., Conteh, L., & Matovu, F. (2005). Using diaries to collect data in resource-poor settings: Questions on design and implementation. *Health Policy and Planning*, *20*(6), 394–404.

World Bank Group. (2016). *World development report 2016: Digital dividends*. World Bank Publications.

Worth, N. (2009). Making use of audio diaries in research with young people: Examining narrative, participation and audience. *Sociological Research Online*, *14*(4), 77–87.

Yin, R. K. (2018). *Case study research and applications*. Sage.

Zhao, Y. (2024). TikTok and researcher positionality: Considering the methodological and ethical implications of an experimental digital ethnography. *International Journal of Qualitative Methods*, *23*, 16094069231221374. https://doi.org/10.1177/16094069231221374

Zimmerman, D. H., & Wieder, D. L. (1977). The diary: Diary-interview method. *Urban Life*, *5*(4), 479–498. https://doi.org/10.1177/089124167700500406

Zundel, M., MacIntosh, R., & Mackay, D. (2018). The utility of video diaries for organizational research. *Organizational Research Methods*, *21*(2), 386–411.

INDEX

A

ability, 9–10, 30, 35, 73, 78, 105–6, 114, 129–31, 139, 216–17, 220
access, 9, 55, 70, 73, 77, 99, 102, 104–6, 109, 130, 132–34, 136, 153
accounts, 159, 163, 165, 169, 172, 174, 178, 180, 186, 191–92, 194, 200
participant's interview, 174
across, 12, 162, 185, 192, 208–9, 211, 215–16
activities, 10, 32–33, 56, 88, 119, 122, 174, 187–89, 221
actor network theory (ANT), 87
actors, 3–4, 87, 169–70
additional challenges for participants, 113
additional time for analysis, 191
advancements, technological, 66, 218, 220
agreement, data process, 138
Alaszewski, 20, 36, 68–69
alignment, research question-analysis, 162, 182
Analysing Dynamic Qualitative Data, 195, 197, 199, 203
analysis, 24, 96, 114, 155–56, 158–61, 163–69, 171–73, 175–83, 188, 190–91, 193, 196, 205–6, 219, 221
discourse, 162, 166, 195
first-pass, 39
narrative, 167, 169–70, 192
nexus, 175
analysis approaches, 164, 166, 169, 178, 180, 185, 216
qualitative, 171, 196
traditional, 172, 180, 216
analysis methods, 156, 162, 179–80, 182, 186, 191, 210, 219
traditional qualitative, 156, 163, 172, 185, 216
analysis of QDM data, 191
analysis of qualitative diary data, 155
analysis processes, 15, 169, 171, 176, 201, 208, 219
analysis to textual data, 173
analytical approaches, 96, 155, 161–64, 167, 171–72, 178, 205
traditional, 173, 216
analytical approaches for QDM data, 167
Analyzing Data, 15, 90, 155–83
anonymity, 38, 42, 45, 85, 91, 93, 102, 110–11, 118–20, 123, 152
anonymity and privacy, 85, 91, 111
answer, 7, 10, 20, 25–26, 33, 35, 38, 53–54, 85–86, 105–6, 204, 208, 214–15
ANT (actor network theory), 87
anticipation, 30, 199, 201–3
anticipation of next day, 199, 202–3
app-based diaries, 1, 29, 94, 127–28, 130–31, 133–38, 140–41, 145, 147, 149–50, 152–53
app diaries, 45, 58, 128–32, 138, 140, 150, 214
app diaries in Chapter, 58
Approach & Rationale, 80–81
approaches, 20, 22–24, 32–36, 51–53, 59–60, 83, 106–7, 120–21, 161–65, 167–68, 171–72, 176, 178, 180–83, 185–88, 191–92, 205–6, 208–9, 215–17
proceduralized, 169, 171, 176

261

apps, 78, 127–54, 218–19
　developing, 140, 150
　employing, 128, 218
　platform-based, 129, 138, 141
　smartphone, 127, 154
apps for data collection, 218
apps for diary data collection, 128
apps in QDM research, 218
artifacts, 94, 114
attention to video diaries, 113
audio, 69, 74, 79, 121, 128–29, 135, 143, 147, 149, 151, 158
audio and video diaries capitalizing, 107
audio and video diaries capitalizing on young people's familiarity, 107
audio data, 102, 181
audio diaries, 51–52, 66–71, 74–78, 81, 86–88, 94, 107–8, 113, 166
audio diaries in research, 81
audio diaries in work psychology, 71, 81
Audio Diaries in Work Psychology, 72
audio diaries to conduct research, 67
audio diary research, 75–76
audio recorders, 61, 67–68, 73
audio recording devices, 67, 79
authors, 41, 133, 146, 166, 168–70, 174–75, 177
availability of private spaces for participants to record, 112

B
balance, 25, 38, 41, 95, 97–98, 145, 177, 190
　work-life, 89
Bates, 103, 106, 117, 119–22, 125
benefits, 7, 16–17, 19, 29–30, 42–43, 51–53, 55, 66–67, 75–76, 89, 104–5, 109, 122–23, 127–30, 150–51, 172–73, 185–86, 209–11
　across, 185–86, 191, 198, 205–6
　data-focused, 212
　ethical, 78
　important, 12, 36–37, 39, 53, 85, 104, 128
　often-cited, 110
　significant, 132, 138, 140, 211
benefits for participants, 70

benefits of audio diaries, 75
benefits of participant reflexivity, 43
benefits of photo diaries, 89, 94
benefits of written diaries, 55
benefits of written diaries in terms, 55
benefits of written diaries in terms of allowing time, 55
bespoke apps, 129, 133, 135, 137–38, 140–41, 143, 145, 150–51
bespoke apps report, developed, 132, 137
Braun, 165–67, 183–84
Braun & Clarke, 161–62, 164, 166–67, 193

C
cameras, 92, 103, 107, 112–13, 116, 120–22, 131
capabilities, 132, 135, 146, 150–51, 166
capturing video diaries, 108
cases, 21–23, 35, 39, 56–58, 60, 68, 71, 73, 76–77, 112, 115, 204, 206
Case Study, 60, 65, 70, 89, 93, 97, 101, 117–18, 122
Cassell, 15, 18, 21, 41, 43–44, 47, 49, 69–72, 78, 88–92, 95–96, 98, 100–102, 109–10, 213
Categorical theme, 201, 203–4
categories of apps, 129, 141
challenges, 4–5, 8, 13–14, 19–22, 27–28, 51, 53, 56–59, 73, 83, 85–86, 104, 109–10, 112, 127–30, 150–51, 155, 210–12
challenges of traditional ethnographic research, 14
challenges of traditional ethnographic research and participant observation, 14
chance, 26, 28, 116, 176
change, 10, 12, 16–17, 26, 30, 33, 162–63, 170, 177, 199–201, 208, 211, 215
Chapter
　preceding, 127–28, 155, 214
　subsequent, 25, 52
checklists, 16–17, 152, 180

children, 4, 8, 63, 87, 91, 98, 107-8, 116, 119, 168, 175, 190
choice, methodological, 17, 85, 180
clarity, 31, 97, 101-2, 195
Clarke, 165-67, 183-84
clear data management process, 214
code data, 196, 204
collection, in-depth analysis post-data, 159
Colom, 128-34, 140
Colón Cabrera, 90, 165-66
columns, 157, 196
combination, 23-24, 32, 34, 162, 165-67, 173, 178, 182, 191, 196, 208, 215
company logos, 91-92, 99
comparative analysis, 188-90, 206
comparison of pen-and-paper diaries, 135
comparison of pen-and-paper diaries and app-based diaries, 135
completing private diaries, 45, 74
completion, retrospective, 53, 56-57, 68, 131
completion of video diaries, 110
complexities of diary data, 186
complexity of diary data, 173
complex relationship, 98
compliant, 138-39, 147, 151, 154
Concluding Chapter, 213, 215, 217, 219, 221
conducting photo diaries in Chapter, 142
confidence, 107-8, 136-37, 221
confidentiality, 44-45, 48, 116, 119, 138, 213
confidentiality of participant data, 45
conflict, 10, 31, 60-61, 97-98, 100, 187-90, 206
conjunction, 7, 23, 35-36, 39, 163, 205
consent forms, 45, 119-20, 123, 139, 146, 152, 158
Constructivist/ relativist, 194
consult Chapters, 128, 142
contact participants, 33, 140, 213
content, 39, 42, 92, 99, 146, 151, 163, 170-71, 176-77, 195, 198

context, 2-3, 5, 13-15, 17, 42, 45-46, 76, 81, 83, 95-96, 112-13, 119, 160-61, 166, 194-95
context of app-based diaries, 136-37
context of health research and audio diaries, 166
context of work, 188, 192
control, 12, 14-15, 55, 75, 90, 92, 94, 96, 108, 110, 120
convenience, 22-23, 66-67, 78, 130-31
cost of developing apps, 140
cost of developing apps for research, 140
costs, 129, 133-34, 140-41, 145, 150, 152-53, 219
   additional, 73, 150-51
costs to participants in terms of devices, 150
couples, 9, 21-22, 40, 61-62, 74, 89, 187, 189-90, 206
Couples' Decision-Making, 60
Couples' Decision-Making in Instances of Work, 60
creation, 65, 91, 196, 198, 200
Crozier, 69-72, 78, 81
customization, 140, 149

D

daily experiences of work, 89, 99, 209
data, 24-28, 40-46, 58-60, 111-13, 119-22, 127-30, 142-43, 151-53, 155-56, 158-60, 162-69, 173-75, 178-83, 187-89, 191-94, 200-202, 204-6, 208-10, 213-14, 218-20
data analysis, 59, 104
   delay, 132
   enhanced, 219
   subsequent, 159
   usual text-based, 114
data analysis phase, 123
data analysis process, 118
data and analysis, 167
data collection, 7, 14-15, 27-29, 31, 35-38, 41, 45, 47-48, 107, 110, 114, 117, 156-57, 159-60, 218
   multimodal, 129-30, 218, 221
   purposes of, 51, 55

data collection methods, 5, 12, 155, 158, 162–63
  appropriate, 7
  popular, 7
data collection process, 12, 27, 38, 88, 108
data collection tools, 5, 172
data costs, 133
data costs for participants, 133
data files, 160, 181
data for analysis, 96, 122, 160, 181
data logs, 114, 123
data loss, 25, 27, 56, 61, 73, 77, 110, 112, 121, 132, 137, 157, 159
data management, 45, 155–56, 180, 184
data management processes, 156
data organization approach, 160
data privacy, 127, 154
data repository, 160, 181
  participant's, 160
data storage, 74, 112, 123, 152, 219
data storage approach, consistent, 157
data storage for participants, 74
data storage process, 111
data to answer, 25–26
data types, 159
day, 30, 33–34, 57, 60, 62, 71, 74, 142–43, 190, 192, 197–99, 201–2, 206, 209–10
  working, 32, 45, 116
day of entry, 65, 197–98, 201, 203, 207
decision-making, 9, 11, 37, 68, 121, 171, 180, 188–89, 209–10
decision-making factors, 188–89
decision-making processes, 2, 15, 32, 34, 56, 60–62, 95, 143, 187, 189, 192
Decision-Making Processes of Dual-Earner Couples in Incidents, 62–63
Decision Prompts, 181–83
decisions, 8, 11–13, 15, 31–32, 34, 60–63, 74, 76, 96, 99, 134–35, 141–42, 180, 187–90, 192
  methodological, 25, 180
  work-based, 209
decisions impact, 209
decisions in incidents, 189

decisions in incidents of work, 189
design, 3, 5, 23, 25, 29, 33–34, 61, 98–99, 101, 113–15, 118, 140–41, 145–47, 156–57, 215–17
  event-based, 57–58, 60, 68, 97
  mixed, 34, 215
  mixed-contingent, 215
design choices, 47, 152–53
design considerations, 29, 59, 114, 128, 217
design decisions, 215
design diaries, 56
designing, 19, 22, 42, 48, 58–59, 65, 78, 96, 112, 206, 213–14
designing app-based diaries, 147, 149
designing app diaries, 134, 141
designing pen-and-paper diaries, 65
Designing QDMs, 19–49
design stage, 19, 161
detail in Chapter, 45, 123, 187
developers, 139, 147, 149–51
devices, 55, 68, 73, 77–79, 102–3, 121, 130–33, 137, 139–40, 143, 150–52
diagrams, 188–89, 201
diaries, 1–4, 14–16, 24–33, 35–39, 41–42, 44–46, 48–49, 55–59, 61–62, 68–69, 73, 127–53, 157–63, 165–66, 168–70, 178–79, 186–88, 196, 205–6, 212–18
  complete, 42, 137, 198
  completing, 57, 156
  daily, 2, 22, 26, 187
  designing, 142
  employing, 31, 33, 215
  employing audio, 66, 70, 74–75
  event-contingent, 206, 209
  instant messaging, 6
  patient, 169–70
  photo-based, 34, 96
  photographic, 88
  qualitative research, 16
  semi-structured, 27, 35
  text-based, 1, 83, 88, 149, 163
  total, 166
  traditional, 80–81
  unsolicited, 3, 168
  visual, 164, 173, 176–77

Index **265**

diaries and diary data, 218
diaries by viewing entries, 166
diaries entries, 57
diaries for family budget research, 217
diarist, 68, 105, 114, 170, 177
diary completion, 26, 31, 37–38, 42, 45, 57–58, 61, 67, 91, 93, 99, 117, 121–23
diary content, 37, 42, 59, 61, 205
diary data, 39, 157–58, 162–63, 165, 168–73, 178, 180–81, 185–86, 188–90, 192, 196, 208, 216, 218, 220
  analyzing, 59, 166
diary data collection, 39, 41, 128, 156
diary data for analysis, 196
diary day, 159, 181
diary designs, 29–30, 32–33, 35, 59–60, 97, 115, 122, 124, 134, 206, 213–14
diary design worksheets, 19, 221–22
diary entries, 29, 31–39, 46, 57–58, 60–61, 65, 67, 70, 73, 77–78, 156, 159, 198, 206, 209
diary information sheets, 71, 75–76, 79, 99, 115, 123, 152
diary instruction sheet, 28–29, 60, 65, 101–2, 118
diary-interview approach, 4, 36, 39
diary-interview method, 18, 36, 41, 52, 59, 61, 117, 155, 189, 209
diary mediums, 28, 35, 45, 52, 54, 68
diary methods, 1, 49, 51, 83, 217
  app-based, 127
diary methods for particular research projects, 51
diary pages, 60, 65
diary participants, 20, 24, 26, 38
diary process, 47
Digital Brain Switch Project, 105, 117
discourses, 175, 195
dual-earner couples, 21, 60–63, 143, 187
Dual-Earner Couples in Incidents of Work-Family Conflict, 60, 62–63
dynamic participant tracking table, 156

E
ease, 55, 67–68, 70, 79, 87–88, 99, 147, 153, 218
ease for participants, 70
ease for participants and researcher, 70
ease for participants and researcher to access, 70
EDA, 186–89, 191–93, 198, 205, 208–10, 216
emergence, 137–38, 169, 214
emotions, 2, 8–11, 30–31, 43–44, 66, 74, 80, 106–7, 147, 210–11, 213
entries, 24–28, 30–31, 34–35, 57–58, 65, 112, 122, 129–32, 134–37, 142–43, 145, 157–60, 196–98, 201–3, 206–7
  failed, 112
  participant diary, 188, 198
  video, 111, 113, 135
environments, 45, 56, 86–87, 105
equipment, 73, 102, 116–17, 123, 131
ethical benefits for participants, 78
ethics, institutional research, 151
ethnographic approaches, 4, 13, 87, 217
evaluative themes, 202–5
event chains, 187–88
event-contingent designs, 26, 31, 34, 57, 60, 206, 215
Event-Contingent Diary Data, 207
Event-Contingent Diary Designs, 31, 37
event diagrams, 187–91, 198, 208
events, 7–12, 24, 31–33, 40, 57, 59–61, 68, 78, 97, 122, 172, 186–91, 199, 202, 215
  particular, 31, 36–37, 57, 60, 97, 191
  triggering, 60
events/experiences/thoughts/emotions, 7, 162–63, 182, 214
exercise, 80, 123–24, 209
existing apps, 127, 129, 138, 140–41, 146, 149–51, 153
existing apps for qualitative research purposes, 127
experience for participants, 47
experience for participants and researchers, 47
expressions, bodily, 103, 106

F

familiarity of apps, 133
familiarity of apps in recruiting participants, 133
family, 4, 6, 9-10, 45, 61-63, 142-43, 169-70, 206
family conflict diary data, 206
family conflicts, 10-11, 32, 37, 60-61, 147, 187-89, 192
family decisions, 9
feelings, 2, 5, 7, 11, 14, 30-35, 38, 43, 54, 75-76, 106
FFR and bespoke apps, 129, 143
FFR Apps, 136, 140-41, 150-51
field, 4, 88-90, 221-22
Figure, 4, 100, 143-44, 147-48, 157-58, 181, 187-90, 196-204, 206-7
findings, 22, 27, 166, 168-69, 173-75, 177, 179, 184, 186, 193, 204, 208
first-pass analysis of diary data, 39
Fit-for-research, 129, 141
flexibility, 10-11, 29-30, 34, 43, 78-79, 122, 129-30, 135, 165-67, 209, 215
  providing participants, 145
focus, 3-4, 23-24, 68-69, 75-76, 84, 93-94, 101-2, 111, 114-15, 128, 162-63, 169-71, 177, 185-88, 201-2
  across, 162-63, 208
focus groups, 3, 5, 25, 36, 212
focus on photo and video diaries, 84
Frąckowiak, 129, 131-32, 135, 141
frequency, 26, 29, 174, 200

G

GAI (generative artificial intelligence), 219
GAI/LLMs, 219
Garcia, 128-29, 131-33, 136-37, 140-41, 218
GDPR (General Data Protection Regulation), 138, 147
General Data Protection Regulation (GDPR), 138, 147
generative artificial intelligence (GAI), 219

genres, 175-76
geolocation data, 128, 149
grand challenges, 5, 222
grounded theory. See GT
groups, 3, 20, 23, 25-26, 40, 66, 91, 146, 176, 200
GT (grounded theory), 162, 167-69, 171-72, 182-83
guidance, 92-93, 97, 101-3, 117, 119-20, 127, 138, 140, 142, 149, 154-57, 160, 173-76
Guiding, 193-95
GVPA, 176-78

H

Hannah's research, 26, 32, 34
health conditions, long-term, 19, 23, 26, 32, 209
health research, 166
health research and audio diaries, 166
home, 4, 11, 16, 56, 63-64, 72, 74, 115-16, 119, 124, 177-78, 190, 207
hours, 57, 64, 139, 167, 170, 184
household, 45, 61, 74
house on time for work, 32
Hyers, 20-21, 26

I

identities, 38, 55, 105, 107, 116
Iedema, 108-9
Iivari, 103, 107, 175-76, 178-79
images, 87, 89-91, 94-96, 101, 110-11, 135, 174, 176-77
impact, 2, 8, 10-12, 26, 34, 63, 110, 166, 174, 197, 199
Impact of interaction, 199
Impact of interactions/event, 199
Impact on work, 199
Implications for Use of TTA, 193-95
incidents, 31, 37, 57, 60, 62-63, 74, 188-89
individuals, 8, 11, 20-21, 23, 26, 34, 41, 106-7, 124, 187, 189, 192, 209
information, participant-facing, 123, 152

Index 267

initial interviews, 37–38, 77, 102, 117, 136, 140, 189
instance, 2–5, 8–10, 14–15, 21–22, 24–26, 32–34, 38, 40–41, 43, 45–46, 54, 56–57, 59–60, 69–70, 73–75, 77–79, 94–95, 105–7, 111, 118–22
Instances of Work, 60
instructions, 73, 76, 79, 91, 97, 99–100, 114, 119, 121, 123, 130
integrating interview and diary data, 163
intensive investment of participants, 46
intensive investment of participants in QDM research, 46
interaction order, 175
interactions, 3, 10, 30, 98, 107, 116, 161, 170, 195, 197, 199
interactions/event, 199
interest, 18, 21, 24, 30, 33, 41, 43, 165–66, 172–73, 196, 198, 215, 217
interest in audio diaries, 66
interpretive phenomenological analysis. *See* IPA
interval-contingent designs, 29–31, 34, 57, 122, 131, 142–43, 157, 206
Interval-Contingent Diary Designs, 29–30, 34, 79
interview and diary data, 165
interview data, 24, 36, 42, 163, 165, 180, 189, 191, 209, 216
  broader, 191
  qualitative, 189
interviews, 2–3, 5, 7–9, 22, 24, 36–44, 46, 59, 61, 93, 95–96, 99–100, 109, 117–18, 163–65
  integrating, 163
  photo-elicitation, 90
IPA (interpretive phenomenological analysis), 162, 168–69, 171, 173, 184
IWN, 199
IWPN, 199

J
justice, data modalities, 85, 130

K
Karadzhov, 6, 129, 131, 133–34, 173–74, 178
keeping photo diaries, 89, 91, 101
key benefits of diary data, 208
King, 161, 164, 167, 171, 174, 178–79, 186–88, 192, 195, 197–99, 203, 210
King & Brooks, 164, 192–93, 198, 200, 210

L
LAN, 199, 203
large data, 113, 123, 152
large language models (LLMs), 219
Laura, 8, 10–11, 21–22, 37, 45–46, 87, 89, 91, 108, 110, 142, 165, 187–89, 192, 205–6
Laura's research, 9–10, 16, 21, 25, 37–38, 40, 43
Laura's research on decision-making processes, 32
laws, 72, 87, 138, 149
learning, 43, 54, 72, 77, 80, 93–94, 120, 211, 221–22
Leighann's doctoral research, 133, 186
Leighann's research, 11, 30, 39, 47, 131, 192
length of time, 25, 59, 122
level, 8, 20, 23, 44, 61, 103, 188, 196, 198–200, 213, 219
levels of templates, 198, 200–201
life, 64, 89, 95–98, 103, 174, 177
life balance, 62, 95, 97–101, 109
life conflict, 97–99
limitations, 73, 107, 153, 155, 164, 171–72, 180, 185–86, 191, 205, 212
links, 11, 153, 187–89, 192
LLMs (large language models), 219
locus of anticipation, 199, 201–3
Lucy, 63–64, 190

M
macro-templates, 199–200
major themes, 188, 200–202, 204

Malik, 18, 98, 100–101
management research methods, 18, 49
managers, 60, 63–64, 67, 72, 81, 108, 115, 163, 197
matrix, data display, 181, 196
meeting, 106, 197, 199
Mendoza, 132–33, 136–37, 149
meso-templates, 198–201
methodological, 101, 184, 194
methodologies, 17, 41, 61, 99, 161–62, 167, 180, 182
  inclusive data collection, 13
methods, 5, 7, 11, 14, 24, 35–36, 48, 87–88, 108–9, 117, 161–62, 172–73, 182–83, 206, 210–11, 217–18
  time-intensive, 7
  visual, 84
micro-templates, 198–200
mobile data charges, 150
modes, 14, 25, 29, 55, 70, 76, 79, 91, 135, 142, 215–16
modes to complete diary entries by participants, 70
moments, in the, 1, 7, 67–68, 93, 172
Monrouxe, 13, 68–69, 75, 107, 212
Morgan, 3, 219
MS (multiple sclerosis), 166
multimodal data, 96, 114, 129
  rich, 114, 142
multimodal data collection and analysis, 221
multimodal data collection methods, 1
multimodal diaries, 143, 173
multimodal diary data, 153, 173
multiple sclerosis (MS), 166
mundane, 4, 8–9, 32, 61, 88–89, 98–99

N
Nadin & Cassell, 2
Nash & Moore, 103–4, 110, 112
nature of photo diaries, 94
Negative interaction/event, 199
networks, 21–23, 87
Neves, 90, 165–66
new approaches to multimodal data collection and analysis, 221
new forms of diaries and diary data, 218
next day, 199, 202–3
nexus analysis framework, 175
Noyes, 106, 114, 117–19
nurses, 169–70

O
obsessive-compulsive disorder (OCD), 80
OCD (obsessive-compulsive disorder), 80
often-cited benefits of participant reflexivity, 110
Ontology Epistemology, 193–95
opportunity for participants, 70, 136, 213
ordering, 176–77, 196
organizational research, 125, 172
organizational research design, 18, 101
Organizational Research Methods, 18, 101, 115, 125, 183
outcomes, 2, 8, 11, 62–63, 172, 187–89
overarching benefit of app diaries, 128–29

P
participant analysis, 94
participant and researcher, 27, 46
participant and researcher burden, 46
participant and researcher reflexive thinking, 15
participant as researcher, 83
participant as researcher burden, 123, 152
participant as researcher context, 110
participant comfort, 54, 68, 88, 97, 105, 107–9, 112
participant commitment, 26, 29
participant data, 45, 91, 138, 197
participant dropout, 25, 48
participant ease, 67, 85
participant editing, 94, 113
participant engagement, 28, 48, 130, 147, 158, 218
participant entries, 202
participant group, 22, 25

Index 269

participant information sheets, 44–45, 48, 91, 119–20
participant interpretations, 99, 101
participant-led approach, 12, 14, 108, 110, 212, 221
strong, 99
participant-led data, detailed, 35
participant-led design, 3
participant-led nature, 15, 104, 111
participant-led nature of video diaries, 104
participant-led research, 13
participant-led research approach, 17, 58
participant observation, 4, 13–14, 36
participant power dynamics, 90, 108
participant preferences, 103, 165
participant privacy, 48, 74, 78–79, 139
participant recruitment, 21, 33, 109, 213
Participant Reflections on Keeping Audio Diaries, 72
participant reflexivity, 41, 43, 48, 89–90, 104, 108–10
instigates, 15, 43
Participant reflexivity in organizational research design, 18, 101
Participant/Researcher Well-Being, 45
participant retention, 25, 131
participants
 allowing, 77, 107
 asking, 5, 30, 40, 59, 97, 102–3, 118–19, 122, 202
 capturing, 86, 104
 empowering, 12, 108
 enabled, 14, 135
 enabling, 37, 129, 142
 given, 159–60, 198
 help, 32, 137
 impact, 11, 16, 218
 interview, 24, 38–39, 86
 leading, 35, 97
 maintaining, 20, 37, 213
 monitor, 132, 139
 particular, 134, 191
 permitting, 3, 212
 potential, 53–54, 133
 providing, 43, 58, 120, 123, 131, 152
 recruiting, 26, 39, 133
 remind, 131, 143
 seeking, 97
 support, 75, 136
participant sample, 91, 94, 102, 191
 particular, 33, 88
participants and researchers, 77
participants and subsequent resolution processes, 37
participants as researchers, 113, 120
participants benefit, 17
participants choice, 130, 135, 216
participants choice and flexibility in terms, 135
participants diaries, 48
participants for non-research purposes, 143
participants in pre-diary interviews, 32, 79
participants in terms, 90, 108, 150
participants recording, 1, 32
participants to experience, 136–37
participants to record, 7, 29–32, 34, 60, 209, 212
participants to record entries, 112
participants to report, 32, 34, 57
participants to upload video diary entries, 122
participants to use video diaries, 111
participant summaries, 160, 181
 descriptive, 160, 219
participant tracking table, 157, 160
 rigorous, 157
 systematized, 181
participant tracking table ID, 158
participation, 26, 39, 48, 81, 131, 133–34, 137, 139, 143, 166, 218
participatory research, 5, 12
participatory video research, 115, 125
particular benefits for participants, 54
particular times of day, 30, 33
patient diaries and interviews, 170
patients, 169–70
patterns, 12, 79, 88, 176–77, 195, 200–201, 204, 208
Patton, 20, 160–61, 183, 219
Paul, 63–64, 190
pen-and-paper diaries, 51–59, 61, 65, 130–31, 135
 physical, 1, 45, 51–52, 57, 59, 68

pen-and-paper diaries and audio diaries, 51
permission, 62–63, 72, 89, 92, 95, 99–100, 117
personal data, 45, 220
phases, 39, 156, 173, 175, 181–83, 206
phenomena, participant as researcher, 94
phenomenological approaches, 168–69
Philosophical, 161, 193–95
photo and video diaries, 83–84
photo data, 173
photo diaries, 83–90, 94, 96–99, 102, 105, 108, 110–11, 113
 additional insights, 89
 conducting, 142
 considering, 84
 employing, 43, 87
photo diaries and video diaries, 83
photo diary data, 113
photo diary research projects, 84
photo-elicitation, 84, 98–101, 142
photo-elicitation research, 84–85
photo-elicitation to understand experiences of work, 98, 100–101
photographer, 177
photographic data, 85, 91–92, 96, 102
photographs, 83–85, 88–97, 99–102, 135, 145, 173, 175–76
photography, responsible, 92, 99, 101–2
photos, 84–86, 99–102, 124, 128–30, 142–43, 145, 147, 149, 151, 159, 173, 176–77, 213, 216
physical diaries, 45, 53, 56, 65
physicality, 104, 106–7
pictures, 3, 11, 28, 32, 87, 92–93, 95, 97, 99–100, 208, 212
place of work, 56, 124
planned sample size to account for participants, 25
platforms, 23, 147, 149–51
plots, 64, 169–70, 201, 206
police officers (POs), 80
populations, 52, 54, 133–34
 older, 134–35
POs (police officers), 80
position, 93, 176, 193–95

Positive interaction/event, 199
post-diary interviews, 36, 39–41, 43–44, 46, 48, 96, 109, 117–18, 159, 205
Post-interview Diaries, 42
potential benefit of photo diaries, 88
potential challenges, 44, 55, 73, 113, 209–10, 214
potential data loss, 53, 73, 157, 214
potential impact on participants, 41, 43
practical considerations, 19, 59, 75, 96, 111, 114, 137, 141
pre-diary interviews, 32, 36–38, 79, 102, 158
previous chapters, 89, 91, 117–18, 135–36, 205, 211
principles, 5, 193–95
privacy, 44–46, 56, 61, 66, 74, 78, 91, 93, 118, 123–24, 138–39, 143, 151–52
private diaries, 39–40
 keeping, 45, 61
processes data, 138
project, 4, 16–17, 28, 108, 117, 119–21, 124, 141–42, 149–50, 153, 156–57, 181–83, 196–97, 208–9, 222
Project Brief, 80–81, 124, 209–10
project considerations, 17–18
purposes, non-research, 129, 141, 143
purposes of data analysis, 59

Q
QDAS (qualitative data analysis software), 160
QDM Analysis, 155, 164, 167, 219
QDM data, 22, 38, 155, 161, 167, 180, 185, 191, 206
QDM data for analysis, 155–56
QDM-Focused Analysis Approaches, 187–209
QDM project, 15, 25, 47, 152, 156, 213, 221
QDM research, 13, 19–21, 25, 46–47, 127–28, 161, 164–65, 180, 211, 214, 217–18, 220, 222
QDM research projects, 51, 164, 211
QDMs (Qualitative diary methods), 1–48, 51–54, 56–80, 83–84, 86–222

Index   271

QDMs
  photo-based, 85, 90, 93, 98, 105
  video-based, 103-4
QDM studies, 17-20, 23-24, 27, 29, 41,
    44, 58-59, 66, 68, 76-77, 101,
    156, 164-65, 212-14, 216-21
  existing, 164
qualitative data, 12, 18, 155, 183, 186,
    189, 191, 204-5, 211, 216, 219
  longitudinal, 205
  rich, 12, 162, 204, 208, 211, 215
qualitative data analysis, 58, 219, 222
qualitative data analysis software
    (QDAS), 160
qualitative data types, 163
qualitative diaries, completion of, 27-28
qualitative diary data, 9, 12, 155
  interesting, 46
  rich, 208-9
Qualitative diary methods. *See* QDMs
qualitative diary research, 19, 156
qualitative organizational research, 49,
    92, 100
qualitative research, 21, 24, 43, 46, 49,
    58, 154, 164, 172, 182-83, 220
qualitative research methods, 2, 27, 98,
    100-101
qualitative research projects, 42, 156

R
Radcliffe, 5-6, 15-16, 18, 21-22, 24, 27-28,
    35-38, 40, 46-47, 56-63, 100-101,
    155-56, 165, 185-88, 210
  Laura, 62-63
Radcliffe & Cassell, 6, 9-11, 22, 24, 31,
    37, 40, 163, 165
range, 1, 5, 17, 19, 84, 97-99, 115, 161,
    165, 167, 171, 209, 211
rapport, 37-39, 42, 76, 101-2, 117
realities, 84, 87
record entries, 56, 67, 109, 111-12
recorders, 73, 77
recording, 26, 33, 35, 37, 69, 73-76,
    78-79, 103-4, 108, 112, 117,
    119, 121-22
  tape, 71

recording audio diary entries, 75, 112
recording device, 76
recording devices, technical challenges,
    data storage, 104
recording equipment, 77, 118
recording video diary entries, 107, 109
recruitment, 21-22
reflexive analysis of roles in
    participatory video research,
    115, 125
reflexivity, 2, 15, 43-44, 47, 70, 93, 113,
    194, 212-13
relation to audio diaries, 87
relation to photo diaries, 108, 110
relation to written diaries, 74, 76
relative ease of audio diaries, 78
relativist, 194-95
reminders, 28, 34, 75, 131-32,
    142-43, 197
research and participant, 38
research contexts, 2, 13
research design, 21, 41, 47, 53, 85, 128,
    131, 141, 153, 162, 216
  participant-led, 118
  participatory, 3, 5
researched relationship, 46-48
researcher, 2-4, 12-15, 17, 20-23,
    27-28, 32-35, 37-38, 40-42,
    44-48, 57-59, 76-78, 90, 94-96,
    102-3, 118, 139-40, 143,
    157-58, 209-10, 212-21
researcher and participant, 14, 28, 47
researcher/editor, 85, 104
researcher/researched power relations,
    12, 212
researchers and participants, 5,
    129-30, 132, 140
researcher's judgment in terms, 20
researcher's judgment in terms of
    selecting participants, 20
researchers to tailor, 129, 141
research findings, 31, 185
research focus, 58, 185
research methods, 3, 49, 54, 136, 212
  remote, 6, 217
research participants, 13, 15, 49,
    99, 143

research process, 2-3, 5, 12, 38, 41, 43-45, 107, 110, 156, 212, 218-20
research project, particular, 5, 7, 51, 53, 58
research projects, 1-2, 6-7, 16-19, 22, 74, 76, 80-81, 103, 111, 113, 151, 153, 214, 216, 221-22
research purposes, 1, 77, 103, 129, 139, 141-42, 217, 219
research question, distinct, 80, 123, 179, 209
research questions, 7, 12, 19-20, 25-29, 33, 35, 46-48, 53-54, 59-61, 75, 85-86, 97-98, 104-6, 145, 153, 160-64, 177-79, 200-201, 209, 214-17
research questions and rationale, 114, 163
research questions and rationale for selecting video diaries, 114
research team, 90, 95, 113, 117, 120, 134, 136
research topic, 15, 78, 84, 111
retrieve participant data, 214
retrieve photo diaries, 102
retrospection, 7, 30-31, 162
risk, 22-23, 25, 31, 37, 40, 48, 53, 55-58, 73-74, 91, 93, 131, 133, 138-39
risks of participants diaries, 48
Roberts, 103, 108-9
roles, 20-21, 31, 38, 64, 68, 72, 105-6, 115-16, 122, 125, 177-78
RQ, 80-81, 124, 181, 189, 209-10
running dedicated training workshops for participants, 136
Ryan, 54-55, 58, 70

S

sample, 20-26, 29, 61, 66-67, 77, 80-81, 107, 110, 113-14, 124, 130, 133-34, 143, 145-46, 209-10
particular, 53-54, 67, 73, 87, 113
sample size, 20, 24, 141, 150, 153, 167, 169, 214
planned, 25
sampling, 19-23
purposive, 22-23
snowball, 21-23
sampling strategies, 22-23, 48
sampling techniques, 20, 23
nonprobability, 20-21
Saunders, 20, 22, 49
school, 8, 63, 190
Seide, 133, 135, 149, 154
self-editing, 69-70, 75
semi-structured diary questions for participants to focus, 35
sense, 14-16, 29, 31, 38-42, 47, 51, 54-55, 65-66, 69-70, 76, 85-86, 90-91, 103, 105-7
sensemaking processes, 105, 108
sensitive research, 14, 56, 212
services, 149-50
sheets, 71, 142-43
Shortt & Warren, 96, 101-2, 164, 176-78
signal, 32-34, 48, 59, 97, 131, 162, 215
signal-contingent designs, 29, 32-33, 78, 131, 159, 215
significant benefit of app-based diaries, 138
singular data set for analysis, 179
smartphones, 32-33, 55, 61, 77, 102, 130-31, 133-37, 145, 149, 151-52, 173
social action, 87, 175
social science research, 3-4, 16, 20
social sciences, 5-6, 36, 84, 103, 106, 127, 173, 217-18, 220-21
Sociological Research Online, 81, 125
solicited diaries, 1, 4, 107
sources, 178-79, 195
sources of data, 36, 163-65, 167, 171, 178-79, 181, 201
space, private, 67, 112
spacing, 30-31
Spencer, 10, 12, 56, 156, 160-61, 163, 165, 167, 172, 185-86, 192, 195, 197, 199, 216-17
Step, 167, 169, 172, 176-77, 181-83, 186-88, 190, 192, 195-96, 198, 200-201, 204-6, 208
Steps and Decision Prompts, 181-83

Index   273

strategies, 24, 59, 170, 206
strengths, 155, 171, 180, 185-86, 216
students, work experience, 63-64
Study design, 209-10
subsample, 24
subthemes, 200-201, 204
switches, 103, 105, 110, 115-16, 129

T
table, 41-42, 53, 65-67, 79, 85, 101-2, 104, 122-23, 129-30, 150, 152, 177-80, 193, 195-96
tailor, 129, 141, 145, 149-51
taking part in photo diaries, 88
technical challenges, 53, 67, 73, 123, 152
technology, 51, 53-54, 67, 73, 77, 107-9, 115-16, 121, 134, 136, 218, 220
template analysis, 161, 164-65, 167, 182, 186
templates, 165, 171-72, 187-88, 193, 198-201
  methodological, 171-72
temporal unit, 159, 181, 196-98, 201, 206
terms, 9-11, 20-21, 33-34, 37-38, 54-56, 58-59, 65-70, 75-78, 83-86, 97-98, 101-3, 106-8, 119, 121, 130-32, 139-40, 143, 149-50, 191, 213
text, 84-85, 98, 102, 124, 128-30, 135, 138, 142-43, 145, 147, 149, 151, 158-59
text-based data, 93, 96, 114, 123, 173
text-based diary data, 176
text entries, 129, 147, 149
textual data, 161, 164, 173-74, 179, 194
TGIF, 199, 203
thematic analysis, 155, 161, 164-66, 182-83
thematic content, 187, 192, 201, 204
thematic data, 200, 203
thematic template, 163-65, 188, 190
thematic template analysis, 188, 192, 196
thematic trajectories, 194, 200-206

thematic trajectory analysis. *See* TTA
Thematic Trajectory Diagram Based, 207
Thematic Trajectory Diagram Based on Event-Contingent Diary Data, 207
themes, 164-65, 169, 174, 177, 187-88, 191, 193-95, 198-202, 204
  first-level, 164-65
  thought processes of participants, 95
time, 1-3, 10-13, 16-19, 25-26, 29-37, 41, 45, 54-64, 70-72, 83-84, 88-89, 112-14, 140-41, 173-74, 189-92, 196-98, 200-202, 204-9, 211-12, 214-15
  additional, 45, 117, 123, 191, 205
  real, 76, 88, 131-32
time commitments, 26, 59
  additional, 46, 102
  considering participant, 68
time for work, 32
time frame, 31, 34, 114, 182
time-intensive data, 59
time period, 30-31, 46, 97
  particular, 1, 211
times of day, 33-34
topics, 2, 6, 8-9, 15, 24, 27, 39-40, 43-44, 74, 79, 84-86, 88, 104
total diaries for analysis, 166
tracking elements, 147
traditional approaches, 51-52, 110, 171-72, 186
Traditional Diary Methods, 51-81
traditional qualitative analysis approaches, 164, 171
trajectories, 193-94, 200-201, 204, 208, 217
trajectory diagrams, 200-202, 204-6, 208, 210
transcripts of video diaries, 173
transitions, 26, 31, 105, 116, 124
TTA (thematic trajectory analysis), 173, 186, 192-200, 203, 205-6, 208-10, 216
types, 20, 29-30, 32-35, 105-6, 118-19, 129-30, 149-50, 155, 159-60, 163-64, 179-82, 187-90, 212-13, 216, 218-20

274 Qualitative Diary Methods

U
understand experiences of work, 98, 100–101
unfolding processes, 10
United Kingdom, 62–63, 138
upload, 116, 135
Use, 53, 67, 85, 104, 130, 151, 193–94
useful tool for participants, 70
useful tool for participants and researchers, 70
Use of Audio Diaries in Work Psychology, 72
Use of TTA, 193–95
Use Photo Diaries, 85
Use Video Diaries, 104
utility of video diaries, 125
utility of video diaries for organizational research, 125

V
video clips, 109, 175–76
video data, 111, 114, 116, 121
video diaries, 83–84, 103–14, 117–19, 123–25, 128, 173
  complete, 122
  considering, 114
  employing, 108, 113, 119
  inward-facing, 111
  selecting, 114
video diaries capitalizing, 107
video diaries to document, 106
video diaries to garner insights, 107
video diary data, 107, 112–14
  considering, 119
video diary entries, 109, 111–12
video diary instruction sheets, 118–19
Vince, 91–92, 99–101
visual data, 85, 91, 173–74, 177–80, 182
  pertinent elements of, 114, 123
visual diary methods, 83
visualization, 87, 186–87, 200, 208
visual research, 84, 90
voluminous data, 160, 165

W
Warren, 84, 90, 92, 96, 99–101, 176–78, 183
way, 10–17, 26–29, 37, 55, 69–71, 88, 94–96, 108–11, 120–22, 130–33, 145–46, 163–64, 169–71, 173–74, 188–89, 191–92, 196, 208–9, 212–15, 219–20
Welford, 128–29, 132–33, 136–37, 140, 146, 154
WFCs, 60–61
WhatsApp, 32, 69, 128–29, 132–34, 138–43, 146, 149–51
WhatsApp diaries, 142–43
Whiting, 103–5, 108–10, 114–15, 117–18, 120–22, 125
WIM (Work, Interaction, and Mood), 133, 145
work, 6, 8–11, 29–32, 34, 56–58, 60–64, 71–72, 89–90, 95, 97–101, 124, 143, 168, 177, 187–90, 192, 197–99, 202, 206–7, 209
  complete, 190
  daily, 4, 8–9, 37, 74, 97, 105, 187
  early, 4, 52
  existing, 98, 206
  full-time, 177
Work, Interaction, and Mood (WIM), 133, 145
work and family, 61–62, 206
work and family responsibilities, 31, 40, 62
work and family roles, 60, 124, 143
work and home roles, 16, 124
work and life, 89, 177
Work Diary, 71
work event, 11
Work-Family Conflict, 60, 62–63
working arrangements, flexible, 9–10
working hours, 74, 207
  usual, 190
working parents, 67, 124
workload, 72, 197
work on time, 8, 32, 64, 190, 207
workplace, 8, 19, 30, 39, 45, 64, 74, 115–16, 202

workplace experiences, 30, 34
  daily, 18, 49
workplace mistreatment, 47, 217
work psychology, 71–72, 81
work roles, 16, 124
worksheet, 47–48, 152–53, 215
workshops, 136, 146
  running dedicated training, 136
workspace, 56, 115
written diaries, 24, 52, 54–56, 61, 66, 68–71, 74–76

X
x-axis, 201–2, 206

Z
Zimmerman, 3–4, 13, 18, 36, 39, 52, 59, 155, 157, 212, 217
Zundel, 24, 103, 105, 107–9, 111–14, 117, 121–22, 125, 159